By Candlelight

About Janina Renée

As a toddler, Janina Renée was introduced to candle burning in a family ceremony, and she has long appreciated the power of candles in framing memories and providing a core around which traditions can be built. Her observation that some of the major social and spiritual problems of the modern era derive from individuals' struggles with meeting the ordinary challenges of life and work led her to design rituals to deal with these problems. She also designs rituals that help one live with paradoxes, such as a recognition of the impermanence of life versus a sense of wonder and joy in the works of Nature.

Janina holds a B.A. degree in anthropology and is a scholar of such diverse subjects as material culture, folklore, mythology, ancient religion, ritual studies, psychology, medical anthropology, culture studies, history, and literature. Her current research interests include the use of ritualism in nature writing, the ways we ritually interact with material objects, and the role and subject position of high-functioning autistic persons in history, literature, and culture. When she is able to wrest time from work, studies, writing, and family duties, Janina makes forays into the American heartland to explore small towns and cities.

Janina has been a student of folklore, magic, psychology, and ritualism for over thirty years. She has drawn from her knowledge of ritual and symbolism in the writing of her other books: *Tarot Spells, Playful Magic, Tarot: Your Everyday Guide,* and *Tarot for a New Generation.* In some of these books she showed readers how to get more out of their Tarot cards. Here, in *By Candlelight,* she shows readers how to get more out of their candles.

By Candlelight

Rites for Celebration, Blessing & Prayer

Janina Renée

2004 — Llewellyn Publications, St. Paul, Minnesota 55164-0383

FIRST EDITION
First Printing, 2004

Book interior design and editing by Connie Hill
Cover design by Ellen L. Dahl
Cover photo © 2001 by PhotoDisc
Interior art by Kerigwen

Library of Congress Cataloging-in-Publication Data
(Pending)
Renée, Janina, 1956–
    By candlelight ; rites for celebration, blessing & prayer / Janina Renée — 1st edition
        p. cm.
    Includes bibliographical references.
    ISBN 0-7387-0417-2
    1. Candles and lights—Miscellanea.   2. Rites and ceremonies—Miscellanea.   I. Title.
    BF1623.C26R46   2004
    203'.8—dc22   2003071041

Llewellyn Publications
A Division of Llewellyn Worldwide, Ltd.
P.O. Box 64383, Dept. 0-7387-0417-2
St. Paul, MN 55164-0383, U.S.A.
www.llewellyn.com

Printed in the United States of America

This book is dedicated
to the memory of Vivian Elaine Runyon,
also known as "Valiya,"
a beautiful, talented, vivacious young woman.
At a very early age, Vivian decided to dedicate her life
to helping other people feel good about themselves.
She succeeded in reaching out to many,
creating and uniting a large community of friends.
Vivian was killed by a drunk driver in May 2001.

Other Books by Janina Renée

Tarot for a New Generation
Tarot Spells
Tarot: Your Everyday Guide
Playful Magic

Contents

Preface

Who does not take pleasure in lighting a candle? The light. The beauty. The ambience. While many people burn candles just for their romantic glow, candlelighting has long been a spiritual and meditational practice. This ritual act is common to many different religions. There is something very meaningful and focusing inherent in lighting a candle while making a wish or saying a prayer. Indeed, the act of lighting a candle signals a time and space set aside from the stress and bustle of the work-a-day world. The candle effectively creates a small circle of sacred space.

This book contains a wide variety of candle rites—simple, nondenominational rituals that combine spiritually and psychologically meaningful words and actions as they address a number of common concerns. Many of the rituals engage the spiritual world, the interconnectedness of all things, and the ideal of a harmonious universe. Some are prayer-like, for cultivating one's spiritual nature or communicating with higher powers. Others are focused on the self, for purposes of managing one's attitudes, habits, and moods, to improve the quality of daily life. Some of these rituals respond to special needs, such as love, healing, prosperity, and protection. Still others are celebrational, for commemorating special occasions, extending blessings to loved ones, or adding depth or dimension to certain phases of the day or year.

May you find this book both a practical and an inspirational companion as you explore the sensory delights of candle burning.

Introduction

The performance of small personal rituals gives you a means of expressing your spiritual nature, focusing on goals, and adding to the quality of your life. The performance of family rituals and other group rites enables you to make memories, demonstrate your concern for others, and enhance the quality of celebrational occasions. This book, *By Candlelight*, provides ceremonies for both the public and private spheres of life by combining the simple act of lighting a candle with a variety of prayers, blessings, meditations, affirmations, visualizations, and ceremonial actions.

Candle Rites are Easy and Convenient

I wrote this book in response to some of the common issues and concerns that may arise in the course of a day or week. Therefore, most of these rites are designed to be performed whenever you have an immediate need, as long as you have a candle and a place to burn it. These rituals are self-contained and laid out in an easy-to-read format, so all you need to do is flip the book open to a given ritual, light a candle, and recite the words provided.

Most of the rites require the use of just one candle. Usually a simple white candle will do, though a "suggestions" paragraph at the end of each ritual discusses ways in which a rite may be enhanced with additional candles, or how you might choose candles in different colors to fit your purpose. In some cases, you might be able to use the psychological effects of color to tailor the rites to your personal goals, or shift your perspective to key in to the symbolic potentials of different colors of candles you may have on hand. (As an example of color choice, the suggestions section for the rite for "burning anger," describes how you could use a red candle to objectify—that is, make solid or stand for—a hot-headed anger, or you might prefer a white candle to represent the pure energy to which you hope to transform the anger, or a blue or turquoise candle for calm and healing energies to contain it.) Thinking about color choice acts as a focusing exercise, helping you to sort out your feelings and objectives.

Actually, many of the ritual recitations in this book are capable of standing on their own as prayers, blessings, or affirmations, so you could perform them without the candles, (or you could, instead, say them while lighting a stick of incense). However, even though the rites don't call for a lot of fancy candles, that doesn't mean that you can't use and enjoy your favorite candles. If you are a person who loves candles—perhaps even someone who makes your own or likes to browse gift shops for the wonderful array of scented candles and novelty candles that are now available—this collection of rituals will give you an excuse to fully indulge your candle habit. You can also go on "candle quests" by making outings to some interesting new places to find just the right candles for special rituals. You may especially want to go questing to find "presentation candles," which are candles given as special gifts to others, as described in the blessing rituals featured in Section IX.

Again, most of the rituals in this book do not require you to make any special preparations, obtain any unusual ingredients, or go out of your way or to any unusual lengths in their performance. With the exception of certain celebrational rites for different times of the day or year, they also don't need to be performed at specific times (such as certain days or hours of the week, as is the case with the type of candle-burning used in "folk magic"). However, if you enjoy the ritual experience, there are suggestions as to different ritual actions, use of incense and oils, symbolic accessories, candle arrangements, and other enhancements that you can include in your performance if your time and circumstances allow. The appendix provides additional information on candle burning tips, colors, oils, accessories, and practices.

Also: the wording of these rituals is kept fairly short and to the point, but you are encouraged to add on to or modify them, where desired, to better express your own feelings.

Candle Rites are Rich in Meaning

Although the lighting of a candle is such a simple ritual action, it resonates on several levels of experience and meaning. The flame of a candle can represent the fire of life and spirit within each person, as well as each person's ability to bring light to the world. Because some candles look and smell so beautiful, it seems a shame to light them and then allow them to burn down. However, in this way, the act of burning a candle becomes an act of sacrifice. The motions you go through in picking out a candle, striking a match, and lighting the candle help signal your intentions and desires to spiritual forces, as well as your own unconscious mind, which is often referred to as the "deep mind." Even persons who do not believe in anything spiritual may acknowledge the powers of the deep mind to influence one's body, energy levels, moods, attitudes, personal circumstances, and life choices. If you have chosen an especially symbolic candle, or if you anoint your candle with fragrant oils, or if you inscribe your candles with symbols related to your desires,

In this book, references to "the unconscious" do not mean the condition of being asleep or knocked out. Rather, "the unconscious" refers to that part of one's mind and brain that is normally inaccessible, but that can be likened to a vast, complex, and multilayered storehouse and processing center of memories, dreams, emotions, instincts, and motivations. Because the unconscious also has a certain intelligence and determination, it can be approached not just as the place where all of these memories and motivations are stored, but also the person or personnel who organize and maintain them. Ritual is a way of impressing upon the unconscious one's need to make changes in attitude and behavior; in so doing, one alters one's reality. Ritual also makes it possible to draw from the unconscious as a deep source of energy and creative inspiration. The use of the term "the unconscious" can be confusing because different schools of psychology have different preferences in usage, and sometimes this term is used interchangeably with the word "subconscious" (though not in this book). The term "subconscious" is more specifically used to refer to the place that holds short-term memories, older memories that have been reactivated, intuitive responses to current environmental cues, and other mental activities that are operating not too far below your level of conscious awareness—that is, just below the threshold of consciousness.

or if you decorate your candle area with symbolic objects, these actions also underscore your intention.

Gazing into a candle flame is a way of focusing. By concentrating upon the flickering light of a candle, you can shut out the distractions around you and align the powers of your mind and body with your goal. Your concentration, combined with the relaxing and refreshing sight and scent of the candle, can help you ease into the "alpha state," which is rejuvenating as well as conducive to creative insight. You further engage the powers of your deep mind through your interactions with your candle. Depending upon your need and the nature of your rite, you can see the candle as "a physical representation" of a prayer,[1] or as the embodiment of an issue that you want to burn through, or you can relate to the candle as a friend who takes on your cares and burns them away for you.

> A candle can be viewed as a small hearth, so it is interesting to note that the word "focus" derives from *foculus*, a word for "hearth."

When you are working with candles, you are also working with the power and symbolism of Fire. (I capitalize this word to distinguish Fire as a metaphysical force from more ordinary references to fire.) Fire has long inspired images of spiritual devotion and passion. For example, Marianne Williamson describes spirituality as "an inner fire, a mystical sustenance that feeds our souls," and states, "The mystical journey drives us into ourselves, to a sacred flame at our center."[2]

Fire also plays a role in legend and lore, as its actions were of interest to early natural historians. Some perceived Fire as a living being, and it is one of the four elements of ancient science (five elements in the Chinese tradition). Elemental theory is no longer used in modern science, but poets, philosophers, and mystics find the workings of elemental Fire, Earth, Water, and Air to be a useful and inspirational way of perceiving, organizing, and experiencing reality. Fire is respected for its qualities of energy, warmth, illumination, purification, and transformation. Candle rites, as Fire rites, therefore tend to be positive and proactive, emphasizing light and transformation. (However, I want to point out that some of the rites in this book do take account of what is tragic in earthly life; they don't try to dismiss peoples' sorrows, but they can help work through some darker emotions.)

Many of these rituals engage the powers of elemental Fire as well as the powers of the deep mind through exercises that involve visualization and other types of sensory images. Similar techniques are being used in self-improvement systems, psychothera-pies, alternative healing therapies, athletics, education, creative work, and other fields of endeavor, because numerous clinical studies have demonstrated that guided im-agery can reprogram the brain, exert control over the body, and alter one's personal reality. The effectiveness of imagery both supports and is informed by theories that the brain has a holographic quality, processing and storing information as wave forms. Through carefully chosen, vividly imagined images, we can bring about de-sired changes, because, as Michael Talbot states, "the mind/body ultimately cannot distinguish the difference between the neural holograms the brain uses to experience reality and the ones it conjures up while imagining reality."[3]

Concepts of a holographic brain inform and are informed by concepts of a holographic universe. One of the curious properties of a hologram is that any given part of it contains or reflects the whole of it, and here we approach the realm of magic, as the model of a holographic universe relates to the belief in "the interconnectedness of all things" which is common to shamanic societies and mystical philoso-phies. A sense of this interconnectedness is applied in different forms of folk magic, where people try to bring about changes in their lives by using symbolic objects and/or going through motions that symbol-ize their goals. We can bring about seemingly magi-cal changes in our own lives by creating harmonious conditions that resonate throughout our webs of re-lationships. Therefore, ideals of harmony and inter-connectedness are invoked in many of the rites in this book.

The holographic brain theory has been advanced by neurologist Karl Pribram, and ties in with the idea of a holographic universe as proposed by the theoretical physicist David Bohm. My scientific knowledge isn't adequate to the task of properly explaining these theories. For more about the structure of reality, see Michael Talbot's *The Holographic Universe*, which is con-cerned with the way these theories ex-plain the paranormal abilities of the mind. Also see Allan Combs and Mark Holland's *Synchronicity: Science, Myth, and the Trickster*, which deals with the way these theories engage the intercon-nectedness of all things.

This is not a book about candle burning as used in folk magic—the rituals here being more spiritual, psychological, or celebrational in nature. Therefore, you don't need to believe in magic or know anything about it. However, I do include some tid-bits of information about folk magic in the end notes and other places where they might be of interest, just out of appreciation for the colorful, multicultural history and lore of candle burning and other areas of folk life.

Rituals Suitable for Most Religious Orientations

The models of a cosmos in which everything is interlinked, and a brain that can be consciously directed to bring about changes, should not conflict with open-minded religious philosophies. For example, if you are a person who believes in one creator God, may He not have designed things to work in this fashion? Why should God therefore resent our trying to enlist our deep minds in summoning energy, effecting healing, breaking bad habits, pursuing success, and so on, as long as we do so in a respectful way that does not harm other people?

Some other beliefs that are expressed in some of these rituals include a concept of a life force that animates the cosmos, and the idea that we are essentially spiritual beings who are born into the human world for some special life purpose. In composing these rites, my personal outlook has been influenced by African, Asian, Native American, old European, and many other wisdom traditions, as well as some spiritual philosophies advanced in the late nineteenth century. The spiritual dimension of existence can be seen as part of a larger holographic reality, and again, I hope this will not conflict with most readers' religions, as most religions believe in a spiritual world, even though they may differ in their beliefs about the nature of the god-force behind it.

Some of the rites in this book are aimed at making an emotional or intuitive connection with nature, and reflect my belief that nature and the things of nature are "inspirited" or "ensouled." As I explain elsewhere, a desire to relate to nature as a living presence, or to honor the spirits of nature and nature's creatures, need not be perceived in a negative sense as nature worship. Rather, it is a simple act of courtesy to show consideration and appreciation for other living things. Although people will differ on the extent to which they feel that animals and other expressions of nature have spirits or souls, such a belief need not conflict with a belief in a creator God. If you would like to perform the nature-oriented rites, just let yourself by guided by your own religious beliefs and sense of relationship to Nature.

In recognition of many different peoples' desires to have a variety of simple ceremonies that can be practiced at home, I have otherwise tried to keep these rites nondenominational. However, you can personalize them to better express your own religious beliefs by the way you preface them. Some of the more spiritually oriented rituals start with invocations that may be worded something like, "I call upon you, my Deity, and upon all spirits of guidance." To adapt these rites for your own religion, use the name by which you address your own god, goddess, or higher power in place of the word "Deity." (For example, "I call upon you, my dear Lord Jesus.") If it sounds better to your ears, eliminate "I call upon you" and just start with something like, "Dear God . . ." or "Goddess of Mercy, as I light this candle . . ." (or however the ritual goes). If your religion has a repertoire of traditional blessings and invocations, you could open with those. In this manner, you can also bring religious intent into some of the rites that do not involve spiritual issues (such as certain rites for self-improvement, seasonal celebrations, etc.). Where spirits are also being addressed in certain rituals, the fact that they are good spirits, such as angels, ancestors, and other friendly forces, is implied in the wording, the nature of the rituals, and your intent in performing the rituals. If you pray to Jehovah, Jesus, or Allah, you might agree that evil spirits would be unlikely to assist a ritual—or even remain in a place—where His name is spoken. Nevertheless, if you are troubled by the very idea of calling on spirits, simply omit such lines when you encounter them.

In addition to substituting your preferred names for Deity, there are other ways that you can rework these rituals to reflect your religious orientation. You can add lines that describe your religious philosophy, and subtract lines that are not a harmonious fit. You can also freely improvise by talking (in a stream-of-thought manner) about your religious feelings; don't worry about whether you are expressing them in a suitably formal or poetic way, just speak from the heart.

The more spiritually oriented rituals may prompt you to reflect upon the words "soul" and "spirit," and what they mean to you. In my rituals, and in my personal practice, I use these terms in a very general sort of way. I do not have any hard and fixed beliefs about the nature of soul and spirit, other than my perception that there is something

Conventional religions have their own teachings about the soul, and some popular writers have added their own ideas. For example, Gary Zukav describes the soul as immortal, with a special quality of light and intelligence, while Thomas Moore writes in a more general sense, declaring that, "It is impossible to define precisely what the soul is. Definition is an intellectual enterprise, anyway. The soul prefers to imagine" [xi]. On the other hand, Buddhist teachings don't recognize the existence of a soul as such; rather, what is reborn is an aggregate of karmic cravings and intentions, (behind which, however, there is a greater mystery of "Original Mind"). It is beyond the scope of this book to go more deeply into concepts regarding soul and spirit.

that soars in us, and something that strives for depth in us, and something that enables us to feel connected with others, as well as connected with a greater mystery that transcends time and space. Absolute certitude about the nature of soul and spirit is not necessary for performing these rites or leading a spiritual life. I therefore leave it to my readers to apply their own intuition or understanding to these terms.

About Performing These Rites

If you enjoy these candle rites, you may want to perform some of them on a regular basis. Including candle rites in your daily routine will enhance your quality of life by providing a few moments of beauty, fragrance, and color. Such rituals also serve as a structure around which you can organize some of life's activities, helping you achieve calm and reflection amidst the chaotic swirl of family, work, and social demands. If you have set up a home altar for personal devotions and meditations, you will find that these rituals provide pleasurable new ways to interact with your altar. (Home altar-making, once limited to certain religious and ethnic groups, is gaining popularity among larger numbers of Americans who have discovered that it is a wonderful means of creative spiritual expression.)

Note that the individual rites in this book can be performed as often as you like. If you are intent on working toward a certain goal you can relight your candle and perform a specific rite until the candle has burned down; you can also start a new candle and repeat the rite—as long as you enjoy the ritual experience. Also, relighting the candle without repeating the ritual words and actions can have the same effect as repeating the rite, because the action of lighting and the sight of the flame will act as mental keys to remind your deep mind of your purpose. However, once you have performed a rite, you do not need to repeat it. If the initial ritual performance has given you the calm, sense of assurance, ability to communicate your feelings, or whatever it is you wanted, that is enough, and you can set the candle aside until the next time you might feel a need to perform the same or a similar rite.

Most of these rites have been written with a solitary practitioner in mind, though a few (particularly those that would be ideal for family participation) use plural terms. However, many can be adapted for individuals or groups by changing the terms "I/me/my" to "we/us/our" and vice versa. You can build on the traditions that you share with family members or others by incorporating some of these candle rites into family routines or group celebrations.

When conducting the ceremonies in front of others, you might want to put a little flair into the lighting and recitation. There are not many things in this life that we can control, but little rituals enable us to weave a web of memory and experience that pulls individuals together and creates a sense of continuity with past and present. As Alexandra Stoddard has pointed out in her guide to *Living a Beautiful Life,* "A ritual is a mini-performance, whether privately performed or shared with a friend, and it has a life of its own."[4] Ritual performance especially makes an impression on children, so it is an effective way of underscoring a family's values and framing special moments in time; the regularity of certain performances also adds to children's sense of security and stability. And here is another way that candle burning can warm your social interactions: when a friend comes to visit, the conversation will naturally drift over to his or her problems, desires, or goals. That's the perfect time to say, "Hey, let's burn a candle for that!" Then, get out a candle, and maybe even some scented oil, and accompany him or her in performing an appropriate ritual. Your friend can take the candle home afterward, and continue to burn it there, with warm memories of your visit.

If you are able to perform certain rituals on a regular basis, you will find that ritual repetition generates and maintains its own current of energy, which can carry you through times of disruption and chaos. However, I do have a little warning about regular practice: because so many concerns can be expressed with candle rites, you may be tempted to keep adding more of them until you become over-programmed. Naturally, it is important to avoid obsessiveness by seeking your ideal balance of activity, and by allowing space for flexibility and spontaneity. While the regular performance of certain rites can add rhythm and dimension to your day and week, the rites are meant to be meaningful and pleasurable, which is something that would be lost if you tried to overdo them. Rather, let your sense of what is appropriate for your own needs guide you in deciding which of these rites to perform often, which you may want to plan for special occasions, which to perform spontaneously or only as a particular need arises, and which to ignore.

By the way, as I was working on this book, I thought of many more needs that could have been addressed and rituals that could have been included, but I had to stop somewhere in order to bring this book to a finish and prevent it from becoming unwieldy. However, if you have some special concerns that are not covered here, perhaps you can adapt the format of some of these other rituals for the purposes you desire. Because making a ritual of candle lighting is so easy and pleasant, you will probably think of many other activities that you could ceremonialize, or ideals that you could affirm in this manner.

A Few Words About the Language in this Book

In composing these rituals, I have tried to use language that is dignified, stylized, and consistent, yet emotionally expressive and easy on the American ear. Where I could fortuitously do so, I have worked in some Celtic word imagery, Anglo-Saxon alliterative or metrical patterns, Balto-Slavic structural forms, and in a few instances, some end rhyme. I hope that this achieves something of a poetic tone without grating on modern sensibilities. There are some people who think that ritual verse should be in rhyme; however, I do not have the rhyming talent of a Kipling, a Frost, or a Dickinson, so I feel that elegant prose is preferable to doggerel poetry. I am also backed by the study of ethnopoetics: in the ritual verses of peoples the world over—not just African, Asian, and Native American traditional groups, but also the older European—we find that systematic end rhyme is often nonexistent, or else an uncommon and relatively recent innovation.

In closing this introductory chapter, I once again emphasize that all of the lines to be recited in these candle rites are just meant to serve as convenient guidelines. If you like them as they are, that's great. However, do feel free to modify the wording, (as well as actions, accessories, and other aspects of these rituals), as much as you like, so that you can better express your personal needs, beliefs, and sentiments.

Rites for the Rhythms & Routines of Daily Life

Certain routines of everyday and household life can be elevated to ritual, enhancing our sense of security and continuity. Rituals also enable us to shift mental gears, or enjoy a change of pace. This section offers some simple prayers and practices to add meaning and dimension to your day or week.

1

Greeting the New Day

Candle burning is often regarded as something to be done at night, after the fall of darkness. However, lighting a candle can also help you welcome the new day, and it especially brings cheer to dark winter mornings or overcast days. For help in starting your morning in a positive frame of mind, you might choose one of these simple candle rites:

1. To give thanks for a new day, light a candle while saying:

   As I light this candle,
   I give gratitude for this new day,
   and the gift of grace
   that makes my world anew.
   O let the fire of enthusiasm
   and the light of clarity
   flow now through my being.
   Thus do I set my mind and heart
   on a life of purpose,
   on a life of blessing.

2. I think the most magical time of day is the hour before dawn. If you are able to rise early enough to watch the dawn break, you can give a special salute to the Dawn, whom many peoples have regarded as a lovely goddess. You can greet her by lighting a candle and saying:

   Lady in the form of light,
   I praise your radiant beauty.
   As you open the gates of morning,
   your vibrant colors energize my being
   and gladden my spirit.

You help me to love life
   and welcome change.
You inspire me to fill my own world
   with light and color.

3. If you feel pressed for time in the morning, your devotion can be as simple as lighting a candle and saying these lines from the fourth-century prayer of St. Ambrosius:

   Oh Light, shine upon our thoughts and scatter the sleep of our mind.[1]

4. For a simple ritual to connect with the world of Nature, you could light a candle as you say:

   I greet this blithe and beautiful Morning,
      as I welcome the shining Star of Day.

   Actually, you don't even need to light a candle—you can simply greet the Sun with these words; this is something nice to do when you step outdoors.

5. Here is a rite that you can perform by lighting three candles, in turn, to activate the power of three Suns: the Sun in the sky, the Sun that is the molten core of the Earth, and the Sun which is within you (astrologically, as well as in the "hara," or solar plexus energy center).

   I light this candle
      to honor the Sun in Heaven.
   I light this candle
      to honor the Sun within the Earth.
   I light this candle
      to honor the Sun within me.
   You remind me that I, too,
      am a being of light
      with the power to craft my day.

A Christian could use four candles, opening with a larger candle to honor the Son of God.

Suggestions

Morning devotions can be performed at a homemade altar, or before a window, or at your breakfast table. You could use a white candle to represent the spectrum of possibilities that the day contains (also: "white dawn" is a term used in Romance language poems, called "albas," and in the Slavic countries, one speaks of "the white day"[2]), or use a yellow, orange, or golden candle for the Sun. For special use with dawn rites, you might first want to observe the colors of dawn, noticing the beautiful shades of yellows, oranges, reds, and pinks that bleed into the blacks, grays, purples, and indigos of the fading night sky. Then go on a candle quest

Adjusting our attitudes to welcome change and seek creative inspiration will activate Dawn's blessings and opportunities, and may help mitigate the sadder implications of rising each morning a day older, to face the loss of youth and many other things that we have loved. This dark side of the Dawn is expressed in the Rig Veda: "Ancient yet newborn, . . . she wastes the life of man." [Quoted by Basham, 141.]

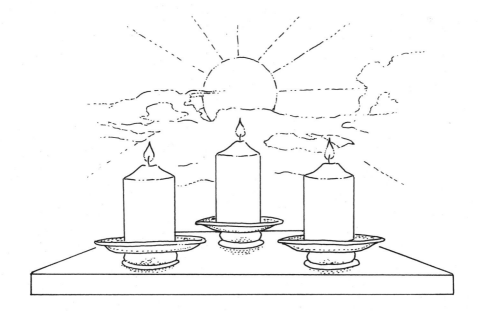

to find candles in one or more of these shades. (If you wish, you could group morning-colored candles in a half circle around your breakfast or focus area.) If you can choose scented candles, or use anointing oil or incense, perky citrus scents like orange, lemon, petitgrain, and tangerine are good for generating morning energy. Coffee-scented candles would also be delightful for awakening your mind in the morning.

Also: after performing these rites, you might drink a glass of orange, apricot, papaya, mango, or some other fruit beverage that echoes the warm tones of Dawn's palette, as a way of drinking in her power. You can assist the Dawn's quickening effect by doing a dance or some graceful stretching exercises to get your body in motion and stoke your metabolism.

2

A Prayer for Guidance

There are times during the day when we may need some help making decisions or avoiding some problem. When we are very busy or very tired, we may also feel that we have lost sight of our purpose. On a larger scale, we may also experience this loss of direction at certain junctions along our life paths. Therefore, the following rite calls for help in finding some direction and focusing on the needs of the moment, while also keeping sight of the bigger issues. Whenever you feel the need, light a candle and say:

> I call upon you, my Deity,
>   and upon all spirits of guidance,
> you, who would see me fulfill
>   my own best destiny,
>   in harmony with the living universe.
> Hear my prayer, for I would open
>   my mind and heart to wisdom,
> that I may manage problems,
>   and make wiser decisions.
> Please help me be receptive to inspiration,
>   that I may bring creativity and skill
>   into all that I do.
> Please help me perceive the energies
>   at work in the world around me,
> that I may set priorities, avoid troubles,
>   and recognize opportunities.
> And please help me be sensitive
>   to the needs of others,
> so that I may know when I am most needed,
>   and give blessings where I can.

When you perform this rite, it is a good idea to follow it by sitting for a few moments in silence—not thinking about anything or expecting anything, but as a way of signaling that you are in a receptive state.

Also: when you are seeking guidance in relation to larger life issues, think about how you might make the time to get away from home or work to perform this rite in some other location—for example, at the seashore, or in a country cabin, or even in a local cemetery, or some other place that is outside of your normal, everyday boundaries, (but where it is permissible to burn candles). Sometimes the act and the fact of "dislocation" help us put things in perspective. Many creative thinkers have deliberately removed themselves from familiar environs in order to provoke insight.

Suggestions

Choose a candle in any shape and color that helps you concentrate on your desire for guidance. White can symbolize pure intentions, blue denotes receptiveness and contemplation, and yellow is for mental illumination. If you choose candle scent, anointing oil, or incense to enhance this rite, use any uplifting fragrance; you could try cedar, juniper, lavender, benzoin, or sandalwood, as these help us become more receptive to positive spiritual influences.

3

For Blessing Your Space

People who enjoy burning candles may have an intuitive perception that they provide more than ambience. With ritual intent, you can use their warmth and light to bless your personal space and cast a protective glow about it. This is the sort of rite that many people perform on a regular basis to promote serenity, though it can also be used after (or in anticipation of) unpleasant experiences, quarrels, or visits from negative persons. When you want harmony and security around you, just light a candle and say:

> *I dedicate this candle*
> > *as a blessing for this space.*
> *Let its light and warmth and pleasant fragrance*
> > *extend to every corner of this place.*

Gaze at the candle flame and visualize its circle of light pulsing and glowing and expanding, sending its rays of golden-white light outward to warm and bless and caress the room or house that you occupy, as you say:

> *All beings who enter here,*
> > *who enter this sphere,*
> *may their hearts be light,*
> > *and their minds be clear,*
> > > *and their spirits uplifted.*

Visualize the strength of the light building and expanding to charge the atmosphere and create a circle of protection. Image any negativity that may be lingering in your area (or trying to enter it) as a grayish mist that is easily pushed away, dissipated, and dissolved into nothingness by the force of the expanding light, as you say:

This is also a protected space.
Whatever negative energies come into this place,
are broken down, diffused, and purified.
As they are dissolved and expelled,
so are they transformed into wholesome energy
for the benefit of living beings.

End the rite by saying:

So it is, and so shall it be!

Know that you can leave the candle burning or extinguish it if you wish, but your circle of light will remain in place. Every time you relight this candle, you replenish and fortify its blessing energy, though it is not necessary to repeat the ritual affirmations and visualizations every time.

Suggestions for Candles

For this purpose, white is a good color, signifying the power of white light, although pink, peach, yellow, and gold could also aid your visualizations of loving energy and warmth extended outward. You could also use blue to focus on tranquility, or light green for the energy of gentle healing and growth. If you use scented candles, anointing oil, or incense, you could use any fragrance that is pleasing to you or that suggests your ideal of personal space. You might also try cedar, lemon, lemon grass, bay laurel, frankincense, rose geranium, juniper, anise, pine, myrrh, rosemary, and sandalwood, as these are all fragrances that promote a sense of well-being, while also possessing purifying and protective qualities. To accentuate the imagery of a defined circle of blessing and protection, you could keep the candle on a home altar or some other central place, ringed with crystals or a necklace of gemstone beads, or wreathed with symbols of the season.

Also: This is an ideal blessing to perform when moving into a new home. (You can amplify this rite by repeating it in every room, with a candle for every room.) When you visit friends, you could take them a nice candle as a hostess or housewarming gift, and perform this rite upon entering their home if they wish. (Candles make perfect gifts for people who don't need more knicknacks—because they get used up, they don't create unwanted clutter.)

4

Candles with Grace

In households the world over, saying grace is a ritual that promotes gratitude and family unity. As many of us appreciate the ambience of a candle at our table, we can easily combine the grace with the candlelighting. We can use any one of the beautiful graces that have come to us through tradition, compose words expressing our own sentiments, or try the following: when the table has been set and you are ready to begin the meal, light a candle and say,

> *As we* [or I] *light this candle,*
> > *we extend our appreciation*
> > *to our Deity* [and/or to the Life Force of Nature].
> *Through the meal laid out before us*
> *we are connected to a vast chain of life:*
> > *the plants and animals that nourish us,*
> > *and all of the individuals through whose labor*
> > > *this meal is brought to our table.*

Then, pause. Link hands if your seating arrangement makes it convenient do so. Alternatively, if the food is already on your plates, you can hold your hands over the plates in an attitude of blessing. Continue:

> *Now let us return our blessings*
> > *to all who have contributed to this meal.*
> *And as we now enjoy this wholesome food,*
> > *so may it be transformed into vital energy,*
> > > *increasing our health and well-being.*

To return blessings, as suggested above, you fill your mind with gratitude. Naturally, you don't know every individual who contributed to the production of the meal, but a sense of gratitude returns energy to the living universe, which ultimately blesses all beings.

As you begin to eat, you might think about the transformative powers at work—the magic of converting food to energy, stimulating your metabolism and revitalizing your body. If you wish to stimulate meal-time conversation, you might also discuss the ways that our foodstuffs embody the four elements of ancient lore: elemental Earth in their substance and their having been grown in the soil, Water in their liquid forms and life's dependence upon moisture, Fire in the sunlight converted by plants, in the transformative process of cooking, and even in the calories and process of metabolism, and the element of Air, which is also present in metabolic processes.

Suggestions for Candles

To accompany your meals, use candles in any pleasing shape, color, or fragrance. Some gift shops carry candles that are colored and scented like comfort foods, such as banana nut bread, pumpkin pie, oatmeal cookies, hazelnut coffee, lemon chiffon, key lime pie, and so on, so you might want to choose one to complement your menu. For general colors, yellow, pink, peach, and orange rouse the appetite and conviviality, while blues and greens promote a tranquil, contemplative meal. If you use candle scent, anointing oil, or incense, fragrances like cinnamon, ginger, orange, lemon, tangerine, or vanilla might harmonize with your planned dinner.

It is interesting to note that, at the end of meals, people in Roman times brought out a pan of hot coals and sprinkled aromatic herbs on them; they believed this improved digestion (as well as sweetened the air), so there is a historical basis for using scent at the table.[3]

5

A Daily Rite of Return

Lighting a candle is a simple way to separate the portion of your day that is dedicated to career and outer world concerns from that which is focused upon home life and family concerns. This is something you can do immediately upon returning home from work, if you tend to bring the tensions of your work life home with you. Also, as Jane Alexander suggests in her book *Rituals at Home*, lighting a candle "signifies that you have returned the heart to your home."[4] Even if you work at home, a ritual pause adds dimension to your day, dividing it into two different phases.

To perform this homecoming rite, you may wish to change from your work wear into comfortable at-home or evening clothes, thank your pets for looking after your house, put away any other items related to the work day, turn on your favorite music, pour yourself a cup of tea, and then light a candle while you say:

> *As I light this candle,*
> *I give gratitude to my Deity,*
> *   and to my guardian spirits.*
> *I have safely come through my work day,*
> *with another chance to explore the path*
> *   that Life has laid before me.*

Now, you might want to pause to review your day. Think about new experiences and things you've learned. Think about the things you have done well. Think briefly also about areas where you could have been more effective; visualize yourself performing these tasks more skillfully the next time around, then put them out of your mind (following Dale Carnegie's advice to shut your cares in "day-tight compartments"[5]).

Now, try to clear your mind by refocusing on the candle flame. Feel its warmth inside your mind, melting your cares away. Breathe deeply in and out for a few moments, until you feel that you are sufficiently relaxed to redirect your energy to your evening chores or plans. You can say:

I am totally refreshed and relaxed,
ready to make the most of my evening.

Then proceed with your normal after-work activities. You can leave the candle burning if you wish. Its cheerful flame may help dispel some of the gloom brought on by "the blue hour," that twilight time that can be especially bleak on early winter evenings. Also, if some of your family members get home later than you, they'll find the candle's fragrant glow to be very welcoming—something that may become ingrained in memory.

Suggestions for Candles

Use any candle color, shape, or fragrance that you find cheering—perhaps warm colors in the winter and cool colors in summer. To help you make the transition between the two phases of your day, you might try candle scents, oils, and incense that are reputed to be "energy balancing," such as lavender, palmarosa, vetivert, sandalwood, and rose geranium.

6

A Candle Rite for Young Families

When I was very young, my mother created a special ritual for the Christmas season: she decorated the dresser (which my brother and I shared) with Christmas candles, knicknacks, and other ornaments, and for a number of nights she lit the candles while we all sang carols. Memories of this little ritual are among my brightest images of family togetherness. Since children cherish such candlelit moments, you might want to burn candles for your own children—not just at Christmas, but other times as well. While lighting a candle, you could say some words like:

> *As this candle casts its circle of light,*
> *so may our family circle*
>> *be blessed and protected.*
> *May we always love and cherish each other.*
> *May we help each other*
>> *through all of the joys*
>>> *and challenges of life.*
> *So it is, and so may we always be.*

When it is time to put out the candle, you could say,

> *It is time to put out this flame,*
>> *and give this candle its rest.*
> *May its light continue to glow*
>> *in our hearts and minds.*

Note that this ceremony can be performed at any time of day, and could be used to signal the beginning of other types of family rituals or activities. However, as with this and any other candle rites you may perform in front of children, make sure that your children understand that they are not permitted to light candles themselves (unless supervised by an adult). Also, so that your children won't be tempted to mimic you by trying to perform rituals by themselves, do not leave any candles or matches within their reach. If performing a candle rite in a child's room, extinguish the candle as soon as the rite is finished.

Suggestions for Candles

Seasonal candles, such as those in the shape of Halloween pumpkins or Christmas trees, are perfect for entertaining children. There are also novelty candles shaped like teddy bears, ducks, mushrooms, stars, and many other delightful forms. For candle scent, fragrances like grapefruit, mandarin, tangerine, lavender, rose geranium, and vanilla are pleasing to children.

7

An Evening Routine

Little rituals can help you wind down your evening. I don't recommend burning candles just before bed, because you could drift off to sleep without extinguishing them. However, a short rite performed a little earlier in the evening enables you to assess your day, plan your tomorrow, and turn your mind toward regenerative rest. Once you have finished your evening's chores or activities, pause to light a candle, and say:

> *The cares of the day-world*
> *are now set aside,*
> *forgotten in the softness*
> *of the lowering darkness.*

Now, visualize yourself drifting off to sleep, sleeping soundly, and then awakening full of energy and ready to tackle all of your next day's duties. Visualize yourself going through an ideally productive day. Then, return your attention to the candle, and say:

> *Be with me please, my Deity,*
> *and all my guardian spirits.*
> *May I be protected throughout the night,*
> *and awaken fully refreshed,*
> *and eager to greet the day.*
> *And as I ask this for myself,*
> *so may all beings everywhere*
> *find rest and comfort.*

Then, put the candle out and engage in some relaxing wind-down activity, such as reading a book or watching your favorite TV show.

Persons who are prone to insomnia will find that evening rituals (performed consistently, at the same time each night) help control the problem by adding to the signals that tell the brain that now is the time to start releasing its sleep-inducing chemicals. Children also benefit from such routines. An hour before bedtime, you could gather your children and perform a shortened version of this candle rite by changing "I/me/my" to "we/us/our," and omitting the lines about cares and work (if these are not relevant to your children), as well as the visualization. You could use this rite to begin your children's bedtime story time. In her book of family rituals, Margie McArthur suggests lighting a candle at the beginning of your children's story hour, and then putting it out afterward, as a way of framing this special time together.[6]

Wishing happiness (in this case rest and comfort) for all beings is a Buddhist custom. For those who might raise the objection that this and similar references in this book would mean wishing success to criminals, other evildoers, and even demons, I must point out that in Buddhism, the attainment of happiness assumes the attainment of virtue—so a wish for happiness is also a wish for goodness.

Suggestions for Candles

The warm glow of a candle will help you relax. Candles and holders decorated with moons and stars would be a nice touch. You might want to use blue-, green-, or turquoise-colored candles, and scents that are popular in relaxation blends, such as lavender, ylang ylang, vetivert, tangerine, chamomile, marjoram, nutmeg, clary sage, palmarosa, and rose geranium.

8

Bathing by Candlelight

The candle-lit bath is an image of romantic luxury that is often portrayed in movies. However, there is no reason why you can't indulge yourself in such a bath—perhaps after a rough day, or to savor the moments when you find yourself with a little free time. To make a little ritual out of the bath, you will want to set the mood. Set a candle or candles near the tub, but in a safe place. You may want to turn off all other lights, play soft music, burn incense, and assemble your finest botanical bath products. You can also add fragrant herbs to the bath (such as chamomile, lavender, rosemary, marjoram, sage, or thyme) by tying three to four tablespoons of them sachet-style in a muslin bag, a square of cloth, or an old nylon sock that can be tied to the faucet (for the water to run through) when the bath is being poured. It may seem like you are steeping yourself in a cup of tea, but that's okay. If you have essential oils, you can add a few drops after the water has been poured, so the essence won't be dissipated in the steam. (Avoid oils known to irritate skin—see appendix D for a list). In her book on essential oils, Colleen K. Dodt[7] devotes a section to the use of oils in baths; some of the oils that she recommends are rosemary, lavender, lemon, peppermint, ylang ylang, patchouli, bergamot, frankincense, and rose geranium. She suggests that these oils be used sparingly, and that it is helpful to dilute essential oils in a carrier oil, or in a quarter cup of milk or cream before adding to the bath.

When ready to bathe, you can light a candle or candles, and say,

> *The flame of this candle*
> > *lights a time and a space set aside,*
> *a time and space*
> *for comfort and renewal.*

Then, as you are relaxing in the water, you may also want to say,

> *As this water flows over me,*
> > *my cares are washed away.*

Envision the spiritual essence of the water penetrating and purifying your every cell, and carrying away all worry and impurity. (A purifying bath is known as a "lustral bath.")

By the way, as a loving gesture, you can also prepare candlelit baths for your lover, and for your children. My friend Margie McArthur used to make a ritual of her children's bath time. To help them wind down for the evening, she would also arrange "grounding" stones such as obsidian and hematite around the edge of the bathtub.[8]

Suggestions for Candles

Use any pleasing color or candle scent. You can coordinate your candle fragrance, and incense if you wish, with your other bath products.

9

A Dream Candle

When dreams, as messages from the unconscious,[9] are acknowledged, the unconscious will reward you with even more interesting dreams and possibly some synchronicities in the form of fortunate coincidences. Therefore, when you have been presented with a meaningful dream, you can say "thank you" for this gift by lighting a candle upon waking. (This is especially effective on dark winter mornings.) As you light the candle, you can say something like:

> *I thank you for this night of dreaming,*
> *and beg the gift of understanding.*
> *May questions be answered,*
> *wishes fulfilled,*
> *and wonders revealed.*

Then, if you keep a journal, write down or tape record the details of your dream. Also, think about whether you can incorporate something from the dream into your day—for example, if the color blue somehow figured in your dream, you could wear a blue shirt that day, or if you dreamed about walking in the woods, stop by a local nature park. As Henry Reed, author of *Edgar Cayce on Channeling Your Higher Self* has pointed out, "Bringing something out of our inner experience outward into our lives completes a circuit of energy."[10] Extinguish your candle after about ten minutes, or after you have completed your journal entry, so you can turn your thoughts to the needs of the day.

Suggestions

Some good colors for dream candles are indigo blue for visionary power, blue green for regenerative fantasy, or silver for the mysteries of moonlight. Candles in the shape of moons and stars can be used to hint at the realm of dreams. If you use scented candles, oil, or incense, you could use rosemary, clove, ginger, clary sage, or juniper, as these are good fragrances for refreshing your memory. (However, you may prefer to omit the oil and incense if you are slow to wake up or eager to record your dream.)

10

A Rite for Incubating Dreams

You can perform a little ceremony, using the same dream candle mentioned on the previous page, to "incubate" your dreams. Sometime during your day or evening, in some quiet moments, you can light the candle and say:

I call upon the powers of my Deep Mind.
Please grant me a dream of wonder,
that my questions be answered,
and wishes fulfilled.

If you have a special question or concern that you'd like your unconscious to go to work on, state it aloud and/or write it down (preferably on a piece of fancy stationery) and set it under the candle. Later, you can fold the piece of paper and place it under your pillow. Then place a pen and more paper by your bedside, so that you will be able to write down whatever you remember of your dreams immediately upon waking.

On the other hand, if you would like to experience lucid dreaming, where you are aware that you are in a dream and have some ability to control it, gaze into the candle flame as you say,

As I dream,
so may this flame appear to me,
a reminder of my power
to shape my fantasies.

Continue to gaze into the flame until you can hold it in your mind, with the understanding that the candle will appear in your dreams to alert you that you are dreaming.

Whatever your goals, you can put the dream incubation candle out after about ten minutes, as that is enough to send your message to the unconscious. Perform these rites well in advance of bedtime, and never allow a candle to burn while you sleep.

Suggestions

Some good colors for dream candles are indigo blue, blue green, and silver. If you use scented candles, anointing oil, or incense, you might try cedar, juniper, frankincense, sandalwood, or patchouli to help you connect with your inner world, nutmeg or clary sage for vivid dreams, or melissa (lemon balm), which is reputed to induce golden dreams.[11] (You could also sip some lemon balm tea.)

It is just as effective to do this ritual earlier in the day, because the dreaming mind is more likely to respond to issues that have been brought up and set aside, than issues that have been worked over before going to sleep.

If you want to create a dream altar, objects in the shape of moons and stars would be appropriate, as would glitter and confetti, sprinkled about to represent the glamoury[12] of dreams. Gemstones such as amethysts, moonstones, and clear quartz crystals can be scattered on the altar to enhance your dream world connection. You can include images of wise men or women (for accessing the wise one within), as well as angels or other types of guardian spirits. Jungian analyst and *cantadora* Clarissa Pinkola Estés personifies the intelligence that generates dreams as "the Riddle Mother."[13] If this has resonance for you, and you have some artistic talent, you could make a doll or statue to represent your concept of the Riddle Mother (or, if you prefer, "Father"). Also, you might include some objects or symbols that relate to past dreams (for example, if you sometimes dream about bears, you could place a teddy bear on your altar).

Rites for Self-Improvement & Mind-Body Connection

Through rituals, we can influence our unconscious minds to effect important changes in our attitudes and behavior. Indeed, the very lighting of a candle signals a commitment to action. The rites in this section combine candle lighting with visualization and other psychological techniques for self-management.

11

Self-Confidence and Success

Success, and the type of confidence that generates success, isn't entirely based on individual effort. While it is important to cultivate diligence, skill, and know-how, so much depends on one's connection with other people. Most successful people display a genuine liking for others. Because they know that most people are friendly and understanding, they are willing to take chances, to express themselves, and to let their light shine in front of others.

Here is a ritual to turn up your inner light and radiate it outward, trustful that the light within others will respond. Light a candle and contemplate its flame. Imagine that the flame is pulsing and growing. Now, place both hands around the base of the candle, and imagine a tiny seed of a flame igniting within your being—perhaps in your solar plexus area. Breathe in and out in a comfortable but rhythmical manner, imaging that seed flame within you as pulsing and growing, growing a little larger with every inhalation. Say to yourself:

> *Light within me, glowing and growing.*
> *Warmth within me, glowing and growing.*
> *Radiance within me, glowing and growing.*

Feel the light. Feel the warmth. Feel the radiance. Then, image that flame grown so immense that it suffuses your entire body and being, and sends its light radiating outward. Imagine yourself as a sun, a star, whose light enlivens the world around you. Then, say to yourself:

> *My light sent outward*
> *lights up the light within others.*
> *My warmth sent outward*
> *warms up the warmth within others.*
> *I walk in light, I extend my warmth,*
> *for I am a radiant being.*

When you feel you have concentrated on this visualization long enough, extinguish the candle or let it burn if you wish. Later, you will be able to amplify your confidence and charisma by mentally recalling the image of the candle flame, and then picturing your own star flame. If you wish, you can practice turning on the radiance by going to some public place and walking about while doing this visualization. You could also try this at work. If you own a business, visualize people drawn in by your own light, and by the light with which you infuse your product and service, through the love and care you put into it. As you do so, maintain an open, welcoming attitude toward other people, seeing the good in them, seeing the inner beauty.

Suggestions

Use any candle you prefer; a candle that glows in a soft, warm shade of pink, peach, yellow, or orange would create an image of radiance, while a gold candle denotes public recognition. For candle scent, oil, or incense, use orange to promote communication, vanilla or ylang ylang to enhance attraction, coriander, bergamot, bay laurel, West Indian bay, rose geranium, petitgrain, lime, myrrh, or lavender for a sense of confidence and well-being, other traditional "success" fragrances like cinnamon, frankincense, or ginger, or any fragrance that boosts your sense of self-esteem.

12

A Candle for Managing Stress

Candle burning is a practice that has become popular with persons of both sexes, and of all ages and walks of life. When you ask people why they like candles, they commonly respond that the presence of a lighted candle reduces stress. Here is an exercise that takes the stress-relieving powers of a candle a step farther: you pour your stress into the candle to be burned up, then take some good energy back from the candle, to relax and revitalize you. Light the candle and say,

As I light this candle,
my stress flows from me,
flows from me, and into the candle,
burned off, transformed,
converted to light and warmth.

Then clasp your hands around the base of the candle or its container, and visualize your stress as a gray mist that flows from your body and into the candle. Continue grasping the base of the candle while breathing in a relaxed and rhythmical manner. Maintain the visualization until you feel that a significant amount of stress has been released. Then, let go of the candle, and cup your hands over it, a few inches above the flame (at a safe distance, but close enough to feel the warmth), while saying:

I draw from this candle,
its comforting warmth,
warmth that flows to every cell,
relaxing, restoring, reviving.

Concentrate on the sensation of warmth, feel it drawn through your fingertips, into your hands and arms, and through your body. Warmth pours into every tense or tired muscle, relaxing it, reviving it. Warmth suffuses your entire body, filling you with the glow of well-being. When you feel that you have had enough, extinguish the candle or allow it to continue burning if you enjoy the ambience.

Later on, if you are at work or elsewhere, you can recall the image of the candle flame, picturing it changing to a ball of energy that spreads warmth to your tensest areas, or just gives you an over-all sense of comfort.

Suggestions

Any candle will help reduce stress, but you may prefer shades of blue or green for relaxation, or yellow, pink, or peach for comforting warmth. Also, some may choose to perform this rite with two candles: one for releasing stress and one for drawing warmth. If you can choose candle scent or anointing oil, or use incense to accompany this rite, this is a situation where the powers of aromatherapy can be especially helpful. While any pleasing fragrance seems to alleviate stress, lavender is the aromatherapists' top choice, because it is both relaxing and reinvigorating. Some other fragrances with these qualities are patchouli and ylang ylang. Vanilla, bergamot, cedar, orange, tangerine, sandalwood, clary sage, marjoram, and rose geranium have also been recommended for stress relief.

13

A Candle for Burning Anger

Anger is a good thing when it drives us to action against evil and injustice. However, whether it is justified or not, anger is counterproductive when it clouds objectivity, clear thinking, and decision making. Anger can also poison the spirit. If this is a problem for you, you can transmute anger by giving it over to a candle. To do this, take an inscribing tool such as a small knife, a nail, or an awl, and, in very small lettering, cover your candle with words or symbols describing the nature of your anger. (If you use a jar candle, just inscribe the exposed portion.) Then, light your candle while saying:

Into this candle I pour my anger.

Grasping the candle with both hands, visualize your anger as a stream of energy, flowing out of your body, through your hands, and into the candle. When you feel you have achieved a clear visualization, continue:

As this candle burns,
my anger is transformed
into pure life energy.
May it serve for truth.
May it serve for wisdom.
May it serve for justice.

If after saying the last words above you do not yet feel calmed, continue to repeat the last three lines until they reverberate like gongs in your mind. Then you can close by saying something like, "So it is and so shall it be." Then, go wash your hands with scented soap, in cool water. It is good if you can allow the candle to burn down completely. If not, you can put it out and relight it later. It is not necessary to repeat the ceremony itself, unless the anger wells up again.

Suggestions for Candles

You may want to choose a candle in a color that objectifies your anger—that is, makes it visible and solid to your eyes. Thus, you could use red for a hot-headed anger, or black for frustration with immovable obstacles. On the other hand, if your anger is tangible enough for you, you may prefer a white candle to represent the pure energy to which you intend to transform it, or blue or turquoise for calm and healing energies to contain it. For candle scent, oils, or incense, strong fragrances are recommended. Patchouli is good because it is said to calm anger and quiet wrath,[1] petit-grain "calms anger and reestablishes trust,"[2] and neroli transforms negative emotions. Also, because simmering anger is a form of self-jinxing, you may want to try scents that are traditionally used for hex-breaking, such as anise, bergamot, rose geranium, vetivert, lemon verbena, pine, or rosemary.

14

An Exercise of Will

Throughout life, a person needs to summon will power for many things: breaking bad habits and instilling good ones, sticking to diet and exercise, tackling unpleasant chores, dealing with difficult people, learning to say "No" to the excessive demands of the outside world, and much more. Fortunately, in the cultivation of self-betterment, there are many techniques that you can add to your repertoire of self-motivation devices, (including some of the other rites in this book). On top of all of these, however, you can overhaul your entire self-image by visualizing yourself as a new or improved person—a person of will. You can work to build up this idea of yourself by lighting a candle and performing a rite such as the following: gaze into the candle flame and say to yourself,

> *Let this flame affirm my purpose,*
> *for I am a man* [or woman] *of Strength,*
> *I am a man of Will,*
> *I am a man of Power.*

Think about the traditional concept of will, which combines a sense of purpose with a solid character and readiness for action. Then repeat:

> *I am a man of Strength.*
> *I am a man of Will.*
> *I am a man of Power.*

Think about people you know who have a high level of self discipline and are quick to take action on things that need to be done. You can also think about archetypal characters who exemplify will power, such as characters from mythology, film, comic books, and so on. Then repeat:

> *I am a man of Strength.*
> *I am a man of Will.*
> *I am a man of Power.*

Now, envision yourself embodying an archetype of will power. Imagine what kind of person you'd be and what you could accomplish if you had the world's most powerful will. Repeat:

> *I am a man of Strength.*
> *I am a man of Will.*
> *I am a man of Power.*

Now, picture yourself going through your day and exercising your will in small ways, such as getting out of bed ten minutes earlier, postponing a snack by twenty minutes, picking up the phone to make an appointment for a check-up that you've been putting off, or chipping away at some other area of resistance. (To aid these visualizations, you could make a list of the things you want or need to do.) After allowing a few minutes for these visualizations, extinguish the candle while saying:

> *I am a man of Strength.*
> *I am a man of Will.*
> *I am a man of Power.*
> *So it is, and ever shall be.*

Know that in having performed this rite, in itself it is an act of will. Because you had to make some effort and set some time aside to do it, this ritual reinforces your image of yourself as a person of will. Also, as you go about your day, whenever you push yourself to do a little more, amplify your sense of pride by giving yourself mental congratulations and reaffirming, "I am a man of Strength. I am a man of Will. I am a man of Power." Dwell on the genuine pleasure you take in your new self-image.

Also: for a symbolic object to help activate your image of Will, you could clutch a bloodstone in your right hand as you perform the visualizations. Bloodstone represents grounded energy and firm resolve.

Suggestions for Candles

To boost will power, use any candle color, shape, or fragrance that you find energizing and uplifting. The color red summons energy, and orange stands for mental power and purposeful action. Fragrances that are especially good for conscious focus and self-control include cedar, coriander, basil, clove, ginger, grapefruit, lime, petit-grain, peppermint, frankincense, and rosemary. You could also sprinkle some allspice over your candle, as it is reputed "to add strength to one's will and determination."[3]

15

Three Rites for Managing Bad Habits

The previous rite, for exercising will power, can help with bad habits. However, following are several ritualized approaches for dealing with certain types of bad habits. Because there are so many different kinds of habits, as well as so many different kinds of people, not all techniques will work for all persons or problems. However, if you do try one or more of these rites (or any of the other habit-breaking techniques that are out there), it is important that you faithfully perform the rites or techniques often enough and long enough to give them a chance to work. Sometimes people will accept defeat, saying "I've tried everything," when in fact they didn't try anything long enough. Also: for this kind of work, it is best to focus on one problem at a time. Even if you have an entire catalog of bad habits, pick one to work on and don't worry about the rest of them while your focus is on this one. (Warning: these rites are insufficient or inappropriate for lethal habits or addictions such as alcohol or drug abuse—for those you should seek immediate professional intervention.)

For Repetitive Behaviors

This rite is for the type of minor habit-behaviors that may recur throughout your day or week. It requires lighting a candle every time you commit the behavior in question, and setting that candle in a prominent place. You could keep one candle on hand and light it every time you repeat the habit, burning it for about ten minutes and then extinguishing it. However, it would be better if you could buy a jumbo box of votive candles or tea lights, especially if you engage in this behavior often during the course of your day (unless you are trying to perform this rite in your workplace, where having one small candle in your cubicle may be acceptable, but having a bunch would make you look weird). The advantage of lighting a candle every time you commit the offending behavior is that it makes the problem, as well as your desire to end it, so much more visible to both your conscious and unconscious minds. If your repetition of the habit results in a large cluster of burning candles, the effect is all the more dramatic.

To perform this rite, light a candle as soon as possible after engaging in the problem behavior (even if this interrupts whatever you are doing), saying:

> As this candle burns,
>> so is this unwanted impulse
>>> purged from my body and mind,
>>> and melted away to nothing.

If you are using only one candle for this rite, extinguish it after five or ten minutes or so, and be prepared to relight it the moment the problem behavior reoccurs. If you are using a group of candles (something you would most likely be doing at home), allow them to burn until you have to leave the house or go to bed. Each day, start afresh, (you don't have to relight candles for the previous day's transgressions). If or when the behavior recurs, start lighting any candles left over from the day before, and add new ones as needed until the problem is under control.

Suggestions for Enhancing This Rite for Working on Repetitive Behaviors

It doesn't matter what color candle you choose; however, white could be used to represent your desire to be purified of the habit. Alternatively, you may be able to come up with a color that in some way represents the habit, such as red if you have a problem losing your temper, or purple if you cuss too much (a play on the term "purple prose"). There may be some other ways to link the candle with the habit: for example, if the problem is nail-biting, you could dig your fingernail into the candle each time before you light it. If you can choose your candle scent, or if you wish to use anointing oils or burn incense along with this rite, you can use any fragrance that you prefer. Because a bad habit could be viewed as a type of hex, you might try some of the scents used in folk magic for unhexing, such as citronella, anise, pine, myrrh, rosemary, lemon verbena, and vetivert.

———————

Two Variations of a Rite for Detaching
from Certain Types of Habits

A number of habits stem from our discomfort with silence, solitude, or temporary in-activity, which breeds the nervous compulsion of trying to fill every moment with some kind of stimulant. This can apply to habits of an oral nature, such as smoking, coffee drinking, and snacking, as well as to other attempts to fill the senses, such as watch-ing/listening to too much TV or radio. There are two ways that you can chisel away at some of these problems: (1) find a substitute stimulant that is more beneficial (or at least has fewer negative side-effects), or (2) reprogram your attitude so that you can be more comfortable with the state of nonstimulation and learn to value quietude itself.

Lighting a candle can help you create space within which you can work on your attitudes and explore the sensation of emptiness. Let's say, for an example, that you are trying to cut back on your intake of caffeine. You could make a decision that you can drink all the coffee you want, but before each cup of coffee, you must first drink a cup of herb tea as your substitute substance. When you have prepared your tea, light the candle, and say something like:

> As I light this candle,
> I signal a space set aside,
>   a time for health and wholeness.

Sit before the candle and sip your tea, while trying to be totally mindful of the act of drinking tea. You can also think about how you are doing something good for your body. If the tea has medicinal qualities, think about these added benefits. Savor the taste of the tea, even if nothing tastes better to you than coffee—even if you don't much like the taste of the tea. (Why do some of us feel that to satisfy our senses, we must always have what we most crave, or that things have to have exactly a certain taste or be a certain way?—that can be another type of unproductive attachment.) When the tea is finished, put out the candle and get yourself a cup of coffee. This way, your deprivation issues won't be able to get too much of a hold on you, since you are giving them some of what they want. Nonetheless, you will find your daily coffee intake will diminish, because a busy person has time to drink only so much fluid in a day. (Do not burn the candle while you drink coffee, because for your pur-pose, only the tea should be dignified and privileged with ritual.)

The second method for detaching from habits like coffee drinking (or certain others) is this: when you feel the compulsion to reach for a cup of coffee (or to indulge in some other habit), stop yourself and wait for a short time (which you have designated in advance) such as five or ten minutes. Light the candle and say:

> *As I light this candle,*
> *I signal a space set aside,*
> *a time and a place for emptiness.*

While you are waiting out this, say, ten-minute period, be mindful of what it feels like to not be drinking a cup of coffee (or doing whatever), even if it does not feel very good to you right now. If your craving is intense, just acknowledge it and say something like, "Yes, I really would like a cup of coffee right now, and I will have one when ten minutes are up." But then go beyond that and say, "I am not drinking anything right now, and this is what not drinking anything feels like." If it does not feel good to you, engage in some contemplation and inner dialogue to investigate the reasons why you think that everything has to feel good. You may surprise yourself by finding that under your intense scrutiny, the not-good feeling dissolves and gives way to an okay feeling. Engage in other self-talk to help you to better accept and explore the experience of nonstimulation. Give yourself a mental pat on the back and pump

up your pride in yourself for achieving ten minutes of stoicism. Think about how it feels good and satisfying to exercise will power and self-control, even if only for a few minutes, and you will gradually find yourself exercising more control over more extended periods of time, and in other areas of life. Extinguish the candle and get your coffee (or whatever) when your time is up.

Also: at other times during your day and week, when you are not engaging in your habit, but are nevertheless enjoying yourself, pause and say, "Here I am, I am not drinking coffee (or doing whatever), and I feel perfectly fine." Concentrate on what feeling good in the absence of the habit feels like, so you can call back the memory of this feeling.

Suggestions for Enhancing This Rite for Detaching from Certain Types of Habits

You can use any color that seems symbolically appropriate for you, or you might try white, dark blue, or black, as these colors represent absence, silence, and nothingness in different cultures. If you use candle fragrance, anointing oil, or incense, you might try some scents that are known for promoting a sense of determination along with feelings of well-being, such as lavender, clary sage, juniper, grapefruit, or petitgrain, in order to emphasize the idea of well being in the presence of absence.

A Rite for Very Resistant Habits
(or Addictions or Obsessions)

When habits or other problem behaviors are rooted at such a deep level that behavior modification or the exertion of will power doesn't seem to be enough, it becomes necessary to seek the help of higher powers. Serious habits can be an expression of underlying emotional issues. For example, a person who snacks too much could be doing this as a form of self-medication, to calm his (or her) frazzled nerves, while outbreaks of cursing could reveal that a person has a simmering rage, perhaps because he feels that circumstances prevent him from taking charge of his life. Naturally, you should get professional medical and psychological therapy for serious habits (as well as addictions and obsessions), while also trying to re-engineer your life circumstances

in order to achieve greater happiness and harmony. But while you are seeking therapy and making other changes, you can perform the following rite to call for some
extra help in breaking your habit or problem behavior.

To perform this rite, you need but a single candle. When ready, light it and say the
following, (or similar words, modified to better reflect your situation):

> *As I light this candle,*
> > *I call upon you, my Deity,*
> > > *and upon my guardian angel,*
> > > > *and all good spirits.*
> *I call upon you too,*
> > *spirits of my ancestors,*
> > > *from whose strengths I would draw.*
> *I call upon you, for I must break free*
> > *of this habit* [or addiction or obsession],
> > > *that causes so much torment.*

Briefly describe the nature of the behavior, then continue:

> *Please help me free my mind,*
> > *that I may see far and soar high,*
> > > *through the bluest of skies.*
> *Please help me free my body,*
> > *that I may know the best and fullest*
> > > *of life's experiences.*
> *Please help me free my spirit,*
> > *that I may drink from the deepest depths*
> > > *of soul-stirring waters.*
>
> *Please hear me, help me now.*
> *And as this candle burns,*
> > *so let my troublesome impulses*

and unwanted desires
be burned off and be as nothing.
Let all harmful habits be gone from me,
gone from me now,
and in the absence of these behaviors,
I celebrate myself as a free and joyful being.

Close the rite by saying:

I know that my Deity and guiding spirits
are ever beside me,
and I thank you for hearing me, and helping me.
So it is, and so shall it be.

Then, extinguish the candle, or allow it to burn as long as you wish. It would be well to repeat this ritual every morning and evening. Also, you can burn the candle (without going back through the whole ritual) at regular daily intervals, set aside for contemplating how unproductive or destructive the behavior in question can be. You should do these things even when you are not regularly engaging in the behavior, in order to prevent it from recurring.

Suggestions for Enhancing this Rite

You can choose any candle color that seems suitable. White can stand for the purity you desire, as well as connection with spiritual force. You could also select whatever color could symbolize the habit in question or its underlying source; alternatively, you could choose a color representing the state of mind you hope to achieve by freeing yourself from the problem behavior. If you want to use candle fragrance, anointing oil, or incense, you can use any fragrance that is pleasing or seems appropriate. Benzoin, frankincense, cedar, juniper, bay laurel, myrrh, and sandalwood would be good choices because they promote a sense of connection with higher forces.

16

A Rite to Help Motivate You to Exercise

Most of us know that we should devote time to regular exercise, but sometimes it's difficult to summon the motivation. However, burning a candle while doing some visualizations can help your resolve. To build enthusiasm, it is a good idea to perform the following rite for a few moments each morning and evening, as well as before or in conjunction with your exercise sessions. When ready, light the candle and say,

> *The ignition of this flame*
> *signals my desire to exercise.*
> *Exercise enables me to achieve*
> *my fullest expression of health*
> *and beauty* [or handsomeness].
> *As I light this candle,*
> *I focus my mind on exercise,*
> *I focus my heart on exercise,*
> *and I focus the will of my body on exercise.*

Now, pause to visualize yourself going through all the steps you must go through to prepare for your exercise or sport, whether that requires dressing a certain way, getting out any special equipment, going outdoors or to the gym, and so on. Visualize yourself easily putting aside your other distractions and resisting any temptations in order to do this.

Now, regardless of how reluctant or lethargic you may feel at the moment, visualize yourself performing your exercise skillfully, energetically, and enthusiastically. Most importantly, visualize yourself *enjoying it.* Recall to your mind any past occasions on which you were genuinely enjoying your exercise, and your self-esteem was riding high as a result. Now, visualize some of the end results you are seeking, such as having a toned body and vibrant health, being able to fit into the last pair of jeans you have outgrown, and so on.

Finally—and this is equally important, visualize your choice of sport or exercise as part of *the beautiful life* (not a painful obligation to stay in shape). You can picture yourself as one of the "beautiful people," performing this exercise in beautiful settings. In other words, reframe your mental images to view exercise as a luxurious privilege enjoyed as a part of a smart, sexy, active lifestyle. (Exercise is, in fact, very important to many celebrities and members of the privileged classes, who value the active life and would genuinely prefer to play a game of tennis or soccer than sit in front of the television with a bag of chips; activity is actually a part of their identity.) Other ideals of the good life may focus on some sport or exercise as part of a family or cultural tradition, as part of a life in tune with nature, and so on. Use some mental talk to convince yourself that exercise is essential to your identity and ideal lifestyle, and that you crave it so much that there's nothing else you'd rather be doing.

Now, say aloud:

> *This is the good life.*
> *This is the active life.*
> *This is the beautiful life.*

If you have any special motivational affirmations, you can include them at this point.

If this is just an advance motivational session, you may now extinguish the candle, or leave it burning a little while if you wish. If you are now turning to your exercise, you can let the candle burn if you are exercising in your home, but extinguish it if you are going out. As you extinguish the candle, you can say,

> *Though I extinguish the candle,*
> *my desire continues to build and burn,*
> *and I am ready to start*
> *burning energy and calories.*

As with any good habit that requires a lot of motivation to instill, or bad habit that requires hard work to break, it is a good idea to mentally recite your affirmations and practice your visualizations in any of your off moments: for example, when you are standing in line at the grocery store, when you are waiting for someone in the car, when you are relaxing with a cup of tea, and so on. Then, the lighting of the candle is a more effective final signal of intent, because you have already been training your unconscious mind on your objective.

If you are so busy that you feel you don't have a right to exercise (often the case with housewives and other busy people who can't justify detaching themselves from the 1,001 chores demanding their attention), you must realize that time spent on exercise pays off. In addition to improving your health, exercise boosts your energy so that when you get back to your work or chores, you actually accomplish more.

Suggestions

Choose any candle that you like. Red is an ideal candle color because it stands for high energy and vitality; orange is also good because its combination of red for energy and yellow for mental focus concentrates will power. If you have your choice of candle fragrance, or if you use anointing oil or incense to enhance this rite, choose any fragrance that you find energizing, or try some determined, high-energy scents like basil, bergamot, peppermint, cinnamon, coriander, ginger, lemon, grapefruit, or lime. If you find inspiration in the magic of gemstones, try fingering and contemplating a bloodstone while performing this rite, as its color and symbolism can set your mind on energetic determination. You can also carry it in your pocket for an extra psychological boost while you work out.

17

Health Supplement Booster Rite

An Ojibway (Chippewa) Indian belief holds that the things of nature possess individual "soul-spirits." In the case of medicinal herbs (or other substances), it is believed that healing takes place when the soul-spirit of the person in need connects with the soul-spirit of the herb or other substance that he or she is taking. Among modern practitioners of alternative healing, it is a common practice to "empower" substances, such as herbs, beverages, foodstuffs, and so on, by using affirmations and visualizations to imbue them with energy, encouraging them to better work for healing and other purposes. With these two concepts in mind, we can approach medicines, vitamins, and foods with a magical attitude, activating their healing power and applying them to whichever of our health conditions need attention. Since many of us take medicine or health supplements as part of a regular routine, we can enhance their effectiveness by performing little rituals to direct our unconscious minds to make the best use of these substances. While it is not a necessary part of such rituals, when you are able to include the lighting of a candle, it sends an extra signal to the unconscious that this is something that requires attention.

In *Ojibway Heritage,* Basil Johnston explains that ". . . each plant being of whatever species was a composite being, possessing an incorporeal substance, its own soul-spirit. It was the vitalizing substance that gave to its physical form, growth, and self-healing. This inner substance had a further power. It could conjoin with other members of its own species and . . . with other species to form a corporate spirit" [33]. For this reason, a person picking medicinal plants would say a prayer, like "Your spirit, My spirit, May they unite to make, One spirit in healing" [82–83].

When you want to make a ritual of taking vitamins or medicine, you can do the following: first, light a candle if you are in a place where you can conveniently do so, and hold both of your hands near the flame, though at a comfortable distance. (If you are not using a candle, just go to the hand-rubbing in the next step.) Feel the warmth of the candle as it imbues your hands with power. Second, rub your hands together, feeling the warmth of their friction.

Then separate your hands by a few inches and visualize yourself shaping a ball of crackling golden energy between them, working it up using hand motions, rolling it around between them. Visualize the ball of energy glowing and pulsing and becoming stronger. Feel its warmth.

Now, turn your attention to the substance to be empowered. If you are taking pills, cup them between your hands. If a drink or food item, hold your hands over it in an attitude of blessing. Visualize that ball of energy entering and concentrating itself in your pills, food, drink, or whatever, while you say the following or similar words:

> *This substance is empowered*
> *to work for the benefit of body, mind, and spirit.*
> *My physical being receives its physical virtues,*
> *and my ethereal being receives its ethereal virtues,*
> *as my soul-spirit receives and unites with*
> *the soul-spirit of this substance.*
> *So it is, and so shall it be.*

Once your medicine, herbs, or vitamins have been ingested, the candle can be extinguished, or you can let it burn a little longer to create ambience and impress upon your unconscious mind the healing connections you have made.

Suggestions

Consider choosing a candle in a color that seems appropriate for the health benefits you seek. Among other possibilities, green is the traditional color of healing, growth, and regeneration in the west, while blue is a healing color in Asia. Use red for vital energy, pink, peach, and soft shades of orange for the "glow of health," or white for psychic energy. If you also wish to choose your candle fragrance, or to anoint your candle or burn incense, any scent

In the Mahayana tradition, the Buddha of healing is known as Bhaisajya-guru, sometimes called the "master of medicaments" or "Master of Healing, the Lapis Lazuli Radiance Tathagata." He is portrayed with his lapis lazuli medicine bowl, and in Tibetan artwork, he has deep blue skin. He presides over the Eastern paradise. [See Demiéville; also see Birnbaum 50.]

that is pleasant or energizing is suitable. Because this rite involves eating or drinking, you might want to choose a wholesome fragrance such as vanilla, orange, lemon, or tangerine; these fragrances also have warming qualities and promote well-being.

Suggestions for Beverages

If you are taking pills, you might want to take them with a special drink, out of a special goblet reserved for this purpose. (You could use a goblet coordinated with your healing candle color.) However, there are some medications that can't be taken with certain drinks, (for example, some antibiotics cannot be taken with milk products, some pain killers can't be combined with alcohol, and some herbals should not be taken with blood-thinning medication), so you will want to make sure that whatever you drink is appropriate. Otherwise, among the healthful beverages, orange juice is good because it is described as "liquid sunshine," though papaya juice may be better for some people because it is easier to digest and is reputed to help against allergies. Cranberry juice has antibiotic qualities; if you are not over-fond of the taste of cranberry, you can mix one part cranberry juice with two parts ginger ale. There are many choices of herbal teas (and many have their own magic), while green and black teas are good antioxidants. And of course, there's nothing wrong with water, flavored, perhaps, with a slice of lemon.

18

A Rite of Healing

One of the most common reasons for performing candle rites is the desire to raise healing energy for oneself and others. At any given time, most of us have someone in our circle of family and friends who could use some healing, and many of us also have chronic conditions that we are concerned about. Consequently, there has been much experimentation in the area of ritual healing, especially since the efficacy of prayer, meditation, and visualization in healing has been backed up by clinical research.[4]

The following candle rite uses a general purpose visualization that can be applied to many different types of conditions. Although it is written as a ritual for self-healing, you can perform it on behalf of other people by changing some wording and forming a strong mental image of the other person when visualization is called for. Also, feel free to change any other wording and choose the visual images that best suit your condition, as well as your spiritual orientation. When ready, light a candle and gaze into its flame as you say:

> *I call upon you, my Deity,*
>> *and upon all angels of healing,*
>>> *and helping spirits,*
>> *and the forces of good energy and growth*
>>> *that give life to this Universe.*
> *I also call upon the powers within me,*
>> *as I ask for healing.*
> *Please help me build the energy I need*
>> *to heal* [describe the afflicted body part or system,
>>> or the nature of the illness].

Look at the image of the candle flame until you are able to hold it within your mind. Now, transfer the image of that flame, visualizing it glowing deep within your afflicted body part, if there's one particular area that needs healing. If your illness affects several systems or is a whole body illness, just picture the flame (or a ball of white light or other healing color) deep within your body; in keeping with some Asian traditions, you may want to picture it within your solar plexus, about two inches over your navel. Then say:

> *The healing energy glows*
> > *like a starseed within me.*

Taking as much time as you need to visualize things carefully, imagine the flame transmuted into a glowing light within you, pulsating and slowly expanding until its warmth and light permeate every cell of the afflicted part, or every cell of your body. Say:

> *I feel the warmth and vitality*
> > *as the power of healing glows*
> > > *and grows within me.*
> *The power of healing*
> > *radiates throughout me.*
> *Healing that purifies my every cell,*
> > *at the deepest physical and ethereal levels.*
> *Healing that boosts my strength and energy.*
> *Healing that restores my* [name afflicted parts or systems] *completely.*

Continue to visualize the powerful energy that restores your body or its parts to health and wholeness, or visualize other aspects of the healing process at work. For example, if you are fighting an infection, you might visualize the disease/germs as little waxen beads that are being melted and gently expelled by the healing warmth. You can choose any other imagery that you relate to, but make sure that you always picture the healing energies or factors as immensely powerful, and the disease factors as feeble and easily overcome.[5]

When you feel that you have spent enough time at this, you can close the rite by saying:

> *I now close this rite,*
> > *with thanks to my Deity,*

and all helping spirits,
> *for the forces of healing continue*
>> *to rebuild and restore my body* [or afflicted part]
>>> *to perfect health.*

You can extinguish the candle, or leave it burning if you wish. Upon extinguishing the candle, you can say:

As I go about my day,
> *and as I sleep at night,*
the forces of healing
> *are ever at work.*
They continue to guard me
> *against all threats*
>> *to my body and being.*
So it is, and so it continues to be.

It is a good idea to relight the candle or perform other visualizations when you are able to do so (some therapists recommend three times a day). However, even when

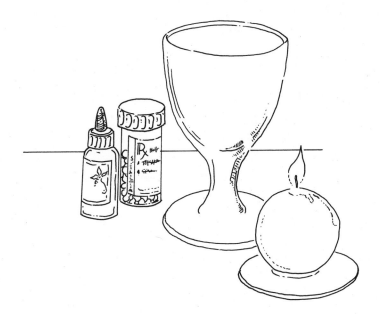

you don't have time to redo the whole ceremony or do other mental exercises, simply relighting the candle will help to fuel the healing energies already at work by reigniting the memory of this rite.

Suggestions

For the purposes of this ritual, a simple white candle will do, because white stands for purity, as well as the white light that is often used in healing visualizations. However, you may choose any other color that you feel is appropriate for the condition in question. Perhaps the most commonly used colors are red for regaining vitality and fighting disease, green for generating soothing energy and the repair of tissues, blue for calming nervous conditions (also the color of healing in Asia—associated with the Buddha of the Eastern Paradise who is called the "Master of Healing"[6]), and yellow for the cheer and confidence to get through surgery or illness. If you want to direct energy toward a condition that is especially difficult or long standing, a large candle or a series of votives may be useful. If you can choose your candle fragrance, and/or if you are using anointing oil or incense to enhance this rite, you can use any fragrance that you prefer, or you might try bay laurel, cedar, cinnamon, eucalyptus, juniper, lemon, lemon balm, mint, myrrh, pine, olive, peppermint, rosemary, or sandalwood, all of which have been associated with health and healing. (However, consult the pages on essential oils and safety at the end of appendix D, as certain oils—even those considered ideal for general healing purposes—have been alleged to aggravate certain conditions.) If you seek healing for a specific condition, you could consult some herbals to see if there are oils (and also incense) made from herbs that are commonly recommended for your condition, as this will help you connect with the etheric essence of the healing herb.

If you have the time and space, you might also want to construct a healing altar. You could include religious icons, a bowl of whatever herbs are traditionally applied to your condition, and gemstones. (If you aren't familiar with crystal and gem lore, you can make an intuitive selection—I have found that suffering persons have a tendency to be attracted to the gemstones most recommended for their condition.) Also, if you have access to Southwestern art catalogs or stores that sell little silver or pewter "milagros," (as votive images of body parts), you might be able to find objects that represent your problem areas. Also, you could improvise—for example, a fancy valentine to represent the ideal health of your heart.

Rites for the Working Life

The need to participate in the work-a-day world and find meaning in our personal occupations is key to our physical and psychological survival, so the rites in this section are designed to make these challenges a little bit easier.

19

A Prayer for Meaningful Work

The Roman philosopher Seneca declared that "Work is the sustenance of noble minds," and the Victorian essayist Thomas Carlyle said, "Blessed is he who has found his work; let him ask no other blessedness."[1] However, when work is stressful, discouraging, or unrewarding, we must find ways to turn it into a creative challenge or an opportunity to serve the Higher Powers—whether we are pursuing long-term careers or just biding time until finding better work. Prayer and ritual can turn work into an opportunity to be in the employment of the Higher Powers. To cultivate this frame of mind, light a candle and say:

> As I light this candle,
>   I affirm the dignity of work,
> that I may burn with enthusiasm
>   for my own work.
> I call upon my spiritual forces:
> please help me achieve my best performance
>   by helping me align myself
>   with the creative life of the universe.
> Let me realize my own work
>   in the working harmony of the universe.
> I give gratitude for chances
>   to explore my potentials,
> and I ask for greater opportunities
>   and deepening experiences.
> Let my work forge stronger connections to others;
> through my work, may I bring joy to others,
>   and make a difference in this world.
> As I do my work mindfully and skillfully,

> *so let my labor be valued,*
> *and abundantly rewarded.*
> *And as I make my work*
> *a unique expression of who I am,*
> *so may I have an abundance of energy,*
> *ideas, and resources.*

You may want to customize this ritual by adding some affirmations citing specific qualities or perks that you want to bring out in your own work (for example, "My job enables me to travel"). The ritual art of affirmation involves making positive statements, stating the things you desire as already manifested—even when they are not "true" in a literal sense. This is a magical mindset that enables you to access and reformat your holographic reality. Even if you are in an exploitative job, reframing your attitude can give you the insights you need to bring about changes or locate better opportunities, and it creates an aura about you that makes you a more desirable candidate for promotions and other jobs.

If you do not have a job, positive affirmations about working or a ritual such as the one above can magically prime the pump for employment. Also, you could perform an act of "imitative magic" by getting into part-time volunteer work, especially work that is close to the type of employment you seek (for example, if looking for work as a musician, you could give free performances at community centers), as this serves as a living affirmation that you have work.

Suggestions

Use any color or shape of candle that suggests the type of work you do, or the type of work you wish to do, (such as yellow for mental work, green for health care, and so on—see appendix B for color symbolism). A green candle can represent steady work, a white candle is good for opening to all possibilities, and a multicolored candle could stand for work that enables you to express many different aspects of yourself. If you choose candle scent, anointing oil, or incense to accompany this rite, use any pleasing fragrance, perhaps a high-energy fragrance like orange, lemon, lime, cinnamon, clove, ginger, bay laurel, West Indian bay, peppermint, patchouli, or vetivert, or try rose geranium or ylang ylang, both of which have been recommended for job seekers.[2]

20

Refocusing Yourself after
Life's Minor Disruptions

No matter how well you plan your day, interruptions are sure to take place. There you are, humming along nicely, then some person, situation, or event intrudes, requiring you to drop everything. When you finally get back to your work, you may have lost your place, your mood, your will, or the clarity of mind to follow through (especially if you had put a lot of time and energy into getting psyched up for some task that was tedious or unpleasant). It's no wonder that one of life's greatest frustrations is not being able to finish what you started.

The following refocusing rite can help restore your concentration. Once the interrupting element is gone and you are ready to get back to work, light a candle on the table before you. Pause for a moment to remind yourself what it was you were supposed to be doing, then visualize yourself going back to your task, and going through all of its necessary motions. Now, gaze into the candle flame and start counting backward from 200 (which may take about ten minutes) or from 100, depending on whether you feel that a longer or shorter transition period is needed. As you do so, empty your mind of all other thoughts except the counting and the sight of the candle and flame before you. (If you prefer, you can close your eyes while counting, but try to hold the image of the candle and flame in your mind.) Know that when you complete your count, your mind will be sufficiently cleared and ready to shift your full attention back to its necessary task. You may then extinguish the candle or allow it to continue burning if you'd like a little extra help in reminding you to stay focused.

Suggestions

Since disruption can be a daily occurrence, you might want to get a big candle for this one, and keep it near your work area. Any candle will do, but it is nice if you can find a multicolored candle with interesting swirl patterns or other colored designs, because lines and patterns have a way of fascinating the unconscious mind; gazing at them can actually help you relax and refocus. You can also put a plain candle into an ornate patterned glass holder to get this effect. If you can choose your candle fragrance, or if you are using anointing oil or incense to enhance this rite, any scent that helps you relax and focus your mind is suitable. You might try rosemary or basil, which are famous for sharpening the mental faculties, or lavender, which simultaneously relaxes and re-energizes the mind; ginger, clove, petitgrain, and peppermint are also good for mental clarity.

For those who like to work with gemstones, you can perform the same rite by concentrating on the lines and swirl patterns of an agate, rather than on a candle. This is something you can keep in your pocket and do at work or in other places where you can't have candles.

21

Simple Exercises for Energy and Inspiration through the Power of Color

The challenges of our daily life and work require energy, inspiration, motivation, and enthusiasm, but too often these things are in short supply. Fortunately, some very potent qualities of energy can be summoned by concentrating on pure, vivid, intensive colors—and this power of color is something that can be activated with the help of a candle.

Following are some exercises to help you experiment with color visualization. You may want to try different colors on different occasions, in response to different needs. You can strengthen your concentration by repeating affirmations or key words. You can also visualize yourself breathing in the chosen color; this is a technique recommended by Raymond Buckland, who says, "When working with projected colored light, it is advantageous to visualize the very air itself as being colored and hence to breathe in that colored air."[3] If you are a person who finds pure color visualization difficult, you may find it easier to visualize some familiar object in the desired hue.

When you do these exercises, you could set a timer for a specified amount of time, perhaps five or ten minutes, if your time is limited. Otherwise, you might try a technique that I find very effective: make a firm commitment that you will sit in place and continue the color visualization until your energy is so thoroughly recharged that you actually feel moved, that is, seemingly compelled by some greater force, to get up and attack your work with full focus and enthusiasm. Don't worry that you'll be sitting there all day. Trust the magic of color. You will know that the technique has worked when you suddenly find yourself doing whatever it is you need to be doing, without having thought about getting up.

For these exercises, choose brightly colored candles, and if you can find candles whose colored wax is translucent enough to "glow" when the flame is lit, this will enhance your ability to immerse yourself in the color. Also, you can create a focus area, surrounding your candle with other objects in your chosen color, such as flowers, gemstones, colored glass bottles and vases, and so on.

A White Candle for White Light

White light is the energy most commonly used in visualizations for healing, protection, spirituality, and so on, because it represents the purest qualities of light itself, and all of the colors that light contains. When you want to summon your inner spiritual force to purify and harmonize your energy nature, while also charging yourself with a renewed sense of possibility, light a white candle, and say:

> *White light, bright light,*
> *Spiritual Power flows through me.*
> *I am transformed by the essence*
> *of pure white light.*

Then, concentrate on the candle and on the idea of white light, until you can hold white light in your mind. Visualize yourself breathing in the white light. Know that as it fills your consciousness, it transforms your entire being.

Note that because white contains all colors and allows other colors to be projected upon it, you can also use a white candle for the other exercises in this section, when you lack candles in the colors you desire. You just have to use more imagination to visualize the other colors in your mind.

A Red Candle for Fast Energy

Red is considered to be the most energizing color. When you need some pep, light a red candle, while saying:

> *Red hot, red blood, vital power.*
> *Energy flows through my blood and body.*
> *Energy flows through my mind and spirit.*

Then try, quite literally, to see red. Fill your consciousness with the color red, as you also visualize yourself inhaling it. Because of its association with blood, you can visualize red energy circulating through your blood stream to infuse all of your body systems with its fullest potency. To help the energy circulate, you might try doing some simple arm exercises, such as raising your arms while spreading them arc-like, to touch your fingertips over your head, (for about sixty repetitions). You can also boost your energy by gently pinching and pulling your ears. (Reflexologist Mildred Carter states that the reflex points in your ears "will stimulate a renewed flow of life force into every part of your body when pressed, pulled, and massaged."[4])

An Orange Candle for Creative Will

The color orange combines thought (yellow) with energetic force (red), so it is a color that you can use for will power or creative determination—something you may need when you face difficult tasks or difficult people. Light an orange candle while saying:

> *Vital, creative, vibrant,*
> *the power of mind and body*
> *are focused through my will.*

Then, concentrate on the color orange. Savor its stimulating effect as you visualize yourself breathing it in and holding it in your mind.

A Yellow Candle for Mental Power

Because yellow is the color of mental activity, promoting the ability to awaken the mind, concentrate, and make connections, it can help students, creative people, and others who work with their minds in one way or another. Light a bright, sunny yellow candle, and gaze at its yellow glow while you say:

> *My mind is filled with yellow radiance.*
> *My mind is awakened with joyous aliveness.*
> *All my being is filled with light.*

Now, hold the bright, glowing color yellow in your mind; breathe it in, and allow it to flood your consciousness.

A Green Candle for Regenerative Energy

When you feel so depleted that you need to restore yourself at a very deep level, choose a bright green candle. Light the candle and contemplate it for a moment. Then say:

> *The greening power of the Life Force*
> *refreshes me completely.*

> *I am fully renewed and relaxed.*
> *I am alive with the energy of life.*

Then, fill your mind with the color green. You can also mentally repeat some key words like "refreshed and relaxed," or you could repeat the word "viriditas," a term used by the twelfth-century mystic, Hildegard of Bingen, to denote "the greening power" which has been described as "the energy of life which comes from God, the power of youth and of sexuality, the power in seeds, the reproduction of cells, the power of regeneration, freshness, and creativity."[5]

A Blue Candle for an Even Quality of Energy

If your problem is not a lack of energy, but too much nervous energy, select a blue candle. Blue is a versatile color with a range that includes turquoise blue, light sky blue, and indigo, so use your intuition to decide which you are most attracted to (lighter blues help relaxation and ease worries, greenish blues have a healing quality, darker blues promote concentration). Light the candle and say:

> *My mind is calm and clear.*
> *My mind is calm and focused.*
> *Bright as a bright blue sky.*
> *Clear as clear blue water.*

Then, close your eyes and concentrate on the ideal of blue that you have chosen. You could also repeat key words like "calm and focus," or some evocative phrase, such as "the blue sky."

A Purple Candle for Acting on Your Ideals

As the color that combines vision with action, purple can help you with the energy and determination to go after your dreams. When you need extra encouragement to prove yourself, light a purple candle while saying:

> *My visions are powered*
>   *with the energy of my imagination.*
> *I am a dreamer and I am a doer.*
> *I bring my dreams to life and fullness.*

Then, immerse yourself in visualizing the color purple, breathing it in, and allowing its inspirational power to carry you away.

Suggestions for Fragrance

Because odor stimulates important areas of the brain, most pleasant fragrances are energizing. (At the same time, they can be soothing and relaxing because they have a "balancing" effect.) Thus, for scented candles, anointing oil, or incense, you could use any preferred fragrance, or one that is especially reputed for its energizing qualities, such as rosemary, ginger, basil, peppermint, lemon, or vetivert. Where possible, you might want to use fragrance with distinct color associations, such as vanilla for white candles; cinnamon for red candles; citronella or lemon for yellow candles; orange, tangerine, or ginger for orange candles; lime, eucalyptus, pine, or mint for green candles; or lavender for purple candles. Also, if you experience "synaesthesia" (which is the perceived blending of the senses), or if you know someone who does, you might be able to discover some new color-fragrance associations.

In choosing key words for visualization and meditation, I like to use words that have layers of meaning. In addition to evoking an ideal of calm and clarity, as well as many other images, "the blue sky" also resonates to the healing poem of that name by Gary Snyder [*No Nature* 76–80].

22

Rite of Procrastination

This rite uses the human tendency to procrastinate, that is to put off doing certain chores, in a novel way. However, I want to emphasize starting out that I am not promoting procrastination as a way of life. If you don't want your problems and anxieties to build, it is important to take care of items of business, chores, and other obligations as soon as they crop up. However, even the most organized persons sometimes have things that they keep putting off. Therefore, when you recognize that the time has come to get on to something that you have been delaying, you can perform the following rite to help you build the resolve. You will find that when you finally stop procrastinating about a matter and get out and *do it*, the store of mental energy that has been building around your continually postponed intention is suddenly released, lifting your spirits, and possibly even generating some good luck.

Part of the psychology and playful magic of this rite is that you don't immediately commence on whatever it is that you have been avoiding. Rather, you write down what needs to be done, lay out whatever materials are needed for your project, announce your intention to carry through by performing the simple candle ceremony provided, and then, before you actually get started on the thing you've been putting off, you go do something else—something just for fun. In this way, you will have made something of a deal with your child self, that part of you which wants to play and balks at work. You are indulging its whims, and the result will be a reaction in the unconscious, an exchange of energy, which will subsequently carry through to complete the thing that needs doing.

Depending on the nature of the job to be completed, this rite can be performed in a day or distributed over several days' worth of time. However, if the job is so big that it is likely to take several days to do, it may be better to break it down into steps or components, and perform a new rite for each phase of the process. If there are actually a number of things that you have been putting off, you should perform this rite for only one chore at a time;

do not plan to dispatch a bunch of odious chores in one session. However, if after you've performed your designated chore, you find that the momentum automatically carries you forward to take care of a few other things—then by all means, go for it!

To prepare for this rite, first select a candle that you can expect to burn longer than the amount of time needed to complete whatever it is that you need to take care of.

Next, get out one of your best pens and a sheet of fancy stationery, then write down, generally, what it is that you need to do. It is best if in writing it down, you can also break the chore down into its smallest components and arrange them in list form.

Then, prepare a special area (preferably clean and free of distraction) in which to perform your task, and lay out any tools or materials you will need. For example, if you need to write a long letter to a relative, set out your stationery and then address and stamp the envelope for good measure.

When ready to perform the rite, light the candle and say aloud:

> *I light this candle*
> > *to affirm my desire and intent to*
> [describe the task you need to perform].
> *The time is right, and I am ready.*
> *As the candle burns, my energy builds.*
> *Ere this candle burns out, the deed is done.*

Put the candle in a place where it can burn safely. If you need to go to bed, leave the house, or otherwise leave the candle alone for a while—it's okay to put it out. Just say:

> *I extinguish this candle*
> > *for the time being,*
> *but the energy continues to build.*
> *When I return,*
> > *I shall rekindle the flame,*
> *and the power goes on building.*

Now, go do something that you enjoy. Something just for fun. Something that wastes time. Something that you would normally feel guilty about doing. Don't worry about the other thing, the task that you need to perform. *Trust* your unconscious to go to work on it. *Have faith* that the energy will mount, and it will get done. Don't be surprised if before you're through goofing off, you find yourself mysteriously compelled to dig into the project about which you are procrastinating. You may even astonish yourself by completing the task before you know what happened. If not, spend a few more hours playing around, but set an alarm clock or timer to go off at a designated time, after which you resolve that you will return to your project.

If your candle should burn out before you complete your task, just dedicate a new one, repeat the words affirming your intent, and keep going. If you finish your chore before the candle is gone, extinguish it, save it, and use it again, the next time you need a push to get something done.

Suggestions

An orange candle will work well for this rite because orange represents will power, combining the color qualities of thought and action. Otherwise, you can choose a candle in whichever color, for you, symbolizes the nature of the task you want to perform. Some examples might be pink for initiating social contacts, black for dealing with obstacles or difficult persons, and yellow for studying for an upcoming exam or research project. Alternately, if you have an old candle that has become rather smuddly looking with the passage of time, this rite is a perfect opportunity to burn it up. The idea of clearing out something old and jaded will support the idea of clearing out old business. If you want to dress your candle, use any oil that is pleasing to you, or try something with a reputation for energizing, such as peppermint, orange, lime, basil, grapefruit, coriander, cinnamon, or ginger. You can also burn incense of the same kind (or any scent pleasing to you), play music, and do other things to create the sense that this is a time and place set aside for a special work.

23

A Candle for Honoring Your Competition

Competition is one of the hard realities of the modern workplace. Whether you are self-employed, or work for a large corporation or institution, or whatever your occupation may be, the need to stay competitive may well be one of your prime stress factors. Fortunately, you can rise to the creative challenges that competition presents by striving for greater innovation and excellence, by acknowledging the ways in which your competitors excel, and by having faith that if your competition edges you out in certain areas, you will be able to carve out new and better niches for yourself. Whenever you feel threatened by the forces of competition, you could light a candle and say:

I honor and bless my competition.
There is room for all of us in this world.
There is prosperity for all of us in this world.
Let my competition be my inspiration
to strive for excellence.
Let my competition be my inspiration
to express my true creativeness.
Out of this competition,
may new ideas be born.

Naturally, you can modify the above wording to better describe the qualities that you want to evoke.

Suggestions

White is a good color for candles because it denotes purity of intention. Alternatively, you might choose some color that you associate with your competition, (for example, colors from company logos). If you use candle scent, oils, or incense, some fragrances suitable for high-minded purposes include cedar, juniper, benzoin, bay laurel, clove, sandalwood, sage, frankincense, and myrrh.

Rites for Problem Situations & Personal Sorrows

Despite the desire to stay positive, we all must deal with minor aggravations and nagging worries, as well as the things that are genuinely tragic in human life. However, candle lighting has long been a gesture of hope and comfort, and this section contains candle rites for working through some common sorrows.

24

Burning Through Your Troubles

From time to time we all have problems that come up and have to be dealt with, obstacles that have to be overcome, sorrows that have to be acknowledged, and hard times that just have to be lived through. At such times, burning a candle while trying to put your anxieties into words can be comforting and therapeutic. The following rite is designed to help you objectify your problem or problems by assigning them to a candle, to symbolically burn them away. At the same time, it is a way of giving your cares over to the Higher Powers and calling upon your guiding spirits to help lighten your stress, give you fortitude to do what must be done, and encourage matters to work themselves out.

When ready to perform this rite, light a candle while saying:

> *As I light this candle,*
> *I give my problems over to the Higher Powers,*
> *to the Living Universe.*

At this point, you may visualize your problems transferred into or embodied by the candle or envision yourself as having put this problem aside by giving it over to the candle. Then say,

> *As this candle burns,*
> *So let this problem* [describe problem]
> *be burned and dissipated.*
> *So is it diminished.*
> *So is it worked out.*
> *So is it forgotten.*

It is best if you then leave the candle burn for as long as possible, extinguishing it at night or when you leave your house or premises, and relighting it the next day or upon your return, until it is burned down completely. Meanwhile, take whatever physical actions are necessary to deal with your problem, but beyond that, don't worry about it or think about it any more than is necessary.

Suggestions

To perform the above rite, select a candle that can symbolize your problem or sorrow. A white candle is suitable because any image can be projected onto it like a movie screen, blue can stand for the blues, black and brown can stand for impenetrable obstacles, and red for anger. Also, if you can find candles in muted or murky tones such as avocado, mulberry, cinnamon, and so on, these are good at representing the turbid feelings that can accompany problem situations. If you can choose your candle scent, or if you use incense and anointing oil, you can use any strong or pleasant fragrance, because the diffusion of scent further symbolizes the release of troubles, to be dissipated by the atmosphere. Neroli (orange blossom) and mandarin are considered superior for transforming fear and worry, and returning hope. Because of the desire to banish troubles, you could also try fragrances used in folk magic for "unhexing," such as anise, citronella, lemon verbena, clove, rosemary, myrrh, pine, and vetivert.

> I do this kind of ritual for myself often enough, and I know it sounds funny, but I find that when I'm picking out and purchasing my candle, I can already feel my ball of stress dropping to a lower level of my stomach—perhaps because my unconscious, as well as spiritual powers, are already starting to process the problem.

Although, like most of the rites in this book, this one is designed so that you can easily and readily perform it with any candles that you have on hand, you will find this particular ritual experience more cathartic if you go out and buy a special candle for this purpose. The act of going forth to seek just the right candle to embody your problem turns into a quest that adds extra energy and psychological significance.

25

A Rite for Banishing Negativity from a Place

Sometimes unpleasant experiences or encounters with negative people can leave an "icky" feeling in a place. Also, sometimes a person's own fears, doubts, and sorrows can generate an atmosphere of gloom that seems tangible and as menacing as some sort of toxic cloud. Fortunately, candle burning is a time-honored method for dispelling such energies. For negative energies of a fairly mild nature, it can be enough to light a candle for blessing your space as described on page 9. However, if you sense that the negativity about you is thick and tenacious, the following rite can help you clear the air. This rite can be performed using only a candle, though there are a number of additional motions that you can go through, depending on how much time and privacy you have, the nature of the space that you need to cleanse, and your own intuitive assessment of how much is necessary. (Note: this rite is primarily designed to dispel negativity from an area; if you feel a need to purify your person on a deeper level, see the rite for purification on page 129.)

It is good if, prior to this rite, you can scrub your hands, arms, and face, or even take a bath or shower, while visualizing the power of elemental Water washing through your ethereal self, washing away any negative energy that is clinging to you. Then, to begin the rite, light a candle and say:

> As I ignite this flame,
>> and light this candle,
> the power of elemental Fire suffuses me,
>> to purify and protect me.

Cup your hands near the candle flame. As you feel it warming your fingers, visualize a warming energy spreading through your hands and arms, spreading through the rest of your body, through skin and bones and blood. While doing so, breathe deeply and rhythmically, in whatever manner is comfortable and relaxing for you. As the warming energy spreads, you can picture any of the negative energy that has touched you as a gray mist that is pushed outward and away from you, as power is exhaled through your pores. However, the elemental warmth stays with you, its radiance creating a protective glow around you. Then say:

> *As this candle burns,*
>> *the power of purifying Light*
>>> *extends its energy outward,*
>>>> *to protect and cleanse this space.*

Then, pick up your candle and walk around your room or rooms, making a counterclockwise circuit of each room (as your space permits), visualizing the power of Light that penetrates every nook and cranny of the space and expels all negativity. (For some of us, walking counterclockwise may feel funny, like going against the grain, but this is a valid traditional method of undoing unwanted energies or situations.) As you do so, visualize the candle projecting an ethereal light that pulses and glows as it starts expanding outward—reaching into every hidden corner—burning, transforming, and purifying any negative energy, then as it pushes outward until it is totally dissipated.

This candle action will probably be enough to cleanse your space, but if you wish, you can also go through some of the following motions, all of which are traditional methods of dislodging negative energies:

- Slam each door several times.

- Open the doors and windows. (If it's chilly outside, you can close them after a few minutes.)

- Make counterclockwise circuits around the space while clapping your hands, ringing a bell, waving a stick of incense, or fanning (in an office, you might be able to discreetly walk around with a homemade paper fan), while saying (or thinking): "By the power of elemental Air, are all negative energies dispersed."

- Make a counterclockwise circuit while tossing pinches of salt and saying, "By the powers of elemental Earth, are all negative energies dispersed."

- Make a circuit with a spray bottle of air freshener or cologne.

- Give the space a thorough and energetic cleaning. Where you can, cleanse windows and other objects with water mixed with vinegar. You can also set little cups of vinegar in the corners, to dissolve any energies that remain or that try to enter the space.

Substances used in folk magic for purification and unhexing often have antiseptic qualities. Vinegar is a staple of the old folk practitioners, so it is interesting to note that researchers have recently verified that vinegar is a potent antiseptic.

Once you have circled your place with candle light (and gone through any of the additional motions mentioned above), return to the center of your space and say:

> *As this candle burns,*
> *it also blesses this space*
> *and fills it with revitalizing light.*

Then, carry the candle through your room or rooms once again, this time moving through each space in a clockwise circuit, while visualizing it charging the atmosphere with the golden energy of blessing. When done, set the candle in a central space, and allow it to burn for as long as is convenient. If you can, allow it to burn down entirely. If you must leave (or go to bed), extinguish it while saying:

> *I now extinguish the flame,*
> *but its protective power remains in place,*
> *neutralizing any unwanted energies,*
> *and continuing to bless this space.*

You can relight the candle later, for continued protection, but it is not necessary to repeat the ceremony.

Suggestions for Enhancing This Rite for Banishing Negative Energies

Any type of candle will do, but a white candle for purity, yellow or orange for light and warmth, or a red candle for the more aggressive power of elemental Fire, would be most ideal. If you can choose your candle, something with a very strong scent

James van Praagh mentions that frankincense, myrrh, and sage "are sensitive to extremely high frequencies and help to clear out dark energies" [95].

would be effective—for the purpose of banishing, it doesn't have to be a pleasant scent. However, fragrances like anise, lemon, lemon verbena, citronella, pine, clove, frankincense, myrrh, sage, and sandalwood would also be good, as these are used for cleansing, banishing, and/or unhexing.

26

A Prayer for Times of Crisis

The lighting of candles is a tradition that has comforted many people through times of crisis. At such times, the candle is a beacon for calling spirits of guidance, as well as a symbol of hope. Following is a simple prayer that you can say when lighting such a candle. The words are necessarily very general, but you can change them or add words that better express the nature of your concerns.

As I light this candle,
I call upon you, my Deity,
> *and upon all protective spiritual forces.*
I thank you for all of the help
> *that you have given me in the past,*
for you have brought me safely to this day,
> *through many trials and hardships.*
Now, I must call upon your help again,
> *for this is a time of crisis.*

Please bless and protect me, my loved ones,
> *and all of the people I care about.*
Please help us summon all of the wit and energy
> *that we will need to work our way*
> > *through this time of trouble.*
Please help us to see and think clearly,
> *and to be more receptive to your guidance,*
knowing that you are ever with us,
> *and have always taken care of us.*
I thank you again,

> *as I affirm your Presence.*
> *So it is, and so shall it be.*

If the crisis is a larger national or world problem, you might want to set the candle in a window, to share this symbol of hope with others, but do make sure there are no curtains or other flammable items nearby.

Allow the candle to burn for as long as the crisis period endures, replacing it when it burns out. However, you should put it out when you leave your house or go to bed. You can relight it later, but it is not necessary to go through the ritual each time you relight the candle, unless you want to.

Suggestions

Use any candle color that you consider appropriate. White is always good because it represents sincerity. You could also choose a color symbolizing qualities that you require in facing the crisis, such as blue for self-composure or red for energy. If you can choose scented candles, or if you use anointing oil or incense, consider a fragrance that will also help you summon the qualities you need, such as lavender for tranquility, or cinnamon or ginger for energetic endurance. You could also use spiritually uplifting scents such as sandalwood, benzoin, cedar, juniper, or frankincense.

27

A Rite for Dealing with Vain Regrets, Anger, or Shameful Memories

Over the course of our lifetimes, we can do a lot of dumb things and hurt a lot of people. Such regrettable actions may include committing faux pas or other embarrassments, doing unintentional injuries to others' feelings, committing small acts of meanness, or missing important opportunities. Other causes for regret may stem from the inability to defend ourselves against things that other people have done, such as cheating, deceiving, insulting, or otherwise harming us, or other types of situations where we may have felt hurt and helpless. Whenever the memories of these deeds or incidents arise, we can experience anew an upwelling of anger, pain, or shame, and some of us develop strident "inner critics" as a result. In cases where we have harmed others, shame and remorse is a healthy thing, because it encourages us to make amends and changes. Embarrassments, misunderstandings, miscommunications, and emotional bumps and bruises to ourselves and others are also a necessary part of the polishing process that is socialization, and also humanization. Sometimes, however, recurring regrets may haunt us beyond reason. Perhaps we've done what we could to right the wrongs and make things up to other people. Perhaps the regrets are over the sorts of things that cannot be undone, so there's no use dwelling on them. Although we may know, intellectually, that we should put these things behind us, that other people have their own regrets, and that the things we're brooding over may actually be quite trivial, for some of us the mental and emotional self-castigation continues. Because it can be so hard to shut off one's regrets, the following candle rite may be helpful in dealing with such issues.

(Note: I want to emphasize that the purpose of this rite is not to let off the hook of conscience those people who have committed terrible crimes or abuses. Rather, it is intended to give ordinary people relief from an inner critic that has lost its sense of proportion in regard to ordinary transgressions.)

When you feel the need, select a candle for the purpose of burning off some of your vain regrets or other painful memories. You will delegate the job of burning off these negative emotions to the candle, which has the power to transform them into a light and pleasant scent. Before you light the candle, hold it in your hands while thinking of some of your regrets, (or pain or anger), then visualize those regrets flowing out through your hands, through your fingertips, and into the candle, which accepts them as fuel. Then light the candle and recite the following words, which you may modify to be more specific to your situation, or to better fit your religious orientation:

> *I light this candle to burn through my pain*
>   [or guilt, rage, shame, regret, etc.].
> *and give it over to the powers of the Universe,*
>   *to transform it into a blessing.*
> *I call upon you, my Deity,*
>   *and all angels and spirits of compassion.*
> *Help me to release this pain,*
>   *as I acknowledge the need*
>   *to turn compassion toward myself,*
>   *as well as others.*
> *I accept that making mistakes*
>   *is part of the active life,*
>   *and part of becoming a true human being.*
> *Regrettable things happen, and*
>   *leave strong emotions behind them.*
> *Sometimes we hurt other people,*
> *and sometimes they hurt us,*
> *and sometimes things happen*
>   *that are beyond anyone's control.*
> *Therefore, let the spirit of compassion surround me*

with acceptance and forgiveness
for myself as well as others.
And now, as this candle burns,
so help it to release my regrets,
into fire and into air
as warming light and pleasing scent.

Then allow the candle to burn for whatever you consider an appropriate or convenient length of time. Turning your regrets over to the Universe through the burning of the candle and the diffusion of its scent frees you to turn your mind toward other things. When you are ready to put it out, say,

I now put away my regret [pain, anger, etc.].
I have duly acknowledged it,
and accepted it as part of the process of living,
so now it is time to move on.

If you light this special candle whenever you catch yourself giving over to regret, you may find that such episodes will occur less frequently. (It is not necessary to repeat the ceremony every time you relight the candle.)

Suggestions for Candles

You can use any color that seems appropriate to your situation; a pink candle could be ideal, showing the red of anger transmuted into the pink of affection and self-acceptance, while light blue could denote the ability to face past errors with tranquility. For the purposes of this rite, it is also good to choose a candle that will release a strong, pleasant fragrance—likewise if you are using an anointing oil or incense to enhance this rite. You might try lemon balm (melissa), neroli, or mandarin, which have the power to drive cares from the mind, or try pine, rose geranium, or palmarosa, whose abilities to turn compassion toward the self and others encourage forgiveness and acceptance.

On the subject of regrets, here are some other things to think about:

- If your regrets stem from things you've done to give others a bad opinion of you, take to heart the words of Oscar Wilde, who is reputed to have said, "You wouldn't worry what other people think about you, if you realized how seldom they do."

- If you are mentally scourging yourself with recriminations, you may ask yourself what punishment a fair-minded judge would dole out to someone else for the same offenses; in all likelihood, the agony you've caused yourself has far exceeded that.

- As a regular practice, or in combination with this rite, try adding two or three drops of tincture of pine (from the Bach flower essences) to your water or tea. As Mechthild Scheffer of the Bach Centre in Germany has explained, "Pine relates to the soul qualities of regret and forgiveness."[1]

- The fact that you feel remorse for things you've done to others shows that you're a basically good person. Many other persons may do the same sort of things without ever giving them a second thought.

- In cases where someone has done something mean to you but won't acknowledge it, you may be hung up because the pop psychology of the latter twentieth century has told us that confronting other people about their transgressions and demanding their apologies is necessary for "healing." Although this may work for some personality types, it doesn't work for everybody, and often isn't even possible. Be aware that the belief in the necessity of confrontation is not universal: in many other societies, confrontation is viewed as a form of "unskillful speech and action," and it is up to individuals to just get on with their lives.

28

A Candle for Grief

The following is a rite to help you with the process of grieving over some major loss or disaster. This is a rite you might wish to perform following the death of a loved one, the break-up of a relationship, a disabling accident or illness, the loss of your home, job, or business, or the experience of some other catastrophic event or personal defeat. (Although this book has also provided some rites for remembering and blessing our departed loved ones, and these can help to soften grief, this rite gives grieving individuals another means with which to face their darker feelings.) This rite does not try to minimize a person's sorrow; rather, it recognizes the walk through a long corridor of darkness. However, it also calls for a star of hope to light the journey ahead. (This rite takes some of its inspiration from an eleventh-century French prayer calling for a star of light to fill darkened spirits.[2])

When you feel a need to perform this rite, light the candle and recite the following, or similar words, modifying them if you wish to better express your own feelings:

> *I light this candle as I look into a wall of blackness,*
> *into a world of darkness.*
> *In the grip of such sorrow,*
> *I feel that no grief*
> *can be as great as mine is now.*
> *As I acknowledge the Darkness*
> *within and around me,*
> *mere words, the comfort of poets and philosophers,*
> *cannot disperse a grief as great as mine.*
> *Nevertheless, I am aware*
> *that although all life is interlaced with suffering,*
> *it is also necessary to carry life forward,*
> *and I acknowledge that some sorrows*

can diminish with time,

for others have discovered this to be so.

And so I call upon you, my Deity,

and upon all good spirits,

and angels of comfort and healing.

Please be with me now,

helping to light my heart with hope,

and faith, and comfort.

O let your light shine through me and before me

like a star of radiance,

like a star that lights a trail through darkness.

Pause for a moment as you visualize an angel, (or a dewa,[6] ancestor spirit, or other spirit of light) who waits for you far ahead, on a road that winds through a dark and desolate landscape. The angel-like figure holds a star for a lantern. Visualize the light of your candle merging with the light of the angel's lantern. You know that you have a long way to go, but the angel will never be too far ahead of you. Know that other angels and loving spirits are also not far off, walking behind and alongside you, even though you may not see them. Then continue the recitation, saying:

In various Asian belief systems, dewas or devas are god-like beings or spirits who exist in more refined states or dimensions; some nature spirits are also referred to as devas. (The word "dewa" means "shining one.")

Though my walk into the future

may seem a long and lonely one,

let it be a journey of transformation,

opening my heart to all others who sorrow,

and carrying me to that place in the future

where a deeper understanding

will enlarge my being.

Then close the rite by saying:

> *I thank you for hearing me,*
> *and for being with me.*
> *So it is, and so shall it be.*

Extinguish the candle or allow it to burn as long as is convenient, knowing that you have made a connection with the world of Spirit, and with the future. You can relight it whenever you wish, as a way of acknowledging your sadness. It is not necessary to perform this ritual again, unless you feel that it helps you face your feelings.

Suggestions for Candles

A black, dark blue, or other dark-colored candle would be appropriate because the action of burning it symbolizes the act of burning one's way through darkness. Alternatively, a white or yellow candle can be used to symbolize the light of hope. If you can choose your candle fragrance, and/or if you plan to use incense or candle-anointing oil, you could try bay laurel, cedar, copal, cypress, myrrh, patchouli, marjoram, sage, or vetivert, as these fragrances can help a person work through darker thoughts, emotions, and imaginings.

29

A Rite to Call Your Soul-Self
Home to Your Body

Many cultures recognize a condition called "soul loss," which can occur when traumatic events have fragmented a person's sense of being, leading to depression, fatigue, confusion, and a loss of center. Indeed, treating individuals for soul loss is an important function of many traditional shamanic practitioners. I believe that people in our own society can suffer from a form of soul loss, too, and it doesn't necessarily take a specific event or trauma to precipitate it. Certain stressful and dehumanizing conditions of modern work life can cause soul separation by degrees, and extreme dysfunction in family life (as is the case when alcoholics or addicts are present in the home) can have a similar effect. A lifetime of compromise and hardship can also bring about this state of alienation. If this theory has resonance for you because you are suffering from such a condition, you should of course be taking whatever steps you can to get into a better environment or line of work, and do whatever else you can to realign your life with the needs of your core self and spirit.[3] However, if you must bide your time, or if you have recently escaped from a bad situation only to discover that your vitality and sense of self haven't yet been restored to you, then the following rite can help.

This rite is best performed when you have an evening of quiet. When ready, take an incising instrument such as a small knife or an awl, and inscribe your name, many times over, on the surface of your candle (or candles). If using multiple candles (as suggested in the tips for enhancing this rite at the end of this section), light all of the candles except your special essence or astral candle, which you will reserve as your focus. You can arrange the candles in any manner that you wish, perhaps placing one in every corner of the house or dwelling, in keeping with the symbolism of calling your lost bits of soul and self home from the far corners of the physical and astral worlds. Then, set the focal candle in some central place, and light it as you recite the following:

I call myself back to myself:
wandering Soul, and wandering Selves
> *and scattered fragments of Soul and Self.*
I bid you return to me now,
> *Soul, and Self, and Spirit.*
Unite with me, Heart, and Mind, and Body.
Let this candle [or candles] *be your beacon*
> *to guide you back to me.*
I call you through corridors of time,
> *and space, and being.*
Fly swiftly home through days and years,
> *and seasons and cycles past,*
drawn in, gathered in, invited back,
> *home to warmth, and home to love,*
>> *and home to light and comfort.*
You wandering spirits that are part of me,
> *made strong through suffering*
> *and wise through experience,*
are purified now
> *by the light of the flame that guides you.*
Rejoin me now, be one with me,
> *whole in Self and Soul and Spirit!*
So it is, and so shall it be.

Then, allow all of the candles to burn for a while as your resume your normal activities, or settle in for an evening of inspirational reading. You can relight the candles every evening, though it isn't necessary to repeat the recitation ceremony unless you want to. You may burn the candles until they are all burnt down, or until you have achieved a re-energizing sense of reintegration.

Suggestions for Enhancing This Rite

You can choose a single plain candle for this rite. However, it will be more effective if you can gather candles—as many candles as you can get your hands on: old, new, and partially used, of every shape, size, color, and fragrance. Beg candles, too, from sympathetic friends, by explaining your need and condition to them. The act of begging for candles is a Mexican tradition, and adds an important quality of magic that isn't easily explained. However, I believe it has to do with the fact that other people contribute to the construction of one's sense of self, so other people have the power to help repair the self—it's a gift of soul that they are able to give, especially when they are willing to listen to your story. (Later, you will want to keep some nice candles on hand in case your friends need to beg the same of you—or just offer a candle when you recognize the signs of soul loss in a friend.) In addition to whatever other candles you can find, it is good to include one in the color you feel best expresses your personal essence. (If you are uncertain, or don't have a strong color preference, see the chart of "astral" colors in appendix C.)

If you have a necklace or bracelet with beads of different colored gemstones, place it around your central candle to further symbolize the integration of many personal qualities, events, and experiences into a unified and harmonious whole. Making a circle of various gemstones will also serve this purpose. If you keep a home altar, you could decorate it with symbols that represent different aspects of your life and selfhood (as most of us have to wear many different hats, and may be many different things to different people). In her book on altars, Denise Linn states that when things representing your different roles and subpersonalities "are arranged in pleasing combination" on a home altar, they "serve as metaphors for integration and harmony."[4] You could include photos of yourself at different ages and at significant stages of your life. You could even incorporate symbols and objects connected with some of your more stressful or traumatic experiences (perhaps enclosed in little boxes), as a way of achieving some acceptance—integrating them so you can move beyond them.

If you can choose candle fragrance, use anointing oil, or burn incense to enhance this rite, choose any scent that is inviting or suggestive of your personal essence, or try anise, lemon, and cinnamon, as these are used to recall wandering souls in Hispanic folk-healing ceremonies.[5] You could also try scents associated with spiritual force, such as cedar, juniper, benzoin, bay laurel, copal, sandalwood, myrrh, and frankincense.

Candle Rites for Special Needs

The rituals in this section engage some of the special concerns of traditional candle burning practitioners, including luck and love. Such rituals call upon the powers of our unconscious minds—as well as our spiritual forces—to help bring about important changes in our lives. Underscoring these rites is a belief in a world in which we all deserve love, happiness, prosperity, and well-being.

30

A Rite for Attracting Luck

Beyond the sort of luck that a person can generate through practical means, such as maintaining a positive attitude, nurturing connections with friends, and striving for excellence, there is a type of luck that acts as a magnetic force. It can attract good things into one's life—including protective influences, social favors, opportunities, and abundance. To cultivate this kind of luck, we can act on principles of attraction, concentrating on luck attracting images and actions. The rite for affirming your good fortune on page 115 will have this effect, but here is another simple ritual, using a candle as a beacon in the same way that a flower acts as a beacon. (This is inspired by the language of Andean shamanism, where the term "flowering" is used in ceremonies for luck.[1]) As you light your candle, say:

> *In the flame of this candle,*
> *a flower of light*
> *draws energy from air*
> *to its circle of fire.*

While gazing at the candle, envision the flame as a flower of fire. Then continue:

> *So is the flame of my spirit*
> *a flower of light,*
> *inviting all good things*
> *to my sphere of life.*

Now, envision an aura of light taking shape about you, glowing, growing, and extending outward so that you can see in it the form of a beautiful flower—perhaps a golden flower of radiance. This is an energy flower of high vibration, (sense the vibration—how it would feel), that attracts positive influences from many different sources. Then continue:

So does my good luck grow.

So does my good luck blossom.

So does my good luck flower.

Leave the candle burning, or extinguish it if you wish, but continue to work on this visualization (with or without the candle) whenever you have a spare moment. Bear in mind that good thoughts and good deeds will make the flower of your spirit more fragrant, attracting greater blessings from the world of Spirit.

Suggestion

Use any shape or color of candle that is potentially lucky for you. You might try a candle in the shape of a flower, or a candle in one of your astral colors (as listed in appendix C). Otherwise, gold, green, pink, and red are luck-attracting colors (in different ethnic traditions), as is white, for white light. If you use candle scent, anointing oil, or incense, use any pleasing fragrance. Some scents associated with luck are orange, tangerine, mandarin, frankincense, cinnamon, cedar, juniper, peppermint, vetivert, and rose geranium. You could also use ylang ylang, whose name means "flower of flowers." To accentuate the idea of flowering, surround your candle area with vases or pots of flowers.

31

A Rite for Changing Your Luck

This book provides several rites for improving one's luck in different ways, including the previous rite for "attracting luck." However, persons who have had a run of really bad luck may want not merely to attract better luck, but to break the cycle of misfortune. We can think of bad luck as a negative feedback loop, so ritual action can take you out of that loop. With the following ritual, you can visualize your bad luck as a substance, and then allow the candle to transform it. This ritual also assures your unconscious, as well as the spiritual powers of the universe, that your bad luck has served whatever purpose it may have served, and that the harmony of the universe will now be better served by a change for the good.

This is a ritual in two parts, so it calls for two candles, one to represent your bad luck, and one for the good luck that you will now invite into your life. Note that the second candle is not to be lit until two days later, to allow the first candle to burn off a bit as part of a transition phase. When ready, light the first candle and say:

> *As I light this candle*
> *I separate myself*
> > *from whatever past luck*
> > > *is bad luck.*
> *Whatever its cause,*
> > *the time for change is now.*
> *Whatever luck is bad luck,*
> *I give it to this candle*
> > *to be burned up, used up,*
> > > *gone forever.*

Grasp the base of the candle and breathe in and out in a rhythmic manner while picturing the bad luck as a gray mist that flows out of your body and into the candle, where it is transformed into light, warmth, and a pleasant scent. When you have spent enough time with this visualization, proclaim,

I open a space, let good luck come in!
With good luck and harmony,
I serve the universe.
With good luck and harmony,
I live in right relationship
with the living universe.

Continue to burn the candle over a period of several days (putting it out whenever you leave the house or go to bed), until it is burned down. Meanwhile, obtain or prepare the second candle, which is to be lit two days after you perform the ceremony with the first candle (that is, on the third day or night). Also, in the days to follow, be creative about priming the pump for good luck by seeking out positive experiences.

On the third day or night, if anything is left of the first candle, light it and repeat the first part of this ceremony. (If the candle has already burned down, that is okay, never mind it.) Then, take the second candle, and perform the ceremony just before this one, "A Rite for Attracting Luck." With most of the rites in this book, it is not necessary to perform the rite more than once, or let the candle continue to burn. However, for the most effective symbolism, it is a good idea to burn the second candle and repeat the ceremony for attracting luck for several days beyond the time that the first candle has been burned down. (This means that for a while, the old and new candles may be burning at the same time.) As for the first candle, once it has burned down, take whatever remains of it to a place that is distant enough to be outside of the area where you live and work, and leave it on a rubbish heap or other place where it can melt into nature.

Suggestions for Candles

For the first candle, the one intended to contain your bad luck, it is good to use a fairly large candle, because your unconscious may balk at the idea that so much misfortune could be properly transformed by a very small candle. (However, it would then be good to use an even bigger candle for attracting good luck.) Use any color that suggests the nature of your bad luck, or use dark or murky colored candles. Alternatively, for the idea of transmuting your bad luck into something good, you might try an orange candle, which is used for changing luck and "opening the way" in some Hoodoo traditions. If you use candle scent, oil, or incense, use any pleasing scent to suggest the idea of something bad transformed into something good, or try a scent used for hex breaking in folk magic, such as rosemary, rose geranium, pine, bergamot, clove, anise, vetivert, or citronella. For the second candle, see the suggestions paragraph for the previous ritual.

Yronwode's Internet discussion sets the history of magical candle burning in context, explaining its early popularity among African Americans, as well as the Hispanic influences [see Internet listings].

Additional thoughts on luck: if you have been unlucky in certain areas of your life, you may nevertheless be lucky in other areas of your life—perhaps in ways that you haven't really acknowledged. (For example, a person could be unlucky in winning at sports, but lucky in attracting good friends.) Do a life review to identify the kinds of endeavors and other things that have been luckier for you, and then concentrate on doing more of those things. As an affirmation, you can repeat the words of Shoma Morita,[2] who asserts that "Effort is good fortune." Also, if by activating other types of luck you are able to let go of some of the desires that have been luck-resistant, you may find that the release of tension effects an opening up, so that luck can flow in through many new channels, enriching all areas of your life.

32

A Candle for Attracting Love

The union of two hearts promotes the harmony of the universe, as well as the wholeness of two individual selves. However, it can be difficult to find a kindred spirit, let alone a suitable mate. To attract a lover who will appreciate and respond to your unique "vibration," you can amplify that vibration by lighting a candle and saying:

In the core of my heart,
a flame burns brightly,
> *burning to give love,*
> *burning to receive love.*
It burns for a love that is pure and true,
It burns for a love that full of passion.

A great love has cosmic implications. As Arthur Versulius explains, "eros is not only an individual urge toward sexual union with another individual, but beyond this a cosmic yearning for completeness that exists throughout minerals, plants, animals, and human beings—and among invisible beings as well, including angels" [70].

Pause to place your hand over your heart, as you think about your heart qualities: warmth, kindness, passion, and a capacity for a very great love. Feel the beating of your heart, and imagine waves of energy that radiate outward, radiating your special warmth, radiating your unique quality of love.

My heart flame's a beacon
> *for the one who is right for me.*
Whether from near or from far,
> *let him* [or her] *be drawn to me.*
Light the path that he may find me.
As I desire, so he desires.
> *And so my true love comes to me.*

Along with this recitation, you might spend some time contemplating what qualities you require in a mate, and, equally important, what you have to offer another person. Also, as Ray Buckland points out in *Advanced Candle Magick*, to attract "someone of the same sensibilities of yourself," you need to think about who you are—so it is a good idea to make a list of your likes and dislikes.[3] Another way to sort out your needs is to write a sample personals advertisement (not for actual publication—unless you want to).

Suggestions

For romantic attraction, a red candle is probably the best, though pink has attractive qualities, and a white candle could suggest opening to all of love's possibilities. A heart-shaped candle will convey a certain ideal of love. For candle fragrance, anointing oil, or incense, you could use your favorite scent (as a way of attracting the right person to you), or use anything that is romantically evocative. Rose, jasmine, rose geranium, palmarosa, and ylang ylang invite lovers, and patchouli, cinnamon, ginger, and vanilla also have powers of attraction. If possible, surround your candle setting with flowers—perhaps orange blossoms or a spray of jasmine.

Also: folk magic provides many candle-burning techniques for attracting love. A common practice is to burn two candles, set far apart, and each day bring them a little closer together. For fun, you could place miniature magnetic Scottie dogs (such as those sold by the Lucky Mojo Curio Company) in front of the candles, and move them as you move the candles closer together.

Magnetic Love Pups," when half an inch away, will "dash at each other and lock with an audible click." (see Luckymojo.com, "Magnetic Dogs").

33

For Strengthening Love

Sometimes you may want to try something extra to rekindle love when you are concerned that your relationship is cooling off, or when you just want to infuse it with a little more passion. To enhance your romantic evenings, you could do the presentation rite, using "a candle for lovers" on page 183. However, if you are self-conscious about performing that rite in front of your mate, or if you want to strengthen love in a mate who is not present, you can also perform it in solitude. Just light the candle and say the same words:

> *I light this candle*
> > *for the love of my lover.*
> *May its flame help fuel*
> > *the fire of passion*
> > *and the warmth of affection*
> > > *between us.*
> *May the light of our love*
> > *be a flame that is ever renewed.*

While doing so, visualize yourself and your mate in your happiest moments, and in your most intimate moments. Vividly imagine the two of you gazing into each other's eyes and connecting on a very deep level—the level of soul. If your mate has actually left, you could also visualize him or her returning and walking through the door in a cheerful, loving, conciliatory mood—and yourself welcoming him or her in the same spirit. (Of course, if you have had a very troubled relationship, especially if abuse, addiction, or cheating has been involved, you would be better off visualizing yourself accepting a break-up and moving on with your life.)

Suggestions

For rekindling passion, red candles are best, though you could use other (or additional) colors for qualities that you want to bring into the relationship (such as blue for fidelity), or burn a candle in your mate's astral color (see appendix C). For candle scent, anointing oil, or incense, use whichever fragrance your mate likes best (you could borrow his or her cologne for this), or try traditional romantic fragrances like rose or jasmine, or lust-arousing scents like cinnamon, ginger, vanilla, patchouli, or ylang ylang. You could also try the old Hoodoo practice of setting your candle in a dish of cinnamon sugar.

34

A Candle for Prosperity

When we embrace a world view of unlimited good, we open many channels for abundance and other forms of good to flow into our lives. We can accept it joyously when we recognize that all of us deserve prosperity, and no one of us—not even one self—is less deserving. You can signal your own readiness for a life of greater prosperity by lighting a candle and saying:

> *As I light this candle,*
> *I give thanks for the natural world's abundance,*
> *and for our worldly society's prosperity.*

At this point, you might contemplate the wonderful abundance we find in nature—from every flower, leaf, and seed, to the sands of the ocean and the vastness of the stars. Also, think about the vast amount of wealth that circulates in the world economy—not to envy it, but to affirm that this awesome plenitude exists, and that all are entitled to participate in the flow of that wealth. Then continue:

> *We live in a world of abundance,*
> *and we are all worthy of prosperity.*
> *So with this light, I welcome prosperity.*
> *So with this light, I welcome abundance.*
> *With prosperity, and with abundance,*
> *I partake in the creative life*
> *of the universe.*

Viewing the circulation of wealth as the circulation of energy, you can picture streams of this energy flowing through your life. Visualize prosperity coming to you through the regular sort of channels that you can imagine, but leave an opening in your imagination, anticipating that prosperity may also come from some unexpected sources.

Suggestions

Use any candle color, shape, or fragrance that symbolizes your idea of prosperity and abundance—a high-quality candle will help bring this symbolism across. In different ethnic traditions, green, red, gold, and yellow are colors of abundance. The most popular prosperity scent is bayberry, although frankincense, allspice, bergamot, cinnamon, clove, nutmeg, pine, mint, and patchouli have also been used for "money drawing" in folk magic. If you have an altar or focus area for your candle, you may want to surround it with coins, jewels, and lots of glittery stuff. (Think about the saying that "gold attracts gold," which has to be appreciated on many levels.)

When you accept that prosperity is everyone's right, there is no need to feel that you are somehow uniquely undeserving, or that you have to convince the Higher Powers by enumerating the reasons why you need financial success and security.

35

A Prayer for Justice

There are times in our lives when we must deal with contentious people, the legal system, or other intimidating bureaucracies. When seeking fair treatment in these kinds of situations, you can light a candle while saying a prayer:

Dear God [or name of your Deity],
I call upon your power,
 for I am seeking justice.
Please let the spirit of Justice prevail,
that all the people involved in this matter
 will act wisely and fairly.

If this is a lawsuit or some other situation where you have opponents, you may add:

In the spirit of Justice,
 may those who oppose me,
  [use their names, if known],
   withdraw their claims.
So may they acknowledge that which is fair.
So may they now do right by me.

If some sort of judgment is to be handed down, you may add:

In the spirit of Justice,
 may those in power
  decide in my favor.
So may I be vindicated.
So may I be fairly rewarded.

Then conclude:

And as I ask for Your help, [your Deity],
    so may the spirit of Justice
        reside in me also.
In my every action and intention,
    may the love of Justice guide me.
In the knowledge that Justice
    upholds the right order of the universe,
so it is, and so shall it be.

You can modify the above wording to make it more specific to your situation, and accompany it with visualizations of justice being served.

Suggestions

Use a white candle for innocence and purity, or use whichever color you believe applies to the situation. (For example, blue could be used where truth or loyalty are in question.) Use any pleasing fragrance for candle scent, anointing oil, or incense. You might try scents like benzoin, bay laurel, cedar, juniper, frankincense, sandalwood, and myrrh, as these promote high-minded motivations.

36

A Prayer for Protection

When we wish for physical protection of ourselves and of our loved ones (and for many of us, loved ones include pets), as well as protection of our homes, our possessions, and our automobiles and other modes of transportation, we can light a candle while saying a prayer. Here is a prayer for general protection that can be combined with a visualization. Light your candle and say:

> *I call upon you, my Deity,*
> *and all protective spirits,*
> *please hear our prayer,*
> *and grant us your protection.*
> *Grant that your protective forces*
> *will ever surround me and my loved ones.*
> *Let us be free from harm,*
> *and guided along the safest paths.*
> *Please build a circle of protection around us,*
> *strong and radiant, glowing with power,*
> *and bright as the light*
> *of this candle flame.*
> *May we be protected at home,*
> *and wherever we go.*
> *And please, also protect our belongings*
> *and the resources upon which we depend.*

Some common visualization exercises involve imaging oneself or one's loved ones surrounded by protective energy, so if you wish, you can add:

> *I thank you for hearing me,*
> *and in my assurance that you are with me,*

I see myself and my loved ones
in your protective light.

Pause and take the time to visualize yourself, your family, your friends, your pets, and the rest, surrounded by a shield of energy. Many people see this energy shield as an egg or cocoon of white or golden light. To extend your visualization, hold both of your hands near the candle and make circular hand motions around it, as if you were molding its radiance into a sphere of energy. While going through these motions, visualize a sphere of glowing light being built around your own body, your loved ones, your home and property, and your car or other conveyance. You can visualize angels or other good spirits helping to envelop you all with this energy. You can also visualize yourself breathing it in as you breathe in the life force of the universe; as you breathe in the energy, it fortifies you from within.

Also: if you have reason to be concerned about the safety of a particular person or pet, you can reword this prayer by saying, "Please grant that your protective forces will ever surround [name], that he [or she] may be free from harm . . ." and then modify the rest accordingly.

Suggestions

White candles are traditional for protective influences, but you can use any color that suggests the nature of the protection you desire. For candle scent, oil, or incense, rosemary, anise, frankincense, sandalwood, myrrh, pine, cedar, cypress, and bay laurel are often used to create a protected environment.

37

Floating Wishes

A charming form of wishing is the old custom of sending a candle down a stream or a river as an offering to the universe. (This practice is especially associated with Midsummer, a traditional time for wishing, as well as a time of year when many of us flock to the water side.) The following rite ceremonializes this beautiful custom, and you can perform it whenever you are near running water.

Get a floating candle, or if you are handy, build a little raft for floating an ordinary votive candle. Inscribe your candle with a "star of creation," which is a six-pointed figure looking like a flower or an asterisk. This represents the matrix of possibilities and opportunities that Fortune holds. Inscribe your candle with any other symbols that you feel are descriptive of your wish. Now, find a spot along a creek or river where you can have privacy as well as easy access. Standing beside the water and holding your candle, say aloud:

This is my special wish!
I give it into the keeping
      of the friendly spirits of nature,
as I send it forth
      into the living universe.

Now, add a few of your own words to describe more specifically what your wish is about. Set the floating candle down in the water. As you watch it being carried away by the current, say aloud:

As this candle is released,
      so is my wish sent forth.
So it is and so shall it be!

If you are ambitious, you can dedicate as many candles as you have wishes. You can also make wishes by floating flowers in the water.

Suggestion

You can use a white candle to represent purity of intention, or pick a candle color that reflects the nature of your desire. If you can choose a scented candle or if you use anointing oil, bay laurel (which is used for wishing[4]), or tangerine, orange, and cinnamon (which are used for luck) would be good fragrances, or you could choose a fragrance that suggests the nature of your wish.

38

Burn-Off Rite

Because I experiment with different candle rites, at any given time I have an assortment of candles dedicated to different purposes. However, as there are many other things going on in my life, I often get distracted for days or weeks at a time, and sometimes forget what certain candles were being used for. Also, there are some candles that I light up every now and then when a particular need arises, but they can become rather jaded-looking with the passage of time. Consequently, it's good to burn off these old candles from time to time; this can symbolize the need to burn through old issues and make room for new beginnings. The following rite can be used for this purpose.

When you decide to do a burn-off, gather your old candles in one place, such as on a table or tray, to be lit all at the same time. Afterward, you can

distribute them throughout your house to enjoy candlelight in every room, or leave them grouped for dramatic effect. It is not necessary to anoint or re-anoint them. Start lighting the candles while saying:

> *As I light these candles,*
>> *their energy is released*
>> *for the benefit and blessings of everyone.*
>
> *All workings are brought to completion.*
> *All troubles are released and forgotten.*
> *All wishes are fulfilled.*
> *And all good feelings are carried forward.*

Leave the candles burning as long as you like. You can extinguish them at bedtime and relight them again the next evening, burning them every evening until the last one has been used up.

Rites for Your Spiritual Being

As symbols of light, warmth, and inspiration, candles are important to many of the world's spiritual practices, including prayer, meditation, purification, and formal ritual. The following section uses candlelight in different ways, to help you engage the spiritual dimension of your existence.

39

A Rite to Affirm the Presence of Deity

If you believe in a personal god or goddess, or if you have some other concept of the creative, animating spirit of the universe as an entity with whom we can make a relationship, a simple devotional practice is the lighting of a "Divinity Candle." This is something that you can do whenever you want to affirm your connection with your deity or other spiritual forces, perhaps while "practicing the presence of God." You can also burn a divinity candle in combination with other candle rites as an extra request for the aid and companionship of Deity in whatever else you wish to focus upon.

To perform this rite, light a candle and say the following, or alter the wording to better express your own religious concepts.

> *Dear God, Great Deity,*
> *I honor you now,*
> > *in all of your names, forms,*
> > > *and manifestations,*
> *whether you are called Lord or Lady,*
> > *God or Goddess,*
> > *Great Father, Great Mother,*
> > *The Eternal One, The Most Merciful,*
> > > *The Most High,*
> > *The Power of the World,*
> > *The Spirit that Moves in All Things,*
> *or by all of the other titles*
> *that people call you*
> > *when they seek to do good,*
> > > *and work for the betterment of self and world.*
> *You have always been with me,*
> > *and you have always taken care of me.*

You are "the fire in the hearth of my heart,"[1]
and I thank you for your Presence,
and ask for your favor and guidance
in all that I do.

At this point, you might want to pause to talk with your deity, going over anything that is on your mind. Allow the candle to burn for as long as you wish.

Suggestions

A white candle is appropriate for this rite as white symbolizes purity and spirit; because white contains all colors within it, it also subsumes all of the powers of creation. However, I also use pink- and peach-colored candles because my experience of Deity is as a warm and loving Presence. Of course, you may use any color that best represents godhood for you. If you can choose a scented candle, or if you wish to anoint your candle with fragrant oil or to burn incense, use any fragrance that you find to be spiritually uplifting. Benzoin, frankincense, cedar, myrrh, sage, and sandalwood are good choices, as they focus the mind on things of the spirit.

When I burn a divinity candle, I experience a Presence that conveys the same sense of warmth and assurance that I have felt ever since my prayers of childhood. However, I have developed an enlarged concept of God, as I have come to understand how as the force for life, creation, growth, goodness, and wisdom in the universe, Deity has manifested through gods and goddesses of all cultures, and how relationship with that which we perceive as the feminine goddess nature is equally essential. When I light my divinity candle, I hold this larger-hearted image of Godhood in my mind.

40

A Candle for Good Fortune

As a thoughtful person, you can find much to be thankful for as you go through your day, and through the year. As a gesture of gratitude, you can burn a special candle to say "thank you" to your deity and your guiding spirits each time that you experience some new stroke of luck, be it large or small. Indeed, one of the best ways to generate good luck is to continually affirm that you are a lucky person. Thankfulness is a magical state because it gives energy back to the universe; whenever we return gratitude, we contribute to a synergy that circulates even more good energy. Therefore, whenever you want to affirm fulfilled wishes, synchronicities, bits of good luck, and other good things in your life, light a candle while saying,

"Good Fortune" is capitalized to represent it as a genuine force or entity, in keeping with the traditions of ancient peoples who sought to cultivate an active relationship with their own "Bona Fortuna."

> *As I light this candle,*
> *I give thanks for my many blessings,*
>> *for I am a very lucky person.*

These three lines alone are enough. However, if you would like a more elaborate ritual, you can add the words:

> *With Good Fortune[3] I have come to this day,*
> *as a person who has grown in love,*
>> *wisdom, and skill.*
> *With Good Fortune I have been greatly blessed,*
>> *for I have* [a] *wonderful* [spouse/children/home/job—*
>> list a few of the things that you are most thankful for].*
> *Good Fortune is with me now and ever,*
>> *as I give gratitude to my Deity*

and engage the living universe
in an exuberant exchange of energy,
in an ever-renewing cycle of blessing.

You may then leave the candle burning, or extinguish it if you wish. You can put it out while saying words like "So it is and so it continues to be."

By the way, each time you perform this rite, you might want to list one or more of your blessings in a "Book of Fortune" (a blank book dedicated to this purpose). Even in a relatively uneventful life there are things to be appreciated, little serendipities, things gained, and recoveries from accidents and illness. Include emotional riches, such as each relationship you have enjoyed, memories of special occasions, and help received from others. Also, write down your achievements and other good qualities. If you don't think of yourself as a lucky person, you may change your mind once you get started on this list. Also, it's okay to go out and manufacture some more luck by participating in pleasurable activities, buying yourself something nice, or seeking out stimulating people. When you have entered 999 blessings, you may experience some special stroke of luck, because 999 is a traditional charm number. Keep your book on hand so that you can read a few pages whenever you are feeling blue, frustrated, or unlucky. You can also recite lines from your Book of Fortune as part of a regular ritual to affirm your luck.

Suggestions

Your candle can be in any shape or color that suggests good fortune and gratitude to you. White is a suitable color because it signifies purity of intention as well as the mystical energy that reflects all of life's possibilities. If you have affinities for Asian culture, you might choose a bright red candle, signifying the most active qualities of good energy and good fortune. Perhaps gold is the color most associated with good fortune in Western culture, though some persons might prefer silver for its mystical associations. Because you might display this candle and use it often, you might also want to decorate it. Consider affixing little sun, moon, and star-shaped sequins or other small charm symbols to it. Alternatively, you could inscribe the candle with a large *X* representing the rune "Gebo," here used to portray the joyful exchange of energy between the self and the universe. If you can choose your candle scent, or if you use anointing oil or incense for this rite, use any substance that is lucky for you, or try bay laurel, West Indian bay, bergamot, juniper, cinnamon, nutmeg, orange, or tangerine, as these have traditional associations with good fortune. If you want to create a special altar arrangement, surround your candle with objects and symbols of things that have been lucky for you.

The rune Gebo means "gift," and with all runes, there are many levels of meaning. [For more about this rune, see Aswyn 36–40.] In ancient cultures, the exchange of gifts established a ritual relationship, and certain mutual obligations were expected. In this rite, energy and gratitude are exchanged for good fortune, and there is also an implicit understanding that the thankful person cultivates a generous spirit.

41

A Rite to Help Prepare for Meditation

The benefits of meditation are well-known. Aside from its ability to reduce stress and promote healing, meditation enables you to achieve greater mental focus and control, explore the nature of your consciousness, and increase your awareness of your spiritual nature. With higher levels of determination and practice, meditation can produce deep states of serenity, and even ecstacy. Indeed, some philosophies teach that meditation consisting of simple mindfulness of breathing, resolutely practiced, can take you all the way to true enlightenment. Unfortunately, many of us find it difficult to get into meditation and to stick with it because our worldly concerns permit us so little free time, and also because it can be such a struggle to keep the mind clear of intrusive, distracting thoughts. The following rite therefore helps prepare the mind for meditation by focusing on what a gift and a privilege it is when we make the time and space to meditate. The act of lighting a candle prior to meditation signals your commitment to time set aside from worldly concerns, effectively creating sacred space. Also, the candle itself can be used as a meditation object, in certain object-focused methods of meditation.

This type of meditation involves focusing on the points where your breath goes in and out, while clearing your mind of everything else. It was taught by the Buddha, who discussed the benefits of "mindfulness of breathing." See the "Kaya-gata-sati Sutta."

In preparation for this rite, think about what you hope to achieve by meditating, in line with your own spiritual aspirations. You can keep some inspirational literature on hand to help remind you why you want to meditate. Consider how the benefits of meditation are so much more valuable than the competing thoughts that want to occupy your mind. Give your mind a little pep talk to the effect that meditation is the object of your mind's and heart's desire, not something it wants to sabotage. Now, light a candle as you say the following or similar words:

As I light this candle,

    I enter sacred time and sacred space.

In lighting this candle, I honor and affirm

    the profound value of meditation.

All of those ordinary thoughts

    that want to flow into my mind,

I say to them now,

    that they will be attended later,

    in their own time and in their own space.

But now is my special time,

    my privileged time,

      my time for meditation.

May all the powers of my mind

    be harmonized for concentration.

May all the longings of my heart

    be fully set on concentration.

One-pointedness is the sole focus of my mind,

    and the object of my heart's desire.

At this point, you may wish to add some lines that are meaningful to your own meditative tradition, if you have one, such as "Let me now be one with Original Mind," or "Let me now be one with the One Who Knows."

Then proceed with your meditation session.[2] When you are finished, extinguish the candle while saying:

I give thanks for the privilege that I have enjoyed,

    this gift of Time and Mind.

And I pledge my commitment to return again

    to this special time and space

      for my regular practice of meditation.

The pledge of commitment to meditation is important; by demonstrating constancy, you reassure your mind of your seriousness of purpose. Even if you don't get quick results, you will come to a day when your mind is ready to go into a deeper state of awareness.

Suggestions for Enhancing This Rite

Your meditation candle can be of any sort or color that you prefer; white symbolizes purity and clarity, light blue represents a calm mind, indigo blue can represent the Ajna chakra (located in the brow area and concerned with clear perception and connection with inner and outer realities), and violet or purple is associated with the crown or Sahasrara chakra (the point of cosmic connection). If you have a choice of candle scent, or if you use anointing oil and incense, use any fragrance that sets a meditative mood, or try sandalwood, benzoin, bay laurel, sage, clary sage, juniper, cedar, cinnamon, frankincense, or myrrh, as these can set the mind on spiritual values and help it turn inward.

Some Thoughts on "Antimeditation"

If you take note of your random thoughts, the idle mental chatter that intrudes on your mind when you are trying to meditate, you will surely find that none of it is very important—not even remotely as important as the things you hope to achieve by meditating. However, as a way of placating your active mind, you can promise it that you will think about these things later, in a sort of "antimeditation" session. You can schedule such sessions as part of a daily walk, or a sitting in imitation of meditation, but with the intention of letting the stream of consciousness flow, rather than trying to hold it back. Let any idle thought enter your mind, and observe it just long enough for it to register before it gets pushed out by the next thought that comes along. (Actually, this practice resembles a type of meditation known as "mindfulness of thought" or using thoughts as objects of meditation[3]; however, I do not dignify it with those terms in order to keep it casual.) Through this practice, you assure the part of your mind that generates these idle thoughts that it will get a regular share of your attention, so that it will be more cooperative about freeing you to still your mind when you want to get down to serious meditation. At the same time, you gain more understanding of your mental process.

42

A Rite to Remind Yourself that
You are a Spirit

Fundamental to many ancient as well as modern mystical systems is the belief that we are essentially spirit beings. As Wayne W. Dyer, the author of *Real Magic,* has said, "If we believe we are souls with bodies rather than bodies with souls, then the invisible, eternal part of ourselves is always available to us for assistance."[4] Some traditions also teach that we have bodies of light as vehicles for our soul-spirits. However, due to the limitations of our flesh as well as the pressing demands of daily life, it can be difficult to hold these ideas in mind. On those occasions when we do feel this awareness of ourselves as spiritual beings, we are inspired and energized, and experience a revitalized sense of possibility.

Following is a rite to refresh your awareness of the freedom, power, and expansiveness of feeling that you can savor by achieving but a moment of recognition and reconnection with your spirit nature. This is a rite that you might wish to perform when you want to regain your spiritual focus—especially if you feel you need extra energy or are stressed, depressed, and weighed down by matter and by the cares of the world. You may also want to do this as a way of gathering your awareness and starting your day out energized, or as an inspirational meditation when you have a little quiet time. The basic ingredients for this rite are a candle and a crystal or gemstone. However, this rite could also be performed with only a candle, by skipping the directions for handling the gemstone and simply focusing on the candle flame.

When ready, light the candle. To connect with your spiritual self, you might first want to connect with your deity, so you may use the following invocation, or compose other words that express your own religious orientation:

> *O Living Spirit of the Universe*
> *You who are the radiant light within me,*
> *and the loving presence beside me,*
> *I thank you for your companionship*

and ask that you assist me now,

in realizing my spiritual nature.

Please help me to be ever mindful

that I am a spiritual being,

that I am a spirit of light.

Next, cup the crystal in both hands and recite:

I am a spirit of life,

with a body of light.

I am of the form and substance of light.

I am a being of energy,

I am a creature of magic.

Visualize yourself as a spirit of light indeed, your body ethereal and luminescent.

Now, turn the crystal over in your fingers, and hold it up to the candle flame, contemplating it with a calm mind. Appreciate the beauty of the stone, which is fascinating even for its imperfections. Visualize the crystal as also pulsating with the same light and power that vibrates through you. Now, hold the stone up in your left hand and say:

Light transforms me.

Light flows through me.

Move the stone to your right hand and say:

Light flows from me,

directed outward,

to give life to my aspirations.

Now, with both hands, press the stone to your solar plexus area (the area above your navel) and say:

I am energized and revitalized.

I am one with my own being

of light and power.
And I revel in the joy of being,
for I am a free spirit.

Remain in this position for a brief period of time, with your eyes closed, and call back to mind the visualization of yourself as a spirit of light, a spirit without limitations. Hold the visualization in your mind, then reopen your eyes when you feel that you are finished and refreshed. Extinguish the candle, or allow it to burn a while if you wish. Slip the crystal back into its bag or container, if it has one, then proceed with your day.

Note that after you have performed this rite a few times, the candle, the crystal, the visualization, and the affirmations become co-identified with ritual intent, and any one of them will serve as a key to revive your spiritual experience. Thus, if you are at work or elsewhere and cannot light a candle or go through the ritual motions, simply close your eyes and visualize your spirit self, or recite the words in your mind, or carry the crystal in your purse or pocket, fingering it when you get a chance. These actions can refresh you, as if you'd performed the entire ritual.

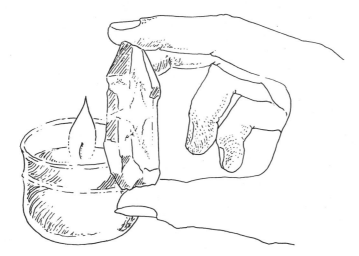

Suggestions for Enhancing this Rite

A white, silver, gold, or yellow candle could be used to represent spiritual light and energy; alternatively, you might want to use a candle in your "astral" color (see appendix C), or any color that you feel best represents your spirit self. If you can choose your candle fragrance, or if you use anointing oil or incense to enhance this rite, use any scent that helps you feel connected to a greater world of spirit, or try a fragrance that conveys a sense of the lightness of being, such as jasmine, neroli, clary sage, mandarin, juniper. If using a gemstone, try a clear-pointed quartz crystal, or any other gemstone that suggests spiritual power to you. (My own preference is a polished piece of rutilated quartz—the fine gold rays within the crystal orb evoke an energetic quality of light for me.)

To help you stay mindful of your spirit nature, you might want to set up some sort of altar or shrine, decorated with symbols and objects that stir you, remind you of who you are, and make you aware of all of your possibilities.

43

A Rite for Spiritual Vision and Clarity

At times when we are weighed down by fear and worry, we need to be able to see things from a broader, higher perspective.[5] Therefore, the following rite helps focus one's sight on the things of the spirit, by requesting the ability to see beyond our worldly illusions, to understand the interconnectedness of all things, and to recognize that we are supported by the Living Universe. To perform this rite, select a candle suitable for contemplation, light it and regard it in a very relaxed manner, with your eyes relaxed (not strained), then recite the following, or similar words that you can modify to better fit your spiritual orientation:

> *As I gaze upon this candle*
> > *I fill my eyes with brightness.*
> *I call upon my Deity,*
> > [and/or upon the Higher Powers],
> > > *please come to me, be one with me.*
> *Please shine through me,*
> > *and fill my eyes and mind with light.*

Close your eyes and hold the image of the flame in your mind for the space of a few heartbeats. Visualize the flame glowing inside your brain, inside your mind. Now, concentrate as you visualize the image of this flame growing brighter, as sparks and rays of gold, silver, blue, and indigo light flare and gleam within it. Visualize this light expanding inside your brain, inside your mind, expanding ever outward, to bathe your eyes in light and to illumine the universe—including your inner, cognitive universe. Then open your eyes and continue to regard the candle flame, while saying:

> *With the eyes of spirit*
> *I see the light within all beings,*
> *that divine spark which animates them,*

and makes me one with them,

and unites us with Divinity.

As the spiritual order becomes clear to me,

so help me to see beyond life and death,

and to recognize the things

which are truly important,

as I understand and celebrate my own place

in the flow of Time, and Life, and Cosmos.

Pause and imagine how it would feel to have a sense of clarity that displaces fear, including the fear of death. Then, close by saying:

The light within my eyes and mind

continues to grow and shine,

that I may always see clearly.

When finished, you may leave the candle burning, or extinguish it if you wish. If you have time, it's a good idea to follow such a ritual by meditating or reading some inspirational literature.

Suggestions

Blue is a good color choice because it symbolizes clear vision and calming insight, but purple, which is the psychic color, and white, which stands for psychic energy, are also appropriate. Yellow, peach, and gold could be used to signify the act of filling the mind with light. If you have a choice of candle fragrance, or if you are using anointing oil or incense, you might want to experiment with benzoin, cedar, frankincense, myrrh, lavender, sage, clary sage, juniper, or sandalwood, all of which promote a broadened spiritual awareness. If you want to add a Caribbean touch to this rite, you can gaze at the candle's flame through a golden ring or earring, then wear it as an inspirational charm.

44

To Help You Trust the Process of Life

Many traditional religious as well as New Age teachings urge us to trust the process of life—that is, to have faith that God or other benevolent spiritual forces are looking after us, that our lives have a plan and purpose, that we will be able to manage whatever challenges may arise, and that everything will turn out okay. However, it is difficult to live without fear and worry if you are starting out on a new path or are making some major life change, or if you have a lot of responsibilities, have to deal with uncertainty, lack money or insurance, or are concerned about your health and security in old age. Therefore, when worries are closing in, you can make a statement of trust by lighting a candle while saying the following words:

> As I light this candle,
> I reaffirm my faith that
> 　　　my Deity [or the Living Universe]
> 　　　　　is taking care of me.
> All of my needs are met.
> My meaningful work is supported.
> Everything works to my benefit.
> Everything works out for my loved ones.
> And a good future is here for me.

Then allow the candle to burn as a comforting image for your spirit, or extinguish it in the knowledge that you will truly be supported. Alternatively, you could use a floating candle, and set it adrift on some nearby stream. By letting the candle go—not being able to see what happens to it—you make a physical statement of trust in your spiritual powers, and in the Universe.

Suggestions for Candles

For candle color, use one of your astral colors (see appendix C), or use white for spiritual power, or any color that, for you, signifies a sense of trust, security, or the presence of God or other spiritual forces that look out for your well-being. If you can choose the candle fragrance, or if you use anointing oil or incense with this rite, you could try bergamot, lemon grass, frankincense, myrrh, geranium, juniper, clary sage, melissa, neroli, mandarin, vanilla, palmarosa, or ylang ylang, as these fragrances ease anxieties while encouraging an optimistic outlook.

Affirmations

If you would like more assurance about trusting the process of life, refer to the works of Louise Hay, who discusses this subject at greater length, and provides meditations and affirmations such as, "I am supported by life. I am neither lonely nor abandoned in the Universe. All of life supports me every moment of the day and night. . . ."[6]

45

Rite of Purification

Rites of purification are a part of many magical, religious, and meditative traditions. Sometimes their procedures for expelling negativity (whether from outside influences or from negative thinking) can be quite long, rigorous, and complex. However, for dispelling some of the negative energies that we may deal with on an everyday basis, candle rites can also be effective.

The following rite for personal purification can be performed at any time that you feel the need for it. This is something you may wish to do if some negative environment, encounter, or other experience has left you with feelings of hurt or resentment, disturbing thoughts or memories, or a general feeling of being contaminated. It can also be used to achieve a state of renewal, (for example, if you feel drained as a result of pouring all of your energies into some major project), and is helpful when coping with illness and the after-effects of illness. Like most of the rites in this book, this ritual is designed as something that you can perform on the spot, when you feel an immediate need. However, if you have the time and are in a place where you can do so, it is a good idea to fast for half a day or so, drink herbal teas (such as burdock, dandelion, ginger root, milk thistle, red clover, thyme, and yellow dock, because these possess both purifying and revitalizing powers), and take a shower or a lustral bath before performing this rite (refer to the rite for "Bathing by Candlelight" on page 19). Set aside a time and space that are tranquil and free of interruption, and dress in clean, loose-fitting clothes.

To perform this rite, select a single candle, but before burning it, ceremoniously wash your hands, as this adds the elemental powers of Water to the ceremony. If you are at work or some other place away from home, an ordinary handwashing will do. However, if you can manage it, wash your hands and face with some special, scented soap, or make an infusion (i.e.,

Plants described as having "antiseptic" qualities are often the same ones used in folk magic rituals for banishing negative forces. Consult your herbals about other herbs with antiseptic properties.

a tea) of cleansing herbs such as rosemary, lavender, thyme, or lemon grass and then pour the warm (but not too hot) solution over your hands while saying:

> *I call upon the power of Water*
> > *to wash through my body and being,*
> > > *and carry away all negativity.*

While you wash, imagine the purifying power of Water as a wave that sweeps through you, carrying away all impurities. Be sure to push up your sleeves so you can wash up to your elbows, and run some warm water over your wrists because this stimulates the blood vessels that converge in this area. Also, it is good if, while you wash, you can rub a pinch of salt between your palms and say:

> *I call upon the power of Earth,*
> > *to break down any negative matters*
> > > *into their purer elements.*

Now, you can anoint the candle, if you wish, then light it. Hold your hands near its flame; they should be at a safe distance, yet near enough to feel the warmth. (If you find it more comfortable, you might want to alternate passing your hands over the flame.) As you continue to absorb this warmth, visualize the purifying energy of elemental Fire entering through the pores in your hands and fingertips. Feel it warming the blood that flows through your hands and fingers, and know that the power of Fire is now circulating through your body, while you say:

> *I call upon the power of Fire,*
> > *to suffuse my body and being,*
> *and transform all impurities*
> > *into pure and wholesome energy.*

If you have incense, light it now, and pass your hands through its smoke while saying:

> *I call upon the power of Air*
> > *to expel all impurities,*
> *and carry them away,*
> > *dispersed as pure energy.*

If you don't have any incense or are not in a place where you can burn it, that is okay; you can say the above words anyway, because the burning of the candle also engages the powers of Air (because a fire can't burn without oxygen).

Return your attention to the candle, and think about how the power of Fire (and Air) radiates through every cell in your body, and through your ethereal body, your body of light. Visualize its purifying effect while breathing deeply and rhythmically. Visualize all negativity being burned off or melted away by the power of Fire. Converted to pure energy, your impurities now flow outward and away with every exhalation, dispersed into the larger atmosphere. Recite the words:

Salt traditionally epitomizes the sustaining powers of elemental Earth, but many traditions also use it for purification. For example, in the Japanese Shinto culture, people sometimes sprinkle salt around themselves as a form of purification after encounters with negative people, places, or events. [See Board of Tourist Industry, Japanese Government Railways.]

> *Everything that does not belong*
> *within my body and spirit,*
> *everything that does not work*
> *for the health of my body and spirit,*
> *is consumed by the power of Fire,*
> *and borne away by the power of Air.*
> *Metabolized by the Living Universe,*
> *it now works for the good of all life.*

Continue to image the sensation of warmth and purification spreading through your body and outward into the atmosphere around you. Feel your body tingling with energy while the Fire tempers and renews everything, restoring it to its most pure and pristine form, even at the cellular and ethereal levels. Finally, say:

> *My body and spirit are purified and renewed,*
> *and I go forward with increased strength*
> *and lightness of being.*

Now, in deference to a West African belief that intensified heat should be modulated with cold in order to restore equilibrium,[7] you can once again wash your hands, this time running cold water over the veins in your wrists, while saying,

> *I am once again restored to myself*
> *And I go forward now,*
> > *with a heart and mind*
> > > *that are calm and cleansed.*

At this point the rite is complete, and you may extinguish the candle, or allow it to burn if you wish.

Suggestions for Candles and Incense

Because of its symbolism, a new white candle would be very suitable. Any shape and size of candle will do, but a jar candle may be ideal, because at one point in the rite you are asked to warm your hands near it. If you are able to choose your candle scent, or if you use anointing oil or incense to enhance this rite, use any fragrance that helps you to feel clean and renewed, or try those that have traditionally been associated with purification rites, such as benzoin, frankincense, eucalyptus, myrrh, rosemary, anise, lavender, lemongrass, sage, and pine.

Rites for the Rhythms of Nature

This section consists of rites for marking the cycles of the Sun and Moon. The rites for the New Moon and Full Moon phases suggest ways of aligning your activities with the Moon's symbolism of renewal, growth, and culmination. The Sun's cycles fall into a natural eight-fold division: the solstices, equinoxes, and the "cross-quarter" days between them. Because there is something intuitively, aesthetically, and archetypally satisfying about an almost-even division of the year into eight parts, we find that many old-world holidays cluster around the equinoxes, solstices, and cross-quarter days.[1] An eight-fold celebrational cycle has been revived by Neopagan ritualists and others. However, as this book is written in a non-denominational spirit, I offer eight rites that relate some common human philosophical concerns to the changing seasons.

Also, for the celebration-minded: you can extend your candle burning enjoyment by thinking of each of these eight year-marks as having its own season or "tide" of almost two weeks, because of all the ancient as well as modern festivals that fall on or around these dates and share some symbolism as well as traditions. This spread of dates also reflects the change-over to the modern (Gregorian) calendar, when the old festivals were off-set by about twelve days, with some countries observing the old style and others the new.

In 1582, Pope Gregory XIII made the corrections that resulted in our modern calendar, but many Protestant countries refused to go along with this until the mid- or latter 1700s, and the Eastern Orthodox churches also resisted. This is why the dates of some Eastern church holidays and others are referred to as "Old Style" [O.S.], and why January 6 is called "Old Christmas," February 14 is "Old Candlemas," and so on.

46

A Rite for Greeting the New Moon

The appearance of the New Moon after its phase of decrease and darkness has inspired human observers as a symbol of hope, renewal, new beginnings, and growth. For this reason, it figures in many folk customs, such as the beliefs that if, upon seeing the new moon on its first night, you make a wish while throwing a kiss to it, or bow three times, or whirl around three times, or show it a piece of silver, your wish will be granted and you will also obtain good luck.[2] The appearance of the New Moon is also important to some religious observances. Because, as "Rosh Hodesh" (or "Cho-desh"), it regulates the Jewish calendar, the Hebrew people once welcomed its monthly first sighting with prayers, celebration, and the sound of the shofar; however, Rabbi Nina Beth Cardin explains that many women are now reclaiming Rosh Hodesh as a time to reflect on women's contributions to Jewish religious life.[3] Neopagans and others linked to the women's spirituality movement also honor the New Moon, which they liken to the Maiden aspect of the Goddess. Thus, Starhawk's New Moon visualization suggests that you, "Feel your own hidden potentials; your power to begin and grow,"[4] while Z. Budapest explores the magical possibilities and exclaims, "The New Moon is quick with results and awesome in her solutions."[5]

The term "New Moon" can be used in two ways. It can refer to the slender crescent that makes a brief appearance in the western sky at sundown, after the dark of the Moon. It can also refer to the Moon and its approximate one-week period between the Dark Moon and the First Quarter. The reason the Moon is little seen at the beginning of this period is because, initially, it rises and sets at the same time as the Sun. However, because the Moon rises about fifty minutes later each evening, we soon come to see more of it.

If you want to align your own activities with the New Moon's energies for increase, renewal, or a change of luck, light a candle and say:

New Moon, Moon of Promise,

your reappearance reminds me

that I can always begin anew,

for although things change,

they also come 'round again,

to a point of new beginnings,

new directions, and second chances.

O Moon of Inspiration,

look graciously upon my dreams.

O Moon of Increase,

look kindly upon my efforts,

as I commit myself

to a new phase of growth.

Of course, you will get the most out of this rite if you perform it outdoors, when the New Moon makes its first appearance. If you wish, you can continue to burn your candle every night through the New Moon phase, then put it away until the next cycle of renewal (or rededicate it with a new ceremony upon the night of the Full Moon).

Suggestions

A white candle may best exemplify the energy of the New Moon, though silver, light blue, or light green candles also hint at New Moon qualities. If performed outdoors, a jar candle is recommended; you can attach crescent-moon-shaped stickers to the jar, or hang a moon-shaped pendant from a cord, and tie it around the neck of the jar. Otherwise, a slender taper would be ideal for its symbolism. For candle scent, anointing oil, or incense, you could choose delicate fragrances such as benzoin, jasmine, grapefruit, mandarin, or rose geranium, or use fragrances we associate with freshness, such as pine, lavender, lemon, lime, and mint.

Diane Stein suggests, "use white candles on the altar for the Maiden Moon, she knows more of milk than of blood yet." See *Casting the Circle* [Freedom, California: Crossing Press, 1990] 75.

47

A Rite for Full Moon Nights

The Full Moon has long enchanted the poetic imagination. The powers of nature are at their peak, and the unconscious mind is open to subtle influences at this time. The Moon's roundness also makes it a symbol of abundance and fulfillment. We can align ourselves with this natural magic by observing the Full Moon phase as an occasion to recite ceremonialized affirmations.[7] Affirmations are positive statements designed to bring about changes in our attitudes, and to manifest things we want to bring into our lives. Based on the theory that the deep mind takes our "self talk" literally and has the power to change our reality, when we recite affirmations we state our desires as if they have already been fulfilled. (For example, one would say "I give thanks for my prosperity," rather than "Some day I will be prosperous," or "I enjoy exercise," rather than "I will stop hating exercise.") To experience the Full Moon's energies, you might want to light a candle every evening upon the rising of the moon; you can include the three nights before the Full Moon, the night thereof, and the three nights following, as you say:

> *Full Moon, Moon of Fulfillment,*
> *your beauty assures me of the enchantment*
> *at work in the world around me.*
> *You remind me that I have the power*
> *to shape my own reality.*

Now, if you wish, you can recite some affirmations that you have composed to fit your own needs. (You can prepare a list of them in advance.) Then conclude by saying:

> *O Moon of Completion,*
> *so it is and so shall it be.*
> *O Moon of Celebration,*
> *I revel in the joy of being,*
> *as I affirm the fulfillment of my desires.*

To add some extra power to this rite,[8] you could write your affirmations on a piece of nice stationery, perhaps ten times each, then fold the paper and burn it in a brazier or other fire-proof vessel; this is a way of giving your desires over to the universe.

Suggestions

White or silver candles suggest the lunar powers, though you can use any color that evokes your ideal of high energy or fulfillment. Large, spherical glow candles would be nicely symbolic. For candle scent, anointing oil, or incense, the fragrances that seem to be most popular for Full Moon blends are lavender, sandalwood, frankincense, lemon, rose, and ylang ylang, though any pleasing fragrance will do.

If you keep a home altar, the celebration of the Full Moon gives you a chance to express your creative imagination. You could decorate it with silver streamers, a strand of white globe-shaped Christmas lights (or, as the British call them, "fairy lights"), round mirrors, white flowers or flowers with globular heads, round white stones, sea shells (especially "moon snails" and "eggshell cowries"), silver coins, and objects that represent or symbolize some things that you would like to bring into your life. If your diet permits, you could also set out a small round cake on the night of the Full Moon, as cakes are used to celebrate the completion of goals. (You might also be able to get "moon cakes" from an Asian grocery.)

If you are a coin collector, you might try to find a Maria Theresa silver dollar; these coins were used as lucky charms by the Gypsies, as well as some members of the old Ottoman Empire, who found the full-figured image of the empress symbolic of abundance.

48

Candlelight for Candlemas

The cross-quarter day that falls about halfway between the winter solstice and spring equinox is often celebrated as "Candlemas" or "The Feast of Lights," on February 2. The astrological half way point is 15 degrees Aquarius, around February 4 or 5. Early February shows great regional contrasts. In more northern regions, it is half way through winter, and though the days are slowly growing longer, they may be some of the coldest and snowiest; in milder climates, it is the beginning of spring and the green world is already renewing itself, so Candlemas can signal the time for plowing and sowing.

The celebrational nature of this season is a mix of traditions. In early February, the ancient Greeks observed the lesser Eleusinian mysteries (around February 1–3) and the Anthesteria (around February 11), both of which honored the return of green life. For the Romans, the days between February 5 and 10 marked the beginning of spring, and they also celebrated the Lupercalia, an ancient festival for purification, protection, and fertility, on February 15. ("February" comes from the word *februa*, referring to ritual means of purification.) Among some Celtic peoples, the cross-quarter day is known as Imbolc ("in the belly") or Oimelc ("in milk" or "ewes' milk") relating to the lambing season. February 1 is also the Feast Day of Bride or Brigid, an important fire festival as well as the first day of spring. Called "Bride of Brightness" and described as the three-fold goddess of poetry, smithcraft, and healing, (though she is also associated with the care of cattle and hearthfires, as well as midwifery), this beloved goddess later became identified with the patroness saint of Ireland.[9] The folk practices surrounding Bride's feast day reveal her concern with the warming,

Bride is pronounced "Breed." Her name may come from a word meaning "bright." As Alexander Carmichael observed, she "is said to breathe life into the dead mouth of winter," and he cites variations of a curious charm, one of which goes, "on the day of Bride, the birth day of spring, the serpent emerges from the knoll . . . " [172]. In the old goddess religions, the undulating form of the serpent and its underground habitation made it a symbol of the earth energies.

quickening, emergent power of the life force. In addition to incorporating the cult of Bride, the early Christian church celebrated February 2 as *Purificatio* or the Purification of the Blessed Virgin, with practices that included the blessing and gifting of candles, as well as candle-lit processions—hence the name Candlemas. The theme of light is also echoed in readings that hail the infant Christ, in his presentation at the temple, as "a light to lighten the Gentiles, and the glory of thy people Israel." St. Blaise on February 3, and St. Agatha on February 5, also share fire festival symbolism,[10] as do several other Christian and Pagan festivals of early February.

In his sermon, "Why do we in this feast carry candles?" Pope Innocent XII mentioned that Pagans made candlelit processions through the city in imitation of the search for the spring maiden Proserpine, and "Because the holy fathers could not extirpate the custom, they ordained that Christians should carry about candles in honor of the Blessed Virgin" [Walsh 168–169].

There are many customs associated with Candlemas. In some parts of England it was known as the Wives' Feast, and for many, it was by this time that the Christmas greenery had to be taken down.[11] Americans know it best as Groundhog Day, from German settlers who passed on the belief that if the groundhog (in Europe the badger) emerges and sees his shadow, we'll have six more weeks of winter. Since Valentine's Day is "Old Candlemas," it can be counted as an extended part of this celebration—and, in fact, in some places February 14 and not February 2 is the traditional date for Groundhog Day.[12] It was also once believed that birds chose their mates on Valentine's Day. This complex of traditions makes Candlemas a festival of fire, purification, and the earth's incipient renewal. (As Chinese New Year tends to coincide with this period, it reinforces this theme of renewal.)

For a simple Candlemas ceremony, you can light a candle and say:

> *May this candle fair and bright*
> *   cheer us all through winter's flight.*
> *Bless us through snow and storm and rain,*
> *   Until the Spring has come again.*

This echoes the old rhyme that reads, "If Candlemas be fair and bright, Winter will have another flight."

Alternatively, in keeping with the more inward qualities of this season, you could try this contemplative rite, perhaps before, after, or as part of a major home cleaning and bodily purification project. Set some time aside to surround yourself with a large array of lighted candles, reserving three of them to be specially lit as part of the ceremony. (If you have but one candle, just modify the words of the ceremony.) Also, you might wish to have on hand some paper and pens, or a personal journal. When ready, light the first candle, and say:

> *As I light this candle,*
> *I pose the question:*
>> *which parts of my life need purification?*

Pause and reflect on this issue. Write down your thoughts, if you want to, or simply sit in contemplation, taking all the time you need to examine this area of your life. Go through the same actions as you light the second candle, saying:

> *As I light this candle,*
> *I pose the question:*
>> *which parts of my life need rejuvenation?*

And the third:

> *As I light this candle,*
> *I pose the question:*
>> *which parts of my life need the fire of inspiration?*

When you feel that you have spent enough time in thought, you can close the ceremony by saying:

> *So shall I purify myself,*
> *so shall I renew myself,*
> *so shall I seek inspiration,*
>> *in time to greet returning spring.*

Extinguish your candles or allow them to burn a while if you wish to enjoy the profusion of lights.

Also, taking inspiration from this season's symbolism of the earth's coming out of her deep, restorative slumber, as well as some Irish and Scottish traditions of "making Bride's bed"—that is, placing a doll made from a sheaf of grain in a cozy little bed by the hearthfire, then welcoming Bride into the house.[13] You could do a variation of this rite: on an early morning, light all of your candles at once, setting them on some very safe and secure surface in your bedroom, then crawl back into your warm bed to contemplate your questions and do your journal writing. (This will be most effective if you do it on a snowy or stormy morning, with a cup of coffee or tea beside you.)

Suggestions

Some favorite candle colors for this festival are white for purity or red for the fire of inspiration; also, green could be used for the promise of early spring, or pink as the affectionate blend of white and red. Because Valentine's Day is Old Candlemas, Valentine candles (and decorations) could be used, too. For candle fragrance, anointing oil, or incense, you might want scents used in purification, such as rosemary, lemon, cedar, or pine (pine boughs were used as "februa"), or use any fragrance that suggests the spiritual qualities of this season.

49

Celebration of Spring

Spring is a joyous time the world over. After lengthening days, the point of equinox is reached (around March 20 or 21, when the Sun enters the sign of Aries), and then the days become longer than the nights. In many cultures, the vernal equinox marked or marks the beginning of the new year.

The Anglo-Saxons saw it as the dawn of the year,[14] honoring Eostre, a goddess of spring, dawn, the east, and fertility, from whose name we get "Easter."[15] We see similar themes in the springtime symbols and festival customs of many countries: new life, sprouting grain, fertility and baby animals, spring cleaning, new clothes, the exchange of colored eggs, and outdoor promenades and celebrations.

You can celebrate the joy of renewed life with a little ceremony, something to do on the days around Easter or the Equinox— perhaps after time spent looking for the birds, buds, and blossoms that herald the return of spring in your own area. Light a candle and say:

> *At this time of lengthening light,*
> *I give thanks for Spring's new life:*
> *snow melting, icy lakes unlocking,*
> *rising rivers and rivulets running,*
> *rainy days, and days of sunshine,*
> *soil warming, soil softening,*
> *animal life awakening,*
> *returning birds and birdsong,*

In Iran, Turkey, Azerbaijan, and related culture areas, Spring Equinox is *Noruz*, meaning "new day"; it is a very festive occasion with pre-Islamic roots. People celebrate with nature outings, picnics, bonfires, purification rites, the exchange of gifts, symbolic foods (dyed eggs and sweets), and the wearing of new clothes [Internet: Price, Payvand's Iran News, Farsinet, and Nakhjavani et al]. Prior to the Gregorian calendar changes, the Romans also began the new year at spring Equinox, as did some other Europeans,

buds bursting forth,
sprouting seeds and bulbs,
the greening, quickening earth.
And as it is in the wide, green world,
so may it be for all of us:
vital, potent, vivacious Life!

Afterward, you may want to think about the marvelous potency of new growth, for when shoots push through the soil and buds open out, they do so with enormous energy, and the sap that rises in the trees also exerts tremendous pressure. Let this inspire you to look for areas of new growth in your life, and to find ways to express your personal potency.

Suggestions

Color choices for candles might include white for purity, green for the return of verdant life, or festive Easter egg colors. Egg-shaped candles would be a nice touch. For candle scent, anointing oil, or incense, the freshness of spring might be evoked with delicate floral fragrances like mandarin, jasmine, rose geranium, or "green" fragrances such as basil, lime, spearmint or peppermint—or try patchouli, which smells like fresh-turned earth. You could place your candle in a bowl of freshly turned earth, or use floating candles (as elemental Water plays a major role in spring's unlocking), or try the Iranian custom of placing the candle before a mirror to reflect more light. Decorate your area with symbols of the season such as eggs, chicks, and bunnies, as well as flowers like daffodils and crocuses, or pussy willows or other budded branches.

Hal Borland comments on the potency of life while describing "the vitalizing current" of "sap rising with incredible pressure, the pressure of spring tides themselves, unseen, unheard, and yet the very flow and surge of all the green life that soon will clothe the earth" [*Moons* 75]. Inspired by this power of green life, the Romans dedicated the month of March to Mars, who also served as an old agricultural deity; the Salii, the warrior priests of Mars, performed leaping dances in mid-March to stimulate the rising growth [James 163–65].

50

A May Festival Candle

In moderate climates, May Day (May 1) signals the beginning of the summer season. (The astrological cross-quarter date, halfway between spring equinox and summer solstice, is 15 degrees Taurus, around May 5 or 6.) Here in the Midwest, in the last days of April, the leaves on the trees are still quite small, and many are pinkish and yellowish tinted, so they create a visual impression of colorful dot patterns. Shortly after the first of May, however, you turn around, and lo and behold, most of the trees are now fully leafed out. Also, the woodland wild flowers are at their peak, garden flowers are in bloom, and the last songbirds are returning.

At this time, the Celts held one of their most important fire festivals, known as "Beltane" (meaning "bright fire"); they made great bonfires, and some would also ritually rekindle their hearthfires.[16] With Samhain (Halloween), Beltane divided the year into light and dark halves, and because such transitional points were very magical, it is prominent in the fairy legends. Around the same time, the Romans had a six-day festival in honor of Flora, goddess of flowers, which they regarded as no trivial thing, as this was one of their oldest holidays.[17] The themes of fertility and festivity survived in customs like the Maypole and May baskets. Through the first half of the twentieth century, youths in many American communities rose early to hang baskets of flowers from neighbors' door handles, and some schools arranged Maypole dances.

A modern celebration of May could take up the themes of leafing, flowering, and brightness, emphasizing the ways that all of us may cultivate unique gifts to brighten the world. (As a verb, "leaf" can mean to "shoot out" or "produce leaves," and "flower" "to develop.") You can celebrate these themes in your own life by lighting a candle and saying:

> As I light this candle,
>   I celebrate the joyful festival May.
> As the green world bursts forth

in leaves and flowers,
and the Sun's light ever increases,
so may I fill my own world
with life, and light, and color.
So may I leaf, so may I flower,
so may I kindle
a flame of brightness.

While thinking about how you could cultivate your own gifts and share them with the world, think about recognizing other peoples' special qualities as well, that each may be valued and encouraged. Perhaps you could also arrange some celebrational outings, as this is a time to be out in nature, doing something playful and active.

Suggestions

A very festive candle would be ideal; you might find a tall one with colorful stripes or swirls suggestive of a Maypole, and surround it with wreaths of ribbons and flowers. For candle scent or oil, floral fragrances like rose, jasmine, ylang ylang, palmarosa, mandarin, or rose geranium would be appropriate for this festival of flowering.

51

A Candle for Midsummer Nights' Pleasures

The summer solstice, the point at which the Sun reaches its highest elevation and gives us the longest day of the year, occurs around June 21. The calendar labels this the first day of summer, though many of us live in climates where the heat of summer, as well as school vacation, is already well under way. In European tradition, this day is celebrated as "Midsummer," and it is rich in folkloric practices. (Sometimes Midsummer is celebrated as late as June 24 or the weekend closest to it, due to historical calendar adjustments and other local traditions.) Across northern Europe, people have honored the Midsummer Sun (in some latitudes the Midnight Sun), with games, dances, songs, and bonfires. However, the turning of the Sun is also tinged with sadness: the days will soon grow shorter, even as the heat grows stronger, in the descent towards autumn. Because it is a special transitional time, Midsummer is also a time to encounter the world of faery, as illustrated in Shakespeare's *A Midsummer Night's Dream*, or the belief that if you stand beneath an elder tree on Midsummer's Eve, you will see the elves ride by.[18]

For us today, summer enchantments may be experienced through little pleasures like vacations by a lake, evening cook-outs, relaxing on a porch swing, or recalling childhood memories of playing outdoors until quite late. If you would like to add a touch of magic to the evenings surrounding Midsummer, you can light a candle (perhaps at "fireflight," the time of evening when the fireflies begin to rise out of the grass), as you say:

> *I light this candle*
> > *to honor the Sun's high days,*
> > *and all of the pleasures of summer nights.*
> *This is a time for celebrations,*
> > *when daylight lingers long into evenings.*
> *And we shall enjoy the sensual summer evenings*
> > *for many weeks yet,*

as we savor the freedom
of the easy summer season.

Also: many Midsummer ritual traditions involve water: gathering alongside it, collecting it, bathing in it, and so on. Aside from the fertility associations, these ceremonies may express the desire to balance the powers of elemental Fire and Water. (We are effectively acting this out when we head for the beach on hot summer days.) In some areas, candle burning is a part of these rites. For example, in the Wachau region of Austria, huge numbers of lighted candles are set on little rafts and sent down the Danube on Midsummer's Eve.[19] If you are spending your time near water, you could try this yourself, by building a raft for your candle, or using a floating candle. Since Midsummer is a traditional time for wishing, you could send your candle off down a stream or river while performing the rite for wishing on page 106.

Suggestions

Yellow, gold, orange, and red are good choices for candle color, honoring the fullest powers of the Sun, fire, and heat; alternatively, to balance the Fire element, you might use a green candle to evoke the lushness of summer foliage, or blue for the pleasures of the Water element. You could carve sun symbols on your candle, or tie a cord with a solar pendant around a jar candle. A floating candle in a decorative bowl would ideally combine the symbolism of fire and water. Create an altar area by surrounding your candle with sun symbols and wreaths of flowers, leaves, and herbs. (Many Midsummer superstitions required gathering nine types of flowers or herbs, which were thrown into the fire or water, or used for decoration, medicine, or magic.) Seashells would be a lovely addition, symbolizing elemental Water; their spiral structures also harmonize the linear and cyclical qualities of time. If you use candle scent, incense, or oil, choose a fragrance that suggests the mood of high summer for you. Lemon balm, ginger, bay laurel, cedar, clove, and cinnamon have all been attributed solar qualities; others may prefer tropical floral fragrances like ylang ylang, mandarin, or palmarosa, or scents that evoke vacations in the wilderness, such as pine, fir, or juniper.

52

A Rite for Lammas

If you enjoy marking the old European festival year, burn a candle for "Lammas" while consuming a piece of fresh-baked bread and contemplating the symbolism of the grain. Lammas, the approximate halfway point between summer solstice and autumn equinox, is celebrated on or near August 1, and can be seen as the beginning of the harvest season. Lammas is an Anglo-Saxon word meaning Loaf-Mass (*Hlaf-maesse*), and refers to bread offerings made to celebrate the first fruits of harvest. This festival also coincides with Lughnasad, the commemoration of a Celtic solar deity. Southern Europeans, including the Romans, also held a number of festivals about this time.

To perform the following rite, set out a plate with a piece of bread or other baked goods. (Baking something, or making a trip to a special bakery, can be part of the celebrational fun.) Something made of whole-grain ingredients would be ideal; a bread with fruit and nuts in it would also be appropriate. If you wish, you can also have beer, wine, ale, apple juice, or grape juice to drink, as these also share the symbolism of the season. If you don't wish to include the eating and drinking, you can still perform this as a simple candle rite, reflecting on the recitations. When ready, light your candle and say:

> *As I light this candle,*
> *I celebrate the Spirit of Life,*

The traditional date for Lammas is August 1, but King George II moved it to August 13 in a calendar adjustment [Walsh 60], putting it close to the August 15 Feast of the Assumption of the Blessed Virgin (known in southern Europe as "Our Lady in Harvest"), coinciding with some Roman festivals [James 237–238]. Lammas as an astrological cross-quarter day occurs when the Sun reaches 15 degrees Leo, around August 8. Due to this spread of dates, we can think of early August as "Lammastide." The Old World celebrated many different agricultural festivals, due to its variety of crops, as well as seasonal differences across its many geographical areas.

> *which animates all things,*
> *and connects us all.*
> *As the mystery of the grain has taught us,*
> *we are all interdependent*
> *and interlinked*
> *through the energy that flows backward*
> *and forward through time.*
> *This energy flows through all the cycles*
> *of life and nature,*
> *connecting us with the world of plants,*
> *and the world of animals,*
> *and the world of the ancestors.*

Take a bite of the bread and a sip of your drink while you ponder these words. Then, proceed with the rite by saying:

> *At this Lammastide, I give gratitude*
> *for the natural world's abundance,*
> *as I take in the power of Nature,*
> *through the grain which is nourished*
> *by Sun and Earth.*
> *O may it be a constant blessing,*
> *for the benefit of myself*
> *and all living.*

Allow the candle to burn while you finish eating, continuing to think about the symbolism of the grain.

Suggestions

Many gift shops sell candles scented like baked goods, such as cinnamon buns or oatmeal cookies. Otherwise, candles in spicy scents and colors associated with late summer, such as gold, yellow, and goldenrod, would do nicely. You could decorate your table with fruits, vegetables, and flowers of the season, as well as other symbols of harvest, such as the wheat weavings called "corn dollies."[20]

53

For Candlelit Autumn Evenings

Each season brings its changes, but the fact of change is dramatically underscored in autumn. After harsh summers, early autumn restores some of nature's green and brings a profusion of wild flowers, such as asters, goldenrod, Queen Anne's lace, gentian, bouncing bet, and more. Those of us who live in northern climates are privileged to see some of Nature's most breath-taking beauty in the vivid shades of red, orange, and yellow of fall foliage. The cooler temperatures invite us to spend more time outdoors, where we may be lucky enough to witness some bird migrations, which is another thrilling, soul-stirring experience. Our senses are further aroused by the smell of wood fires, windfall apples, and the products of the harvest. But as we reach the equinox and look toward winter, our pleasure is shadowed by our knowledge that all of this is transient. So quickly do the trees go bare! Night falls ever earlier, soon many of us are rising in darkness, early frosts blast the autumn flowers, and the chill sets in. Perceiving these changes, one's mind may turn to past loves and lost ones, bringing the realization that, "In all things dear and delightful to me there is change and separation."[21]

If you want to reflect on the nature of change, while at the same time adding a touch of cheer to autumn evenings, you can light a candle (itself an ephemeral thing), and say:

> *I set this candle*
> > *against the lengthening darkness.*
> *Change is everywhere,*
> > *change comes to everyone,*
> > *and truly, all life is change.*
> *So may I honor the seasons of life.*
> *Let me savor the fleeting beauty,*
> > *and yet let go*

> *when time has come and gone.*
> *So may change bring new vitality.*
> *So may change bring added wisdom.*

Suggestions

Use any pleasing candle, perhaps one suggestive of autumn scents and colors. If you want to create a focus area, autumn provides a wealth of decorations: colorful leaves, flowers, seed pods, and produce including nuts, apples, grapes, Indian corn, pumpkins, and gourds.

54

Halloween Enchantments

Halloween is rich in cultural tradition. For ancient peoples in northern climates, this time around late October, early November was effectively the beginning of winter, so they focused on survival preparations. Late harvests were brought in, and because they had to bring their animals into winter quarters, they thinned the herds, then followed with a big feast. They burned bonfires to provide energy for the waning sun, the spirits of Nature, and the souls of the dead, and invited the ancestors to their family feasts. The celebration of Halloween is most deeply rooted among the Celts; this holiday, also known as Samhain (pronounced Saw-wen), was the Celtic New Year. Similarly, various Germanic peoples held "Winter Nights" celebrations in October, combining winter preparations with ceremonies honoring the elves and ancestor spirits who attended to a family's luck. Later, the Church proclaimed November 1 as All Saints Day and November 2 as All Soul's Day (also known as the Day of the Dead), and celebrations throughout the Christian world incorporated many of the old Pagan practices of honoring departed spirits. Different countries' customs have included silent vigils, ringing bells all night, setting out lights to guide the spirits, and spreading a table for the dead. European celebrations of St. Martin's Day (November 11) have also incorporated practices that we associate with Halloween.[22]

Samhain is generally thought to mean "summer's end." (The old European tribes didn't always recognize four seasons: some recognized three seasons, and some simply divided the year into summer and winter halves, for the seasons of light and darkness.) There is some misinformation out there that Samhain was the name of a Lord of the Dead who judged souls on this night. Scholars have found no basis for this belief in Celtic mythology or culture, but trace it back to the fanciful imagination of one Charles Vallency, who wrote in the 1770s. [See Internet: McBain's Etymological Dictionary, Bethancourt, and "The Myth of Samhain: Celtic God of the Dead."]

The North American Halloween was influenced by immigrants from the British Isles. For example, trick-or-treating grew out of the Irish custom of going from door to door to gather contributions for the big feast. However, the nature of this holiday has changed over time. During the nineteenth century, it was most popular with young adults for pulling pranks and practicing divination to learn about future spouses. In the twentieth century, Halloween became more a holiday for younger children, and has undoubtedly done much to stimulate their sense of wonder.[23]

To experience the mystical energies of this season, you can light a candle on All Hallows Eve (and, if you wish, on the nights surrounding it). If you want to keep with ancient traditions of honoring the dead, you could perform the "Rite for Honoring Your Ancestors" on page 213, or the "Rite of Remembrance for the Dead" on page 209. However, if you want to do something lighter, perhaps something that could serve as the focus of a family celebration or kick off a night of party-going, you could perform the following rite, to recover some of childhood's sense of wonder.

> *I light this candle*
>> *in honor of All Hallows nights,*
> *a time when the human world*
>> *can touch the world of magic.*

So at this time,

may we also find wonder

in the mysteries of the universe,

even as we rediscover

the enchantments of childhood.

So may our lives be filled with magic:

magic in our homes,

and magic in our hearts.

Afterward, you might want to set your candle in a jack-o-lantern, or put it in a window (if there are no curtains or other flammable objects nearby), after the old custom of lighting the way for departed loved ones.

Suggestions

For candle shapes, colors, and scents that evoke the fun and magic of Halloween, you can let your imagination run wild. Orange, purple, and black candles will complement many Halloween decorations, and there are novelty candles in the shape of ghosts, skulls, and pumpkins. There are also candles scented and colored like candy corn or pumpkin spice. Other scents hint of Halloween mysteries: sandalwood, cedar, cypress, frankincense, myrrh, clove, patchouli, and vetivert. If you can get it, burn copal, the special incense that Mexicans use for the Day of the Dead.

We can think of the days around Halloween as "Allhallowntide" (an Elizabethan term), because of the festivals during late October–early November that share similar elements. The Roman festival of Pomona, goddess of the orchards, also occurred around November 1, and many Halloween customs were transferred to the British Guy Fawkes Day, November 5, commemorating the foiling of a historical terrorist plot. The cross-quarter day associated with Halloween, that is, the halfway point between the autumn equinox and winter solstice, is fifteen degrees Scorpio, around November 7.

55

Candles for the Midwinter Festival of Lights

Winter is a season when you can burn your candles at both ends of the day, and for many peoples, candle lighting is an important tradition of Christmas, Hanukkah, Kwanzaa, and other world holidays during this time. December truly is the month for a celebration of light, for its days are the darkest, with the winter solstice (which usually falls on December 21 or 22) being the shortest day of the year. Solstice is reckoned as the official beginning of winter, though it is often referred to as "Midwinter" (just as summer solstice is called Midsummer). At this time, the Sun is at its lowest point in the sky, and it rises and sets at its southernmost points. After the solstice, the days will grow longer as the changing angle of the Sun gives us a better quality of light. Ancient peoples may have experienced great anxiety, wondering whether the Sun would actually reach this turning point, or if the world would recede into endless darkness. Hence, many solstice rituals featured such themes as the slumber of the earth, the rebirth of the Sun, the need to light fires to strengthen the newborn Sun, the need to bring in evergreens to shelter the spirits of Nature, and the battles between the forces of light and darkness. The reappearance of the Sun was met with great rejoicing.

Hal Borland says in *Sundial of the Seasons*: "In our latitude, we know that each year brings a time when not only the candle, but the hearthfire must burn at both ends of the day, symbol not of waste but of warmth and comfort. . . ." [258]. Borland also comments on the anxiety over the Sun's return: "Hope and belief are easy in a warm green world, but when the cold days come and the sun inches further and further south, cutting a constantly smaller arc across the sky, the imminence of utter darkness and oblivion seems at hand" [*Moons* 349].

If you customarily light a candle for the nights of December, you can make a ceremony of it by saying:

> The seasons have made their circle,[24]
> and I light this candle
>   to celebrate the Sun's renewal.

As people everywhere illuminate
these long midwinter nights,
so may we all find hope and comfort
in the ever returning light.

Suggestions

Let the traditions of the holiday season inspire your choice of candles. Traditional Yuletide colors are red, white, green, and gold; popular scents are pine, spruce, balsam fir, bayberry, myrrh, ginger, nutmeg, and cinnamon. You might enjoy using a Christmas tree-shaped candle,[25] or other seasonal candles.

Burning a bayberry candle on Christmas Eve or Day is the tradition behind a popular rhyme that declares, ". . . a bayberry candle burned to the socket brings warmth to the heart and wealth to the pocket." (Some variations are, "luck to the home and wealth to the pocket" or, "food to the larder and gold to the pocket.") The same belief has been applied to New Year [Internet sources: "Bayberry candles" and "100% bayberry wax"]. As a holiday scent, cinnamon can "recall the strength and heat of summer." ["Devonshire incense," Internet.]

Rites for Special Days of the Year

This section features some simple candle rites that can be performed on special days, such as your birthday, New Year's Day, and various American public holidays. Due to limitations of space, I have not attempted to include all of the popular or calendar holidays (such as Flag Day, Arbor Day, Mother's Day, Valentine's Day, and so on), just the ones that I thought would best lend themselves to a candlelight type of commemoration. However, if there are other special days that you would like to honor, perhaps you will be able to take some inspiration from the material included here, to create additional rituals of your own.

56

A Birthday Rite for Your Sun-Spirit

Your birthday can be an occasion to renew your spirit of luck, as was done in ancient times. For example, birthday feasts were big family affairs in ancient Rome, and included rituals to honor the individual's special tutelary spirit, known as a man's "genius" or a woman's "Juno" (similar to a guardian angel). Until the emperor Theodosius banned birthday parties in the year AD 392, Roman celebrants wore white for luck, placed flowers on an altar made of turf, burned incense, and made offerings of wine and honey cakes to the birthday person's guardian spirit. They made wishes for happiness, well-being, prosperity, good health, and long life, and asked the genius or Juno to "return often to his [/her] festival."[1] Perhaps the Romans believed that honoring your genius or Juno has an energizing effect. Astrologically, you can relate this regeneration of spirit to your "solar return," which occurs on or very near your birthday, when the Sun returns to the position it occupied on the day of your birth.

To take advantage of this auspicious occasion, you can use the following rite to refresh the "numen" (the psychic energy store) of your Sun and your guardian spirit, which may be synergistically linked to each other. (You don't need to know the exact time of your solar return, performing this rite any time on your birthday is good enough.) Select three candles: a white candle representing the guardian spirit, a gold candle representing the Sun, and an "astral" candle, which is a candle in one of the colors associated with your Sun sign (see appendix C). On your birthday, light the white candle and say:

> *On this day of self-renewal,*
> *I light this white candle*
> > *to honor my personal genius:*
> > *spirit of inspiration, spirit of luck.*

While so doing, envision yourself glowing with light. Next, light the golden candle and say:

On this day of my Sun's anniversary,
I light this golden candle,
   to honor the energizing power
      of the Sun within me.

Envision a scintillating golden ball of energy, generated from within your solar plexus (stomach) area, and filling you with warmth and cheer. Finally, light the astral candle and say,

With this candle,
   I honor the special qualities
      and the needs of my essential self,
   the expression of my own identity,
      my core creativity.

Envision yourself at your best and brightest, doing the things you enjoy with skill and confidence.

You can leave the candles burning for as long as is convenient. Then go about your day, mindful of the auspicious nature of your birthday, a day on which you can really shine.

Suggestions

If you want to choose a scented candle, or use anointing oil or incense, use anything that suggests your personal essence, or try bergamot, bay laurel, West Indian bay, cinnamon, orange, neroli, and rose, as these are fragrances that will boost your birthday luck. You might also want to create an altar or focus area for this rite, using flowers, balloons, a birthday cake, party hats, traditional decorations and party favors, and photos and memorabilia from birthdays past.

57

Welcoming the New Year

A wealth of tradition[2] attends the entrance of the new year as a time for new beginnings, as well as an opportunity to ensure one's luck for the year to come. The following enables you to add ritual to your New Year celebration. Choose the most convenient time to perform this rite by coordinating it with your other activities. You could try it a few minutes before or after midnight on New Year's Eve, or (if you are away from home or go to bed early) at any time on January 1. You can also perform it with your family or group, changing the "I" to "we." When ready, light the candle and say:

> As I light this candle,
> I bid the Old Year farewell,
> with gratitude for milestones passed,
>> and memories cherished.
> And I welcome the New Year in
>> with love and warmth and blessings.
> That the quality of this new year be assured,
> I now dedicate a moment to visioning
>> some ways to make this year 20__
>>> a year of excellence,
>>> a year of fortune.

Pause for a moment to envision the kind of year that you want to have and the kind of person that you want to be. Enhance these visualizations by imagining your objectives charged with energy and bathed in glowing light. Then continue:

> And thus do my wishes for the year 20__
>> take on their own life and purpose.
> So does the year itself
>> take on a glowing life and power:

A bright year, a bold year,

a golden year, a year of magic!

So may this year bring luck,

and peace, and prosperity

to one and all.

Now return to your revelries, or whatever you have planned. You can allow the candle to burn continuously, or relight it every morning to reactivate the magic of your New Year's celebrations. Whether the candle takes a few days or a few months to burn down, you can be satisfied that its flames will radiate your blessings to last the twelve months out.

Suggestions for Candles

Choose any color that represents the quality and luck of the New Year for you. A white candle can symbolize the purity of the newborn year, as well as the broad range of possibilities that the year may bring, as white light contains all the colors of the spectrum. You might also use red or gold, as these are colors associated with good fortune. For candle scent, anointing oil, or incense, use any pleasing fragrance. Neroli would be good for bidding "a sweet New Year," bayberry is a seasonal favorite and also attracts prosperity,[3] and orange, mandarin, or tangerine are harmonious with the Asian tradition of giving these citrus fruits for New Year's luck. For a festive touch, affix twelve sequins to your candle in honor of Janus, the old gatekeeper of the year (whose rites required twelve altars for the twelve months), or surround a main candle with twelve votives. If you have collections that represent the twelve months (such as birthmonth angels) you can arrange them around your candle.

Janus, for whom January is named, was the god who presided over all new beginnings— not merely the new year, but each new day and season, as well as the beginning of every human enterprise; according to Alexander S. Murray, Janus, as "the god of 'good beginning'" was so important that the Romans "placed him on almost equal footing with Jupiter, even giving his name precedence in their prayers" [133, 132]. Because the Romans placed so much emphasis on good beginnings, they were careful to "regulate their conduct that every word and act be a happy augury for all the ensuing days of the year" [Walsh 733].

58

Honoring Martin Luther King, Jr.

Martin Luther King, Jr. was born on January 15, 1929, and is honored with a public holiday on the third Monday in January. Because his philosophy has engaged so many areas of social relations, there are many different themes that we could highlight in commemorating this day. The following is a simple rite to honor those who strive for justice, as well as those who have contributed to building good relations between different peoples. To perform this rite, light a candle and say,

> *On this day, I light this candle*
> *in honor of Martin Luther King, Jr.,*
> *and all others who have worked to bring justice*
> *to the kingdom of culture.*[4]

At this point, pause to think of King and other inspirational leaders who have struggled to improve our society. Then continue:

> *I also wish to honor*
> *all who have extended the hand of friendship*
> *across the boundaries of race and nation,*
> *and class, and religion,*
> *and other divisions of people.*

You might recall to memory some of those persons who crossed social boundaries to give you an encouraging word, help you in some way, or show hospitality, courtesy, or some other consideration. You can complete this ritual by saying:

> *As this candle flame has released*
> *its light and warmth,*
> *so do my heartfelt blessings go forth,*
> *to all good people everywhere.*

If you are a person who has grown up in such circumstances that you have had few positive experiences with members of other groups, let this at least be an inspiration to create positive memories for others.

Suggestions

Considering the desire to build good relations between people of different colors, a rainbow candle might be ideal for this rite. Alternatively, you could burn a candle in warm colors, to symbolize the extension of warmth to others. If you have a choice of candle scent, or wish to use oils or incense, use any pleasant fragrance, or use rosemary for remembrance, bay laurel for honoring heroes, or scents that promote a sense of good will and well-being, such as lavender, bergamot, rose geranium, mandarin, palma rosa, vanilla, and frankincense.

59

A Rite for Earth Day

The gracious Earth provides us with many blessings, and on Earth Day, celebrated nationally on April 22 and internationally as the spring equinox, we can show our appreciation. In addition to other Earth Day activities, we can communicate love and concern for our planet with a little ceremony. The rite provided here starts with a salute which has been lifted and adapted from the Homeric hymn to the Earth. It is best if you can perform this rite outdoors, making an earth-touching gesture as you begin.

> *Greetings, oh well-formed Earth,*
> *you who are the mother of all.*
> *Your beauty nurtures all creatures*
> *that walk upon the land,*
> *and all the move in the deep,*
> *or fly in the air.[5]*

Then take up a candle, light it, and say:

> *O Mother Earth,*
> *As I light this candle,*
> *I honor and bless you now,*
> *for the favor and abundance*
> *that you have given us.*
> *May you have the love and respect*
> *of all of your peoples.*
> *May you have everything that you need*
> *for your own health and wholeness.*

Then, in keeping with the African-American tradition of wishing "from all parts of the world,"[6] you can turn to the east, raise the candle in the form of a salute, and say:

I greet you, lands of the East,
may you always thrive and flourish.

Then, face the south, west, and north in turn, repeating your salutation. You can end this rite by holding the candle at solar plexus level and saying,

Above, below, and at the fiery core,
may all within Earth's sphere be blessed.

Extinguish your candle or let it burn if you wish. If it is an outdoor candle, you could set it on a flat rock surface or a little altar made of sod (preferably in an open, brush-free clearing).

To demonstrate that your good wishes are genuine, you can back them up with some form of action, such as participation in a local clean-up, or by making a donation to an environmental cause.

Suggestions

Use any shape or color of candle that you think appropriate. You may want to use a green or brown candle for earth's green life or basic earthiness, or perhaps a blue candle, since this is often described as the "blue planet," due to its appearance from space. If you are using candle scent, incense, or oils, you could use patchouli or vetivert for their distinctively earthy fragrance, pine for its associations with environmental cleanliness, or any other scents redolent of free nature or your affection for Mother Earth.

The American observance of Earth Day on April 22 arose from the efforts of former Senator Gaylord Nelson (D–Wis.), who began to push for environmental education in 1962; with assistance from governors, mayors, educators, and many others he organized the first national Earth Day event on April 22, 1970. This celebration "was revived on a national level . . . in 1990 and gained support of over 200 million people from 141 countries" [Nelson, Internet]. A similar idea conceived by John McConnell was announced at a November 1969 UNESCO conference. He persuaded San Francisco and some other northern California cities to celebrate their first Earth Day on March 21, 1970. In 1971, the United Nations began its annual Earth Day celebration, which includes ringing the United Nations Peace Bell at the moment of the spring equinox [McConnell, Internet].

60

Memorial Day Remembrance

Memorial Day is held on the last Monday in May, or on May 30. It was instituted shortly after the Civil War, and now honors all who have died in wars since. Memorial Day was also known as Decoration Day, after the practice of decorating the graves of fallen soldiers, but this term has fallen out of usage; whole community participation in graveside ceremonies has also declined in many areas. If you would like to commemorate Memorial Day, consider the following:

For a ceremony to honor certain ancestors or loved ones, you could start by saying,

> [Name or Names],
> *We light this candle to honor you*
> *and all of your comrades.*

For a general ceremony to honor all of the fallen, you could start with,

> *We light this candle*
> *to honor all who have given their lives*
> *for this country.*

Then proceed with the following lines (which have been adapted from Oliver Wendell Holmes Jr.'s Memorial Day Speech of 1884).[7]

> *We honor you,*
> *you, who have been set apart*
> *by your experience,[8]*
> *you, who have taught us that life*
> *is a profound and passionate thing,*
> *you, who have brought to your work*
> *your mighty hearts,*
> *you, the best and noblest*

of your generation.
May you find peace and rest.
May you find new life and joy
in a better, brighter world.

This would be suitable as a ceremony performed either at home or at graveside.

Suggestions

To reflect the dignity of the occasion, plain candles and subdued scents are appropriate. You might choose white for purity, blue for loyalty, or pink for affection. Since crowns of bay laurel were traditionally used to honor heroes, this would be an ideal scent, as would other ennobled fragrances, such as cedar, benzoin, and cypress. In keeping with the idea of Decoration Day, you might want to decorate either the gravesite or your focus area with flags, mementos, and flowers.

61

Candles for the Fourth of July

The July 4 holiday commemorates the signing of the Declaration of Independence in 1776 (drafted by Thomas Jefferson). This is the document that states:

> We hold these truths to be self-evident, that all men are created equal, that they are endowed by their Creator with certain unalienable Rights, that among these are Life, Liberty and the pursuit of Happiness. That to secure these rights, Governments are instituted among Men, deriving their just powers from the consent of the governed . . .[9]

This document has played a very important role in guiding America's history, and setting an agenda that is still unfolding.[10] Unfortunately, the "men" who were created equal were understood by the signers to be white men of property, and certainly not blacks, Native Americans, and women. While some of the founders were more enlightened (such as John Adams, who refused to own slaves as a matter of principle, and whose wife Abigail vainly pleaded that the rights of "the ladies" not be forgotten by the new republic), the fact is that if they had insisted on extending rights to slaves, women, and other Americans who were not being governed by their own consent, most states would have refused to sign, and the union would never have come into being. Fortunately, the wording of the Declaration has enabled subsequent generations to claim a more inclusive interpretation, more genuinely grounded in human rights. It was this broader interpretation that Abraham Lincoln asserted in his Gettysburg Address, and which you may lay claim to in the following ritual. (Note that this is a ritual that you might want to perform in front of your children—perhaps along with readings of other historical documents—so that they will remember something about the Declaration when this subject comes up in school.)

This ritual calls for three candles: red, white, and blue. These colors nicely equate with the three major principles we celebrate, as red stands for the blood of Life, white for Liberty as a state of purity, and blue for the domestic peace that is an important basis of Happiness. To begin your July 4 celebration, you can say:

> *With the lighting of these candles,*
> *I affirm my commitment*
> *to the ideals of the American Revolution.*

Light the red candle and say:

> *I light this candle for Life.*

Then the white:

> *I light this candle for Liberty.*

Then the blue:

> *I light this candle for the pursuit of Happiness.*

Alternatively: if you have but one candle on hand, of any color, you can modify this rite by condensing it to say, "I light this candle for Life, Liberty, and the pursuit of Happiness."

You can conclude here, or you may add some of your own statements about how you benefit from as well as embody these ideals. You could also declare which areas of our national life and conscience still need improvement, recognizing that the American Revolution is an ongoing process.

When finished, allow the candles to burn as long as you wish. As you proceed with your other Independence Day celebrational activities (such as community parades), you might want to think about how they, too, are rituals that affirm certain ideals. As Roy. A. Rappaport has noted, "Ritual contains within itself not simply a symbolic representation of social contract, but tacit social contract itself."[11]

Suggestions

If you want to use candle scent or anointing oil, choose any pleasing fragrance. Vanilla is good for signifying domestic happiness; rose geranium, mandarin, neroli, and lavender promote a sense of well-being; and scents like cedar, benzoin, and bay laurel can convey the dignity of the occasion.

62

A Rite for Labor Day

Labor Day falls on the first Monday in September. We do not usually associate candles with labor or Labor Day with personal ritual, but as the reason for this holiday is easily obscured, I think it well to have some small commemoration. The struggle for recognition of the value of labor is ongoing, and it helps us to better appreciate the dignity of our own labor. And how much of our well being do we owe to the labor of other workers, both past and present! So many of our ancestors have labored under dehumanizing, back-breaking, soul-killing conditions—as do many in the world, still, today. However, even workers who benefit from improved modern conditions may still endure numerous hardships, and deserve recognition for their roles in generating society's prosperity. Therefore, it is a nice gesture to light a candle and say:

> *As I light this candle,*
> *I honor my own labor,*
> *I honor the labor of those*
>   *who have gone before me,*
> *and I honor the labor*
>   *of workers everywhere.*
> *May all labor be recognized and valued.*
> *May all labor be fairly rewarded.*

As you contemplate these words, you may especially want to extend appreciation to the working poor. As cultural critic Barbara Ehrenreich has pointed out, "The 'working poor' . . . are in fact the major philanthropists of our society. . . . they endure privation so that inflation will be low and stock prices high. To be a member of the working poor is to be an anonymous donor, a nameless benefactor, to everyone else."[12]

Suggestions

Note that this rite can be adapted for three candles, or one candle with three wicks. You can use candles in any color that you associate with the idea of labor; otherwise, a simple white candle can convey the dignity of this commemoration; brown, as a color of earth, is also associated with labor; and green could stand for the generative quality of labor. For candle scent, some simple earth scents like pine, vetivert, or patchouli might be suitable.

Hannah Arendt discusses the generativity of labor in The Human Condition. She looks at theories that labor is an important part of the "fertile life process," compares its ability to produce a surplus to "the superabundance we see everywhere in nature's household," and describes labor power as "the specifically human mode of the life force" [106–108].

63

A Rite for Veterans' Day

Veterans' Day was originally known as Armistice Day, commemorating the events of November 11, 1919, when, at the eleventh hour of that day, World War 1 was ended. Since that time, however, many more individuals have been called to serve in subsequent wars and conflicts, so the broader term, "Veterans' Day" was adopted. Although some Americans have ambivalent feelings about our country's involvement in foreign conflicts, it is important to acknowledge the struggles and sacrifices of veterans as individuals, and to welcome their participation in civilian life. If you would like to extend your blessings to veterans, you could perform a simple ceremony on the eleventh hour of the eleventh day of the eleventh month[13] by lighting a candle and saying:

> *As I light this candle,*
> *I honor all of our veterans,*
>   *and thank you for your service*
>   *to our country.*
> *Let the light of this candle*
>   *recall the loyalty you brought*
>   *to your time of service.*
> *Let the flame of this candle*
>   *affirm the energy you now bring*
>   *to the works of peace.*

If you want to honor an individual veteran, perhaps a family member or friend, you could modify the wording and light the candle while presenting it as a gift.

Robert Bly points out that the warrior energy required for military service needs to be remodulated for civilian life, and that veterans must also be acknowledged and reintegrated into society with appropriate rituals. Citing the fairy tale "Iron John," in which the princess rewards the hero by tossing him a golden apple, he decries the plight of Vietnam veterans who were unceremoniously returned and dumped into the streets, and states that they would have been better off "if we had arranged a festival in every small town in the country, in which the veterans had ridden by, and a young woman had thrown them golden apples" [197]. Native Americans have possibly handled this most effectively, honoring their veterans with the presentation of eagle feathers. (And their respect for veterans may be a reason why so many non-Indian exservicemen follow the powwow circuit).

Suggestions

A simple white candle will convey the dignity of the occasion, though a red candle can stand for veterans' readiness for action and sacrifice, a blue candle makes a statement about their loyalty and preservation of peace, and a gold candle proclaims heroism. To pick up on the symbolism of the number eleven, you could make a grouping of eleven small candles. Decorate your candle area with miniature flags and cut flowers, as well as the red paper poppies that are sold to raise funds for disabled veterans. For a choice of candle scent or oil, use any pleasing fragrance. Bay laurel would be ideal for honoring heroes, and other ennobled scents are benzoin, cedar, cypress, and sandalwood.

Poppies recall the blood shed in the fields of Flanders, memorialized in the famous poem by the Canadian poet John McCrae.

64

A Thanksgiving Prayer

Thanksgiving, which falls on the fourth Thursday in November, is the American holiday that preserves the ancient tradition of harvest festivals. In addition to preparing a huge feast of simple but traditional dishes and offering prayers of thanks for this plenitude, the observance of Thanksgiving includes counting our many blessings, such as the rights and privileges that come with living in a free country.

Many Thanksgiving observances also retell this holiday's historical origins, including the fact that the Pilgrim colonists were befriended by local Indians, who taught them survival techniques and contributed food to the first Thanksgiving feast. Today, this memory of friendship between two peoples of different races and beliefs is an important part of the lore and imagery of Thanksgiving. For thoughtful people, this suggests an ideal of how history might have taken a different course, if only more of this nation's forebears had been committed to wisdom, tolerance, and justice. While we are giving thanks for our abundance, we can restore this vision of harmony by making a commitment to see that all people share in this nation's prosperity. Thus, if you plan to set a candle on your Thanksgiving table, you may also wish to include a rite, such as the following:

As we light this candle,
let us give thanks
for all of the good things that we enjoy:
peace, prosperity,
the love of friends and family,
and so much more.
Let us ever be mindful of the blessings
that are here for us each moment,
hour, and day.
And as we express gratitude

for all of this goodness,
and all of the opportunities
that are available to us,
let us also remember our debt
to the land itself,
and to the people of all races
whose personal and historical sacrifices
have laid the ground of our well-being.
May we fulfill our duty
to protect this land and its creatures.
May we truly commit ourselves
to prosperity for all of its peoples.

Perhaps these words will encourage some conversation as to how greater prosperity can be achieved. When too many groups as well as individuals are competing for a thin slice of the pie, the solution may be to involve everyone in baking more and bigger pies.

Suggestions for Candles

You have a wide choice of candles to complement your Thanksgiving feast, as some candle makers produce candles with scents like "cranberry," "pumpkin pie," "apple pie," and "spiced cider," as well as novelty candles in the shapes of Pilgrims and turkeys. Otherwise, use any pleasing color and fragrance—perhaps autumnal colors and spicy scents.

Presentation Candles

Although most traditional candle-burning rites are performed at home, for one's own benefit, it is a nice gesture to present candles to others as special gifts. You can make a ritual of presenting such candles by lighting them while saying a blessing. This is something you can do for different types of occasions or celebrations. It is also something you can do just to bring cheer and pleasure to others.

While presenting gift candles, keep the following points in mind:

- This gesture will make more of an impression if you can present the candle, light it, and say your words of blessing with a flourish.

- After lighting such a candle, set it in a central place where its warmth and cheer can be appreciated—but make sure it is a safe place.

- It is okay if, for whatever reason, someone wishes to extinguish the candle afterward. It is not necessary to keep it burning, because your good wishes will already have been conveyed.

- In preparing such a candle, you can anoint it with oil, to put some of your own energy into it. However, do not light the candle until the moment you present it.

Following are some of the possibilities for candle-giving. (You will probably think of many other types of occasions, for which you can improvise your own presentations.)

65

A Candle for Friendship and Fellowship

Sometimes you may want to give a candle to a friend, or to a group of friends, just for the pleasure of it. While presenting the candle, you could say the following or similar words:

I light this candle
for good times past,
and good times to be.
Let its festive illumination
light up our celebration
of good times shared.

If you make this a regular practice, your friends will find it a reassuring consistency around which group memories can grow.

Suggestions

This is the sort of occasion where you could use whimsical novelty candles, or just use a candle in any pleasing shape, color, or scent. You could choose a peach-colored candle for extending warmth, pink for affection, or yellow for shared joys. For candle scent or anointing oil, lively fragrances like ginger, cinnamon, lavender, lemon, lemongrass, orange, tangerine, and peppermint will all add to the fun with friends.

66

A Birthday Candle

When celebrating friends' or family members' birthdays, the candles don't have to be limited to those on the cake. When you arrive at the party, you might want to light a special candle while saying:

[Name of birthday person],
as candles are part of the birthday tradition,
I light this special candle
to provide some extra power
for all of your birthday wishes.
May its light also illuminate my own wishes
for your increased health, wealth, and happiness,
and the best of everything, always.

You can leave the candle burning throughout the birthday party, and the birthday person can allow it to burn longer if he or she wishes. Since this candle is being used to add to the ambience, you will probably also want to give him or her a personal gift, separately, if this is a party where gifts are being presented.

Suggestions

You can choose birthday candles in the honorees' favorite colors, or astral colors (see appendix C), or whatever colors you associate with them. You could also use white to represent the purity of your wishes for them, or gold for the lucky energies of the Sun (since birthdays represent the Sun's return to its original position at a person's birth). If you can choose the candle scent, or if you want to anoint it with oil, use any scents that are among the birthday persons' favorites, or use bay laurel, West Indian bay, bergamot, cinnamon, orange, or mandarin, as their association with luck extends your birthday wishes.

67

A Candle for Lovers

For a romantic gesture, light a candle when you and your mate have some time set aside for intimacy. You can say something like:

I light this candle
> *for the love of my lover.*
May its flame help fuel
> *the fire of passion*
> *and the warmth of affection*
>> *between us.*
May the light of our love
> *be a flame that is ever renewed.*

You might wish to relight this candle the next morning, just to rekindle the memories of your special romantic evening.

Suggestions

Choose any candle and fragrance that enhances an atmosphere of love, romance, and passion. Red is the most favored color for this purpose; a heart-shaped candle might add a nice touch. Ylang ylang is an ideal fragrance for lovers because it is exotic and deeply sensual (often described as an aphrodisiac), but also classically romantic. Some other seductive scents are rose, jasmine, palmarosa, patchouli, cinnamon, ginger, and vanilla.

68

A Candle for a Couple

To convey your good wishes to a married or soon-to-be married couple, whether privately or at an engagement, wedding shower, reception, anniversary, family gathering, or other occasion, you could light a candle while saying:

> [Names of the pair] *I light this candle*
> *to celebrate your commitment*
> *to love and loyalty.*
> *As this candle burns brightly,*
> *so may the Spirit of Love*
> *continue to grow and thrive between you,*
> *increasing affection,*
> *and renewing passion.*

If they appreciate ritual, the couple could relight this candle later on, perhaps using the rite for lovers on the previous page.

Note: if this candle is intended for a wedding reception, you may want to find out first if the couple has planned to include a "Unity" candle in their ceremony (lighting of a large Unity candle from two smaller tapers, following the exchange of wedding vows) to avoid being redundant.

Suggestions

Use any color, shape, or fragrance of candle that will be meaningful to the couple in question: perhaps an elegant white candle to complement the bridal colors, blue for faithfulness, or red for passion as well as (in Asia) the energetic quality of luck. A delicately colored heart-shaped candle might also fit the occasion. For candle scent or oil, the sweet floral fragrance of ylang ylang stirs passion as well as affection, and neroli speaks of marital fulfillment. Palmarosa, vanilla, rose, rose geranium, bergamot, and frankincense are other scents that promote love and happiness.

69

A Gift for an Expectant Mother

As they slog through the uncertain and highly uncomfortable months of pregnancy, expectant mothers need a lot of encouragement. You can show your concern for a mother-to-be by offering her a candle while saying:

> *I present this candle*
>> *with my congratulations*
>> *for you, the mother-to-be.*
> *May its light provide you comfort*
>> *through an easy pregnancy*
>> *and a safe delivery.*
> *May you have a bright, healthy,*
>> *and loving child.*
> *May motherhood bring you*
>> *an abundance of blessings.*

The expectant mother will be better able to contemplate the glow of this candle, as well as the sincerity of your wishes, if you follow this rite by giving her a foot massage.

Suggestions

Present a mother-to-be with any color or fragrance of candle that she will enjoy. A round or egg-shaped candle would be symbolically fitting. Red is a good color, as it represents activity, the womb, and life within the womb. Otherwise, you might choose comforting colors such as blue for tranquility, pink for affection, or peach and yellow for warmth and joy. For candle scent or oil, use a comforting, uplifting fragrance, such as grapefruit, orange, tangerine, bergamot, vanilla, sandalwood, or ylang ylang. (Also, consult the section on safety at the end of appendix D, as some oils may be harmful for pregnant women.)

70

Blessing a New Baby

When you want to welcome a new baby into the world, whether at a baby shower or a visit to new parents, you can light a candle in front of the parents or parents-to-be while saying:

As you are bringing a special blessing
into this world
with the birth of your child,
so may the lighting of this candle
signal my own best wishes
for your new baby [or baby-to-be].
May this child grow strong in health and wholeness,
well-formed in mind and body,
and radiant in soul and spirit.

Incidentally, in my mother's family it has long been customary to present each new baby with a small pendant charm with an angel image. You could reword the above rite if, instead of a candle, you would like to present an angel figurine or some other type of symbolic gift for a baby.

Suggestions

If you want to be traditional, you could use a blue candle for a boy or a pink one for a girl, especially if this complements the color scheme in the nursery. However, yellow has become popular for children's accessories because it conveys joy and brightness, and has the advantage of being a gender-neutral color. For candle fragrance, scents like tangerine, mandarin, vanilla, rose geranium, lavender, chamomile, and palmarosa promote comfort and well being. (Also: consult the section on safety at the end of appendix D, as some fragrance oils may be harmful for small children.)

71

Blessing a Child

The things that we tell children are very important, because words have the power to bring things into being. If there are occasions when you have some quiet time with your child, grandchild, or some other youngster that is close to you, you can make a little ceremony of blessing. When the mood is right, bring out a candle, and light it while telling the child:

> [Name], *I want you to know*
> > *that you are special.*
> *Let this candle flame remind you*
> > *that you possess an inner light.*
> *May that light within you always respond*
> > *to the light within other people*
> *May that light within you*
> > *always guide you along the path*
> > > *of truth and goodness.*

May that light within you

always provide you

with hope and happiness.

You might want to carve the child's name into the candle. You could even make a little ceremony out of doing so, explaining the meaning of his or her name, or linking the letters of the name with special blessings.

Suggestions

Use any shape, color, or scent of candle that will charm a child. You could also pick a candle in one of the child's astral colors (see appendix C), or choose white for white light and innocence, pink for affection, peach for warmth, or yellow for youth and happiness. Some child-pleasing scents are lavender, mandarin, grapefruit, orange, tangerine, vanilla, and rose geranium. (Also: consult the section on safety at the end of appendix D, as some fragrance oils may be harmful for small children.)

Cautions

With this and any other candle rites you may perform in front of children, make sure that your children understand that they are not permitted to light candles themselves (unless supervised by an adult). Also, so that your children won't be tempted to mimic you by trying to perform rituals by themselves, do not leave any candles or matches within their reach.

72

A Candle for Family Gatherings

To enhance the mood of a large family dinner or get-together, call for everyone's attention, then hold up a candle as you say something like:

Now that most of us are gathered here,
I shall light this candle
as a way of giving gratitude
for our time together.

Now light the candle. If you don't like speeches, you can stop here. Otherwise, continue:

We are people who have a shared history,
and some shared memories,
and shared rituals,
and many other things that connect us.
We may also have some personal tensions,
but, respecting the value of family,
let us all be understanding and forgiving.
So let us now give thanks to our Deity,
and ask that we be blessed and protected,
and that those of us who are absent,
also be blessed and protected.
May we always come together
for memories to make,
and memories to share.

Little rituals like this can provide a framework around which other unique family rituals can be built.

Suggestions

Most festive candles are suitable. A white candle can symbolize unity, pink and peach can stand for affection and warmth, while green may be used to celebrate a family's growth. For candle scent and oils, use any pleasing fragrance. Vanilla stands for love of family, while scents like rose geranium, lavender, orange, ylang ylang, and palmarosa also produce a sense of family well-being.

73

Candles for Get-Well Wishes

To boost the spirits of ailing friends, you can take them a candle, and light it while saying something like:

The light of this candle

> *sets aglow my get-well wishes.*

As this candle generates light and warmth,

> *so may your vitality increase,*
>
> *assisting your full recovery.*

Of course, if you perform this rite for a very sick person, you should make sure that there is a caretaker or someone else on hand who will be able to put the candle out, when necessary.

Suggestions

You might want to use a white candle for the healing power of white light, red for energy, green for regeneration, or whatever color seems beneficial for the patient's physical condition or frame of mind. If you can choose the candle scent or use anointing oil, you might try an energizing, uplifting fragrance like bergamot, rose geranium, grapefruit, lavender, lemon, mandarin, palma rosa, pine, sandalwood, tangerine, or vanilla. (Consult the pages on essential oils and safety at the end of appendix D, as certain oils—even those considered ideal for general healing purposes—have been alleged to aggravate certain conditions.)

74

A Candle for Cheer

When someone you know is in need of a little extra encouragement, you can take him or her a candle, and present it with the following wishes:

> *May the light of this candle*
> > *beam you a ray of hope.*
> *May the warmth of this candle*
> > *bring you a touch of cheer.*
> *May the scent of this candle*
> > *awaken your sense of possibility.*

When you have returned home, the candle may continue to convey your presence by just "being there" for your friend.

Suggestions

Any pleasing candle color, shape, or scent is naturally cheering. Pink, peach, yellow, and softer shades of orange encourage a positive outlook. Some scents that produce uplifting moods are neroli, lemon balm, tangerine, mandarin, bergamot, vanilla, palmarosa, and ylang ylang.

75

A Housewarming Gift

When visiting friends' new homes, you can take them a candle and perform the simple rite for blessing a space on page 9. Alternatively, you could light the candle and say the following words, which are part of a traditional Jewish house blessing used by my friend, Martha Adler:

Light! Forever Light!

For the rest of your lives,

light in your lives

and lightness in your hearts.

If you want to perform Martha's entire housewarming ceremony, you can also present a bag of sugar with the words, "So there will always be sweetness in your life," a box of salt with the words, "So there will always be spice in your life," and a loaf of bread while saying, "And in this house, in addition to the love that nourishes, let there also be the nourishment necessary for body, mind, and soul." (Martha's rite calls for sugar, salt, bread, and some candles to be presented in that order.)

Suggestions

Use a candle in a color or shape that complements your hosts' decor, or use pink, peach, or yellow for extending warmth and affection. In her book *Exploring Candle Magick*, Patricia Telesco suggests that a square candle to symbolize foundations, or a house-shaped candle would make a good "amuletic house candle."[1] If you use scented candles or anointing oil, choose any pleasing fragrance, or try vanilla for domestic happiness, or other scents that promote well-being, such as lavender, neroli, rose geranium, palmarosa, mandarin, sandalwood, or bay laurel.

Some Additional Thoughts on Candles as Gifts

Candles make ideal gifts because while they burn, they create a warm and elegant ambience. However, because they are quickly used up, they are unlikely to be the sort of unwanted gifts that sit around catching dust or clashing with the decor. Also, because high quality candles can be fairly costly, they needn't be perceived as "cheap" gifts, and they provide a luxury that the recipient will enjoy, but might not normally buy for him- or herself. However, it may be wise to avoid giving candles that are too fancy, because then the recipients may be reluctant to burn them, and so they end up as dust-catchers anyway.

Rites for Reaching Out to Others in Spirit

The rituals in this section are premised on the belief that we can communicate good will and blessings directly to the spirits of others, whether living or dead, human or nonhuman.

76

Dedicating Candles to Other People

Our friends and loved ones are often on our minds, because our own lives cannot be meaningful outside of our connections to others. Therefore, we miss them when they are away, and we may worry about their health and safety, their prosperity and career advancement, the quality of their relationships, and their happiness and well-being. Fortunately, we can dedicate candles to the special persons in our lives and keep them on hand, to burn occasionally or to burn often, as a way of sending blessings whenever there is a special need, or just because we want to "beam" them some good feelings. When you wish to create a sympathetic connection with another person, light a candle while saying:

> *As I light this candle,*
>> *I dedicate it to* [name],
>>> *my* [state relationship to you].
>> [Name], *may you be blessed*
>>> *with all my loving wishes,*
>> *and know that you*
>>> *are always in my heart and mind.*

Pause and think warm thoughts about the person in question, concentrating on the qualities that make him or her special to you. Summon your happiest memories and your best wishes for him or her. Then, allow the candle to burn at least twenty minutes, as a way of strengthening the bond. You can keep this and other such candles out on display, or you can store it in a cool place, to be brought out whenever you want to renew or celebrate your connection. Here are some ways that you can use candles dedicated to others:

- Burn the candles to invite the spiritual presence of absent family members to meals, gatherings, or celebrations—likewise for absent friends when you have a group who get together regularly.

- It is pleasant to light such candles to promote sympathetic links when writing letters to friends or family members.

- Use these candles to send your helping energy whenever loved ones are going through hard times, or are just in need of a little cheer.

- If you maintain a home altar, you can keep candles dedicated to your special loved ones on it. As a personal altar serves as an icon of integrated selfhood, the inclusion of candles for others enables you to express an extended sense of selfhood—your "relational" self.

Suggestions for candles

To dedicate a candle to another person, you can choose one in that person's favorite color, or some other color that you associate with him or her. If you know that person's birth date, you can choose an "astral" color, which is one of the colors associated with his or her sign of the zodiac (see appendix C). Otherwise, you might wish to choose pink as a statement of your affection, peach for extending warmth, or white for purity of intention. For added focus, you can inscribe the candles with the person's name, the glyph for his or her Sun sign, or other symbols that would be meaningful to him or her. If you can choose your candle scent, or if you use anointing oil, you could use vanilla for promoting a loving relationship,[1] ylang ylang for creating empathy,[2] orange for maintaining warm communications, or any other scent that is pleasing to you, or a favorite of the person in question.

77

An Appeal to a Hardened Heart

When the soul and spirit of one person can communicate to the soul and spirit of another, it is possible to bypass personal prejudice. The following rite is designed to communicate good will and a desire for conciliation when another person has taken a dislike to you, or is nursing some grudge against you. Perhaps you did something unfortunate to give him (or her) a bad opinion of you, or perhaps it is one of those antipathies that can't be explained. Nevertheless, if it is important for to you to get along, you can try to appeal to his or her better nature.

To perform this rite, choose a candle and inscribe your subject's name on it. If you have a piece of rose quartz, this, too, can be used in this rite. When ready, light the candle while trying to visualize this person as clearly as you can. Picture your subject at his or her very best, being cheerful, friendly, and helpful. Now recite the following:

> [Name], *I call to your mind, and soul, and spirit.*
> *My mind calls to your mind,*
> > *my soul and spirit call to your soul and spirit.*
> [Name], *know that I only seek good will,*
> > *and good will is what I extend to you.*

At this point, hold your dominant hand over the candle flame (at a safe distance), and then place it over your heart. If you have a piece of rose quartz, you can also hold it up to the flame and then enclose it in your hand as you do this. (The rose quartz amplifies the powers of your heart chakra, which is the psychic energy center that radiates affection, compassion, and loving kindness.) Now think warm, kindly thoughts, mentally beaming them to the person in question. Among other things, you can visualize the two of you coming together on very open and friendly terms. At the same time, imagine that the energy generated by your heart chakra is expanding and flowing outward, touching the heart of the other person. Then, continue:

> [Name], *as this candle burns,*
> > *so may your heart be warmed.*
> [Name], *as this candle burns,*
> > *so may your heart be softened.*
> [Name], *as this candle burns,*
> > *so may your heart be lightened.*

You may close this rite by saying, "So it is, and so shall it be." Leave the candle burning for a little while, or extinguish it if you wish. You might want to relight the candle on a daily basis, though it is not necessary to redo this ritual again unless you want to. If the person in question isn't showing a change of heart by the time the candle is all burned down, just let it go for a while. Maybe the time is not yet right for this person to come around. You could try this rite again, after a certain interval of time.

Suggestions

Use a color that links you with the other person or expresses your desire for good will. You could use white for purity of intention, peach for extending warmth, or light blue for serenity and objectivity; alternatively, you might choose your subject's favorite color, or one of his (or her) "astral" colors (see appendix C). Certain candles, which are sold around Valentine's Day and feature solid wax hearts within a matrix of gel, would also be ideal for this rite. If you use candle fragrance, anointing oil, or incense, use any scent that is known to be a favorite of the person in question, or try rose, rose geranium, ylang ylang, orange, mandarin, lavender, vanilla, neroli, or palmarosa, as these scents promote good will and create a favorable impression. Also, you can enhance your focus if you have anything that creates a sympathetic link with this person, such as photographs, belongings, or things that he or she has handled. You might want to experiment with this rite just before dawn, when peoples' minds are believed to be more open to spiritual communication.

78

A Rite for Evoking the Good in Others

For many of us, a major cause of pain and worry is the fear or realization that someone near and dear may be sliding into unethical behavior patterns. Therefore, the following rite is designed to help when someone in your circle, whether a friend or a relative, or a neighbor or a coworker, has been displaying signs of cruelty, failing to do right by others, or possibly even developing criminal tendencies. Inspired by the possibility that one can communicate directly to a person's deep mind, soul, or what is often called the "higher self," this rite tries to evoke the best in another person by generating a sympathetic state through which you can transmit thoughts of loving kindness, compassion, sympathetic joy, and equanimity. (These qualities, known as the Brahmaviharas,[3] are called the "four godly abidings" or "boundless states.") The intention of this rite is to show the other person that it feels good to be good.

When you feel the need to perform this rite, you can select a single candle, or you can use five candles, lighting one as you begin the rite, and then lighting the others in turn, as you go through the next four visualizations. (If you have only one candle, just go through the rite and do the visualizations and affirmations, disregarding the instructions to light the other candles.) To proceed with this rite, inscribe the name of the person about whom you are concerned into the first candle, and then light it, reciting the following words:

> [Name], *as I light this candle,*
> *I call to you*
> *and invoke everything that is good in you.*
> *So also do I call to your soul and spirit,*
> *to your higher self,*
> *to your guardian angel,*
> *and to all spirits of guidance*

> *who care for your well-being.*
> *Please be open to these loving wishes,*
> *and work toward promoting the happiness*
> *which so depends on good thoughts*
> *and good actions.*

Pause and try to form a very clear picture of this person in your mind. Then, you can inscribe the second candle (if you have one) with the person's name, and light it as you continue:

> [Name], *may your mind and heart*
> *be filled with loving kindness.*

Then fill your own mind and heart with images of loving kindness, including yourself showing kindness to this person, and him (or her) showing kindness to others. If you have witnessed him performing acts of kindness on some previous occasions, make these images especially bright and sharp in your visual memory. Then, send a mental affirmation to tell the person:

> [Name], *you are a good person,*
> *and you are loved and supported*
> *by spiritual forces.*

Then inscribe and light the third candle and say:

> [Name], *may your mind and heart*
> *be filled with compassion.*

As you say so, concentrate on the compassion you have felt for any sorrows that this person has suffered, and then visualize him or her reacting with compassion to the suffering of others. If you have seen instances where this person acted compassionately, highlight these images in your mind. Then tell the person:

> [Name], *you are a good person,*
> *and you are loved and supported*
> *by spiritual forces.*

Then, inscribe and light the fourth candle and say:

> [Name] *may your mind and heart*
>> *be filled with sympathetic joy.*

Visualize yourself taking pleasure in whatever successes, achievements, or strokes of luck this person has enjoyed, and then visualize him or her taking pleasure in the happiness of others. Again, if you know of instances where the person has done this, accentuate them in your visualizations. Say:

> [Name], *you are a good person,*
>> *and you are loved and supported*
>>> *by spiritual forces.*

Then, inscribe and light the fifth candle and say:

> [Name], *may your mind and heart*
>> *know equanimity.*

Equanimity is the calm understanding that enables a person to control impulses, manage emotions, deal with everything rationally, discern the difference between right and wrong, and value the path of wisdom. Summon to your mind any images that suggest equanimity to you, such as those of legendary wise men or women, saints, or perhaps serene Buddha-type figures. Then, try to mentally convey this sense of calm, peace, and wisdom to the person you are trying to influence. Envision your subject as the picture of equanimity, responding calmly and wisely to any challenges. Again, say:

> [Name], *you are a good person,*
>> *and you are loved and supported*
>>> *by spiritual forces.*

You may consider the rite closed at this point, saying:

> *So it is and so shall it be.*

Extinguish the candles or let them burn for a while if you wish. You may want to repeat this ceremony (or at least relight the candles) every evening until they are burned down. If the person whom you are trying to influence has not shown a change of heart or tried to turn his or her life around by this time, have faith that some changes may be at work on a deeper level. However, whether this person shows signs of improvement or not, you must be practical, cautious, and realistic in dealing with him or her. Avoid getting into any positions where you could be abused or exploited by this person. This ritual has provided a way that you can show your concern without being taken advantage of.

Suggestions for Enhancing This Rite to Evoke Good in Others

In choosing a candle for this rite, there are many possibilities for the use of color. For the first candle, which can be used to represent the person who is your subject, you could choose his (or her) favorite color, or one of his or her "astral" colors (see Appendix C), or some other color that has strong associations with this person. If you are using a single candle, you could choose white for purity of intention, pink for affection, peach for extending personal warmth, light blue for calm sincerity, or green for the chakra (psychic energy center) of the healing heart. If you are using four additional candles, you could choose pink for loving kindness because it combines action and affection, blue for compassion, yellow or peach for sympathetic joy, and white for equanimity. (Note that my use of color symbolism is borrowed from Western folklore and psychology; it is possible that some Asian groups have associated different colors with these four qualities, but my knowledge of other cultures is not that extensive.) If you use candle fragrance or anointing oil, or if you want to burn incense, you can use any pleasing scent. You might try neroli, mandarin, rose, palmarosa, or ylang ylang for softening the heart and promoting empathy.

Also, it would help your focus if you have at hand anything that reminds you of this person or creates a sympathetic link with him (or her), such as photographs, personal belongings, things that he or she has handled, and so on. In fact, you could set up a little shrine dedicated to this person, surrounding his or her photo with protective religious figures and other images of goodness.

79

Rite for the Newly Dead

Ordinarily, when I think about death, I like to take the attitude of J. M. Barrie's *Peter Pan*, who, when faced with drowning in the Mermaids' Lagoon, proclaimed, "To die will be an awfully big adventure."[4] I wonder what new experiences lie ahead—whether they will involve reuniting with loved ones in some Heaven world, exploring other dimensions of existence, or being reborn in some new time, place, and culture. Some religious and metaphysical teachings also hold that after death our spirits may gain a greater understanding of life's mysteries. However, whenever I have lost someone close to me, it's a different matter because of the pain of loss and a creeping fear that maybe death is truly all there is, and that no reunion will be possible. Even the most religious among us must surely experience moments of doubt. At such times, contemplating the permanent loss of a loved one is even more terrifying than the thought of facing one's own extinction. And yet, the spiritual beliefs of many lands and ages describe rebirth into another body or into a beautiful world beyond. Modern mediums have provided some astonishing revelations, and many individuals' near-death experiences also testify to light and peace and reunion with loved ones on the other side, so we can be hopeful that death is indeed only a transition.

Because our anxieties can be greatest when we have just lost a friend or loved one, the following rite may be helpful in communicating concern and loss to the one now dead, and calling on spiritual powers to protect and guide him or her throughout this transitional period. To perform this rite, light a candle and recite the following or similar words. You can customize this rite by adding your own feelings and concerns for the person for whose benefit you will perform it, and by incorporating statements of your own religious faith.

> *As I light this candle,*
> *I honor and bless the spirit*
> *of my friend* [or loved one], [Name].

[Name], *may you fare well*

> *in this, your soul's greatest journey,*
>
> *in this, your spirit's new adventure.*

[Name],

> *know that all your friends and loved ones miss you;*
>
> *for you have deeply affected all our lives.*

At this point, it is good to pause as you summon your happiest memories of times shared with the departed loved one. Then continue:

> *But* [Name], *I have faith*
>
> > *in immortality, rebirth, and transcendence,*
>
> *and I look forward to meeting you again,*
>
> > *perhaps in a world beyond,*
> >
> > *outside of time,*
> >
> > *and outside of space.*
>
> *And it is my prayer that you*
>
> > *are being guided by other loved ones,*
> >
> > *and other spirits of light.*

At this point, you can visualize this person in radiant spirit form, being surrounded by the spirits of other friends and relatives, and being welcomed into a beautiful new land by shining angels or spirits of guidance. Then proceed:

> [Name], *as I think about you now,*
>
> *I offer a prayer for your well-being:*
>
> *I call upon you, my Deity,*
>
> *who is manifest in all of the good, loving,*
>
> > *and protective powers of the universe.*
>
> *And I call to all angels of guidance,*
>
> > *and to all good and protective spirits.*
>
> *Please go to my friend* [Name],
>
> *and give his* [or her] *spirit strength*

in this, his [her] *time of transition*
into the ethereal state,
into the world of spirit.
Please help [Name] *and protect him* [or her],
that he [she] *may readily go forward*
into a better state of existence.
And please,
for the sake of we who remain behind,
grant us a word or sign of comfort,
that we may renew our faith
and look forward to reunion
with all of those whom we have loved.

Then, close the rite by saying:

Until we meet again,
so it is, and so it shall be.

You can extinguish the candle, or allow it to burn if you wish. You can relight the candle or dedicate a new one each evening if this gives you comfort.

Note: in my paternal grandmother's family, there was a belief that the spirits of the dead walk the earth for forty days and nights before making their transition—during which time, they may contact the living to take care of unfinished business. This is, of course, just one belief among the world's many beliefs about passing over. However, you may wish to perform this candle rite every night for that length of time, or for whatever length of time your personal religious, family, or cultural traditions may deem significant. Having a fixed period of time in which to send good energy and prayers on behalf of the dead is psychologically reassuring, and contributes to the sense of closure when the period of devotion has been fulfilled.

Suggestions for Enhancing This Rite

A simple white candle is appropriate because it symbolizes spiritual essence and the state of purity and freedom to which the soul returns in death. However, a candle in a color that was a favorite of the person you are honoring, or an "astral" candle based on his or her sign of the zodiac, would also be good. (See appendix C.) If you wish to choose a scented candle, burn incense, or anoint the candle with oil, you can use any pleasing fragrance—especially if you know a fragrance of which this person was fond. You could also use spiritually protective fragrances such as frankincense, myrrh, lemon, lemongrass, rose geranium, rosemary, or sandalwood; or try copal or cypress, which are traditional for mourning. You can further dedicate the candle by inscribing into the candle, with a knife or incising tool, the person's name along with words and symbols that express your bond of affection with the person. It is also helpful to decorate your focus area with photos, belongings, and other objects that give you a sense of connection.

Riva says that lemon fragrance is "[u]sed by mediums as an aid in calling the spirits," and can be used to "entice protective spirits into the home" [78]. Greer suggests that lemongrass can be used "to help in spirit communication" [62].

80

A Rite of Remembrance for the Dead

In words of comfort, we are often told that our departed loved ones are never truly dead as long as we keep them alive in memory. While I believe in a survival of the spirit that doesn't depend upon the actions and remembrance of the living, there is something to the power of memory. The following candle rite is designed to help maintain a sense of spiritual connection with loved ones by rekindling memories. It can be performed whenever you feel like it, or on significant occasions such as certain anniversaries, or on All Hallows Eve, which is a traditional time for remembering the dead. This rite includes a ritual action that you can perform to achieve the materialization of memory through the power of the written word. At the appropriate point in the ritual, you can pause to write down at least one memory of the person that you wish to honor. This is inspired by the African word "nommo," a concept that expresses the idea of calling lost ones back into life through the power of the word.

When you are ready to perform the rite, light your candle and say the following, or similar words that you have modified to fit your own sentiments:

> *I dedicate this candle to the memory of* [Name],
> [state the person's name and relationship to you].
> [Name], *I want you to know that I miss you and think of you.*
> *The memories of the times we've shared are very important to*
> *me, and I feel that some part of you*
> *has become a part of me*
> *by living in my memory.*
> *There are so many things that I appreciate*
> *when I recount the memories that I have:*
> *not just big things, but little things,*
> *such as your unique personality,*
> *your acts of consideration,*

the ideas and values you believed in,

your [here you can add some of your own sentiments

to personalize the rite].

If you had some quarrels or personality conflicts with this person, you can add:

[Name],

I realize that there have also been some problems between us,

but those memories are fading,

and they cease to mean anything to me.

Continue:

Your good qualities shine all the brighter,

and I see them now,

enveloped in the golden light of memory.

At this point, pause to recall at least one happy memory. Add strength to the memory by visualizing it, and "turn up the light" in your visual memory by imagining the details growing brighter and more vivid. Then, if you wish, you can perform the following action, saying:

To honor our relationship,

I will now write down a memory of you.

Write down one small memory vignette on an index card or in a journal kept for this purpose. If you do this every now and then, you will eventually have recorded a collection of positive memories. If they are memories of a family member, you will have compiled something valuable for your other relatives.

Then, you can close the rite by saying:

I now close this rite,

by sending you love and blessings.

You are always with me,

And I am confident that my warm thoughts of you

> *will accompany you now, in whichever world*
> *your spirit resides.*

At this point, you may leave the candle burning or extinguish it, to be reused the next time you perform this rite. You can conclude the rite by saying:

> *Until we meet again,*
> *so it is, and so shall it be.*

Suggestions for enhancing this rite

In selecting a candle, white is an appropriate color because it symbolizes the purity of the spiritual state, though gold is also good because the ritual makes a reference to the golden glow of memory. A candle in a color that reminds you of the person you intend to honor would also be suitable. If you know that person's sign of the zodiac, you can choose an "astral" candle for him or her, based on the chart in appendix C. You can further dedicate the candle by inscribing into it, with a knife or incising tool, the person's name along with words and symbols that express your bond of affection with him or her. If you can choose your candle scent or want to use anointing oil or incense, you can use any pleasing scent—especially if you know of a scent that was a

favorite of the deceased person. You could also try rosemary, for though it can have a medicinal smell, it has strong folkloric associations with remembrance. Other fragrances that stimulate memory and/or are considered to be welcoming to spirits are cedar, cinnamon, clove, juniper, cypress, frankincense, lemon, lemongrass, and sage.

When you perform this rite, it is also a good idea to set out some photos or other belongings of the person in question, as an aid to memory. If you intend to do this regularly, you might want to keep some of these mementos in a small decorative box, along with the candle dedicated for this purpose.

81

A Rite for Honoring Your Ancestors

Many traditional societies use ritual to maintain relationship with the "ancestor world," because they believe that the ancestors maintain their concern for the human community. The ancestors' participation in human affairs is illustrated in Chinua Achebe's description of the traditional village; he relates: "It's a world of men and women and children and spirits and deities and animals and nature . . . and the dead—this is very important—a community of the living and the dead and the unborn." Because of this interdependence of the physical and spiritual worlds, Achebe states that, "whatever you did in the village took this into account."[5] Such a belief is often labeled as "ancestor worship," but folklorist Clarissa Pinkola Estés asserts that it should more correctly be called "ancestor kinship."[6] Cross-cultural anthropologist Angeles Arrien cites beliefs that the ancestors take an active interest in us as individuals, explaining that, "ancestor spirits are invested in seeing the current generations and the generations to come fulfill their dreams or life purpose." In our own lives, she emphasizes the need to "bring forward the good, true, and beautiful" in a family lineage, and she suggests that the "ancestors" to whom we can look for guidance are not just our blood relatives, but also "inspirational historical figures."[7]

Many modern ritualists seek inspiration from the ancestor world, and some burn candles to communicate their respect. The following is a simple rite that you can perform whenever you want to strengthen your own connection. Light a candle and say:

> *O my forebears, O my ancestors,*
> *You whom I have known and loved,*
> *and you who have gone before,*
> > *with names and lives unknown to me,*
> > > *yet alive within my body,*
> > > *and within my family's traditions,*

let the warmth of this flame
convey my blessings.
At this time I honor you
and claim the best from you,
that everything good be preserved,
and that every good thing be remembered.
O my ancestors,
in whichever worlds you wander,
may your ways be blessed.

Allow the candle to burn as long as you wish. For a Caribbean touch, you could also set out a goblet of fresh water, perhaps adding a drop of rum, lemon juice, or anise extract, as tradition holds that spirits find this refreshing. As you go through your day, you might want to think about the ways that your ancestors' lives have informed your own.

Malbrough has an effective rite for "[b]ridging the gap of communication with the ancestors" [57–65]. Budapest provides a meditation for reaching your ancestors [Goddess 122-25], and RavenWolf suggests greeting the ancestors as part of regular devotions, observing that by burning a candle in their honor, you are "[m]ystically lighting your path across time" [18–19, 88].

Also: traditional peoples often call on the ancestors for help. For example, Malidoma Somé relates that his people, the Dagara of Burkina Faso, make such petitions, opening with words like, "I greet you, spirits of my ancestors; I greet you spirit guides, friends of the invisible. . . ."[8] Of course, in those societies the obligations go both ways. It is pleasant to think that we westerners, too, could receive blessings from the ancestor world, but for many hundreds of years we have done little to send any good energy back. Positive rituals like this one can help, and I think that we can also nourish our ancestral spirits by thinking lovingly and kindly of those we have known, reminding ourselves of the good qualities that we have inherited or claimed from them, achieving a better (but forgiving) understanding of their failings, striving for accomplishments that they can be proud of, and filling our lives with joy and celebration, so that the spirit community won't just be burdened with knowledge of our problems.

Suggestions

Use any color candle that helps you focus on your ancestral connection. A white candle can symbolize the whole spectrum of ancestral gifts and blessings, as well as the state of purity to which most souls return in death. Yellow or peach would be good for extending warmth and affection, while silver could symbolize the ethereal qualities of the world of spirit. For scented candles, anointing oil, or incense, you can use any pleasant fragrance. Lemon, lemongrass, and copal have been associated with spirit communication, and frankincense, myrrh, rosemary, rose geranium, anise, sandalwood, and cypress are known as spiritually protective fragrances. To aid your focus, it helps to set up an altar area with old photographs as well as heirloom objects. (You could keep these objects in a special chest, to have on hand for this purpose.)

82

Dedicating a Candle to a
Special Place in Nature

Sometimes a beautiful spot in nature—some place that has the inspirational qualities of a shrine—may affect you so deeply that you want to make a gesture of appreciation, to acknowledge the tranquility or power that you experience there. When communing with Nature in this manner, you can light a candle while saying:

> *I honor the spirit of this place.*
> *I honor the peace, freedom, beauty,*
> *and wildness of this place.*
> *O may this place*
> *be ever blessed and protected,*
> *O may all life in this place*
> *continue to thrive and flourish.*
> *So it is, and so shall it ever be.*

It goes without saying that you should only perform this rite in places where there is no fire hazard, and that you should choose candles (such as jar candles) that are safe and appropriate for outdoor use.

Also: it is a human instinct to affirm our interconnectedness by leaving offerings at sacred or numinous natural sites. Offerings have included milk, honey, grains, flowers, wreaths, ribbons, beads, coins, gemstones, tobacco, and incense. Instead of burning a candle, you could perform the above rite while presenting such an offering, provided there are no rules against leaving objects, (or concerns about disturbing the ecological balance of the site). Indeed, the energy and verve that you put into your performative words and gestures can be more important than the type of offering you leave (and you can say these words of blessing even if you have no candle or other offering to leave), because, as the poet Gary Snyder has pointed out, "performance is currency in the deep world's gift economy."[9]

Suggestions for Candles

Choose any color candle that seems appropriate to the place in question, though green for life, growth, and regeneration, may be ideal. If you use anointing oil or scented candles, any pleasant fragrance will do, especially if its scent harmonizes with the surrounding environment. You could try patchouli for its scent of freshly turned earth, vetivert for its earthy-woodsy fragrance, or other woodsy scents such as cedar, juniper, pine, or balsam fir. You can also use incense in some of these fragrances. When incense is burned out of doors, the scent isn't entirely dissipated—some of the scent will linger.

Further Thoughts

When Pagans, poets, and philosophers make ritual greetings or offerings to special features of Nature such as trees, rocks, springs, and so forth, they are sometimes accused of "idol worship." But consider this: when you send your aunt a thank you card because she gave you a nice birthday present, do we call that "auntie worship"? No, we call that "good manners." By the same token, gestures of appreciation for nature help us show respect, affinity, and kinship. They also demonstrate our commitment to a moral universe that includes other beings beside our own kind.

The word "numinous" applies to things, places, or experiences that possess a certain power or soul force, so people perceive that they have a mystical quality. The power that inheres in a place or object can be referred to as its "numen." The ancient Romans believed that people could refresh the numen of a place or thing through a ritual infusion of energy.

83

A Rite for Honoring Domestic Spirits

In the worldview of many traditional peoples, the universe is intensely alive with spirits and spiritual forces, including those that inhabit certain places or are embodied by physical things. Out of a desire to live in good relationship with this in-spirited world, many folkloric traditions have sought ritual means of promoting the well-being of spirits associated with human households. These domestic spirits can include the spirits of the land upon which one lives and the spirits associated with different features of the house, and also ancestor spirits, the spirit guardians of individual family members, and any other spirits who take an interest in a particular household. If you would like to perform a rite to maintain a friendship with your own spirits of home and place, you can burn a candle while saying:

> *With light, and warmth, and fragrance,*
> *I honor the spirits of this place:*
> > *spirits of this land and its creatures,*
> > *spirits of this house and household,*
> > *and spirits with ties to our family,*
> > > *be that through blood or bonding.*
> *May we all thrive and prosper together,*
> > *as we respect and bless each other.*

You might want to assign a special time for performing this rite, such as every morning, or every Monday (a day whose planetary powers are focused on the home), or the first day of the month, or once a year on the anniversary of the day you bought or moved in to your home, or at whatever intervals seem appropriate to you.

Also, if your house and home haven't been very happy or fortunate for you, even if there are tangible reasons why this is so, you may be able to improve your condition by nurturing the spirits of your house, and the spirit of the house itself. When we act as if there are spirits and a spirit of the house, even if we don't believe in them in an entirely literal way, we develop a more engaged relationship with our home and land, and become more sensitive to maintaining the overall harmony.

Suggestions

Use any color or shape of candle that harmonizes with your sense of your home place. White signifies purity and unity, pink and peach suggest the glow of well-being, blue can represent domestic tranquility, and green stands for growth and prosperity. If you use scented candles, anointing oils, or incense, use any pleasant fragrance; some fragrances that can be used for blessing household spirits include vanilla, lemongrass, rose geranium, sandalwood, cedar, bay laurel, anise, and frankincense.

If you don't always feel like burning a candle, you can perform this ritual while simply lighting a stick of incense. Also, this is the kind of rite that you might enjoy performing at a little altar or shrine in your home or garden, one that has been constructed to celebrate a household extended to include all friendly beings and essences who inhabit your space. Such an altar might display photos of family members as well as ancestors; interesting stones, nuts, feathers, or other natural items found on your property; a miniature house (reminiscent of the "spirit houses" of Thailand); miniatures of some birds and animals that share your land; and/or fruits and flowers from your garden.

84

The Death of a Pet

The loss of a pet can be mourned as deeply and genuinely as the death of another human person, especially because of the pure and uncritical quality of love and companionship that animals provide. Unfortunately, due to their relatively short lifespans, those of us who keep pets must grieve over many such losses during our own lifetimes. To help express your concern when a pet has died, you can light a candle while saying the following or similar words:

> *I call upon you, my Deity,*
> *and all protective spirits,*
> *you who watch over the lives of animals,*
> *and have the power to guide their souls*
> *to a better life and a better world.*
> *Please be with my loved one, [name pet].*
> *Please comfort him [or her], and surround him*
> *with love and light and warmth.*
> *Please help him find a new home,*
> *in a place where love and happiness*
> *will ever attend him.*

As you go over these words, you could also visualize angels, departed family members, or spirits of Nature leading your pet into a beautiful sphere of light, knowing that spiritual forces will be looking after him, for James van Praagh, who has written about his experiences as a medium, claims that there are "animal caretakers" on the other side. He says, "These keepers are generous, loving souls who watch over our pets until a family member with strong love ties to the pet joins it in the spirit world."[10]

Suggestions

Any pleasing candle will do. A white candle can stand for innocence and purity, pink and peach for affection, and green for rebirth and the freedom of nature. Simple nature scents, such as pine, cedar, juniper, cypress, balsam fir, or sage would be suitable for candle scent, oil, or incense. If you are burying your pet in your own yard, you could leave a jar or vigil candle by the graveside.

85

A Prayer for the Animals

The lives of animals are fraught with hardship and danger, for they must compete to find food while trying to avoid becoming prey to others. Added to their travails is habitat destruction, as well as torture at the hands of some humans.[11] Even dogs, cats, and other house pets are not free from suffering, for only a very small minority of them find good homes.[12] Although struggle is an unavoidable part of most animals' lives, here is a prayer that requests, nevertheless, that animals may also have some comfort. You can light a candle while saying,

> *Dear God,* [or name of your Deity],
> *I call upon you,*
> *and all the protective spirits of Nature,*
> *please bless the lives of animals,*
> *that each may have a share*
> *of joy and contentment.*
> *And as the well-being of animals*
> *so depends upon the actions of humans,*
> *please turn human hearts to works of kindness.*
> *Inspire them to do right*
> *by the animals in their lives,*
> *and to improve the lives of animals*
> *in the larger world.*

Then, if your religious views include an idea of souls or spirits for animals, you can add:

> *Dear God, as you bless the lives of animals,*
> *please also bless their spirits,*
> *so that they may know a greater share of happiness*
> *in a life beyond pain and struggle.*

Your intentions in saying the last lines of this prayer would of course be guided by your religious orientation. For example, some persons who believe in reincarnation may hope for the intervention of celestials (such as Kuan Yin, goddess of compassion), in easing animals' spirits into improved conditions of rebirth, while persons who believe in an all-powerful creator god might plead that he provide some heaven world to compensate animals for their suffering on earth.

Suggestions

Use any candle you think appropriate. A white candle could stand for the purity of your intentions, while green represents the earth's blessings of life and growth. If you use candle scent, anointing oil, or incense, use any pleasing fragrance. You could try sage, which promotes contact with the animal powers, or use simple nature scents such as pine, fir, cedar, juniper, or patchouli.

86

A Prayer for Good Government

In many homes, congregations, organizations, and communities, prayers for the blessing and guidance of political leaders are traditional at election times, national holidays, and other ceremonial occasions. Some groups and individuals include wishes for the wise management of government in their regular devotions. The following candle rite also expresses such wishes, and you can perform it at special times or as a part of your regular practice. Light a candle and recite the following or similar words, which you can modify to better reflect your own religious and political orientation:

I call upon you, my Deity,
    and the guardian spirits of our society,
you who teach that Justice and Wisdom
    reflect and support the right order of the Cosmos.
Please give your blessings and guidance
    to our country's leaders,
    and to the leaders of this world,
    and to all others who influence public policy.
May their hearts be filled with compassion,
    their minds with wisdom,
        and their souls with light.
May they always act from honesty and integrity,
    avoiding temptations to corruption,
        and all other unethical behaviors.
Please help them to see through fear,
    intolerance, prejudice, and partisanship.
May they dedicate themselves to the needs
    and concerns of all our people,
        hearing each voice,

and understanding each person's point of view.
And as I ask these qualities for our leaders,
so may I also embody them myself.
So it is, and so shall it be.

You may allow the candle to burn as a long as you wish, and relight it whenever you want to express concern for society's well being.

Suggestions for Enhancing This Rite for Wise Government

A white candle is a good choice for this ritual because white stands for the clarity of mind and the purity of intention that we wish to see our leaders embody. However, you could also choose pink for love of country, blue for peace and loyalty, or any other color that has symbolic meaning for you. You may even be able to find candles in the colors of your country's flag, and it can be uplifting to reflect on its symbolism. (Different countries ascribe different meanings to their national colors, so the color coding is not completely standardized; when the United States Congress adopted its Great Seal in 1782, it fixed its color symbolism with white standing for purity and innocence, red for hardiness and valour, and blue for vigilance, perseverance, and justice.) If you can choose a scented candle, or if you wish to burn incense with this rite or anoint your candle with fragrant oil, use any scent that is pleasing or meaningful. Because vanilla stands for happiness in domestic life, its scent could convey the sense of the country as an extended family. Bergamot, rose, rose geranium, palmarosa, lavender, lemon, neroli, mandarin, and lemongrass promote a sense of security and well-being. Benzoin, cedar, juniper, bay laurel, sandalwood, and myrrh encourage nobler intentions.

87

For World Peace

The aggressive side of human nature is such that whenever we think we can enjoy a "peace dividend," a new war starts up somewhere. Or perhaps I should say a renewal of conflict erupts somewhere, due to the cyclical patterns of history. Is working for world peace, therefore, a futile effort? Maybe not. Many philosophers have taught that our own states of mind and strength of character can influence others in direct, as well as in mystical ways. For example, when Confucius expressed a desire to live among some eastern tribes, his friends responded, "How can you? They are savages." He replied, "If a higher type of men dwelt in their midst, how could their savage condition last?"[13]

To aid the work of peace, you can try the following rite, which can be performed any time this desire is uppermost in your mind—perhaps after hearing disturbing news about world events. By fixing your mind on peace, it radiates outward from you to influence the interpenetrating physical, mental, and spiritual planes. If rituals such as this make it possible for many individuals to focus on peace, the collective will can be empowered. When you wish to perform this rite, light a candle and say:

> *As I light this candle,*
>> *I call upon the Spirit of Peace,*
> *You who have been portrayed*
>> *as a gentle dove, and a serene Goddess,*
>> *and in many other beautiful and noble forms.*
> *I ask you to reside with me*
>> *and bless me with all the ways of peace.*
> *Peace be in me, and with me, and about me.*

At this point, pause to place your right hand over your breastbone, and envision waves of loving energy flowing through you, inward and outward, transforming your being and charging the air around you to create an extended aura of peace and harmony. Then continue, saying:

> *Let Peace flow inward*
>> *and outward,*
> *Let the Spirit of Peace bring harmony*
>> *to all around me,*
> *and extend forever onward*
>> *to transform the world*
>>> *with loving Presence.*
> *Let all peoples' minds and hearts*
>> *be filled with the love of Peace.*
> *Let all peoples' actions*
>> *be fixed on the works of Peace.*
> *Thus will harmony renew the Earth,*
>> *and gladden the heart*
>> *of the great World Soul herself.*

Pause to envision the entire planet bathed in the glowing aura of peace. Then, close the rite by saying,

> *So it is, and so shall it be.*

You can extinguish the candle now, or allow it to burn as long as you wish. Relight the candle any time that you are concerned about world affairs. It is not necessary to redo this ritual every time—simply relighting the candle is enough to reactivate your wishes for world peace.

If you want this rite to have a more lasting effect, it's important that you model these ideals in your own life. Promote the idea that reconciliation and harmony are more important than individuals' differences, and that you will only support peaceful solutions to problems. To further honor the Spirit of Peace, let go of some grudge or engage in some kind of action to promote peace and harmony, whether it be in your family or community, or in the larger world. Even a small action or gesture of friendship or conciliation will function as an act of imitative magic, affecting the well-being of the cosmos. If nothing else, you can make a donation to some organization whose activism is making a difference.

Suggestions for Enhancing This Rite for World Peace

A white candle is appropriate for this ritual, symbolizing purity of intention and the white dove of peace. However, other soft colors such as light blue for serenity and peach for loving will can also be used. If you can choose your candle scent, or if you anoint your candle or burn incense, rose geranium, palma rosa, frankincense, myrrh, chamomile, clary sage, neroli, mandarin, and vanilla would be good fragrances because they promote a sense of good will and well being.

Also: as a person dedicated to peace, you might wish to perform this ritual annually, on the festival of the Roman goddess Pax, which is January 30. (Even if you don't believe in this goddess in a literal sense, you can appreciate the ideals she stands for.) Pax had her own temple and was pictured standing upon armor and holding a palm branch. The Greeks knew her as Eirene, and along with the goddesses Diké (justice) and Eunomia (wise legislation), she presided over civil order. She also presided over festive amusements and celebrations.[14]

Candle Care
and Safety

Following are some tips for getting the maximum life and enjoyment out of your candles, as well as for burning them safely. (Some of these tips come from Wicks'n'Sticks, the Bridgewater Candle Company, House of Wicks & Wax, and Genwax.[1])

If you burn candles often, you can collect matchbooks (and ask friends who travel to collect matchbooks for you), because it's fun to use matches from interesting and exotic places.

When candles, especially taper candles, don't fit snugly in their holders because the holder cups are a little too wide, you can drip some wax into the bottom of the holder to secure the base of the candle. You can also crinkle small strips of tinfoil and wrap them around the base of the candle for a more snug fit. Also, dipping the bottom end of a candle into hot water can soften it so that you can pinch it if it needs to be narrowed, or push it down to widen it. You might want to put a few drops of water, some dish soap, or a little cooking oil into the bottom of votive or other glass holders, as this makes it easier to remove the spent candle stubs.

A huge number of house fires are caused by candles, so never use candle holders that could tip over easily, or that are made of flammable materials such as wood. Make sure to place your candles on a heat-resistant surface, such as a thick slab or coaster of marble, stone, or tile, or a tray filled with sand, even if they are in holders. Certain large pillar candles are designed to stand alone, but other candles, such as votives, require appropriate containers to prevent too rapid burning and pooling. Candle holders should be capable of withstanding high heat. It goes without saying that you should never set a candle anywhere near curtains, beds, sofas, lamp shades, plants, or other flammable items. (Even if your candle isn't right "next" to a curtain, make sure it is nowhere a curtain could blow across it.) For candle groupings, leave at least an inch of space between them. If the candle sits on a shelf or counter, there should be plenty of clearance space for heat to rise without scorching or sooting anything above it. Also, keep your candles away from children and pets, and do not set them on anything that could be knocked over.

A tall flame is usually caused by a long wick; because it shortens the life of the candle and causes uneven burning as well as blackening of the glass in jar candles, it is good to keep the wick trimmed to one-quarter inch. If your wick should break, carefully scoop out some of the wax around it to expose the right length. Try to keep the wick centered to avoid uneven burning or damage to the holder. Remove any charred wick or other debris that falls inside the wax pool. Also, be sure to keep your candles out of drafts, as these cause smoking, flickering, dripping, and rapid and uneven burning. If some drafts are unavoidable, turn the candle about a quarter turn from time to time, for a more even burning along its sides.

After performing some of the rites in this book, you may wish to leave your candle burning for the psychological reassurance or ambience. However, lit candles should never be left unattended. Extinguishing the candles when you want to leave the house or go to bed will not disrupt whatever good energy your ritual may have generated. You can always relight the candle later, if you want to.

It is normal for a certain amount of wax to remain around the sides of jar or pillar candles after burning. However, burning candles for a least two to three hours at a time (or at least long enough for the candles to form an interior well of molten wax) will prevent an excessive amount of wax from remaining, and also promote more even burning. (However, for pillar candles, Wicks'n'Sticks recommends that, "Subsequent burns should be less than three hours to prevent the development of 'gutters' that allow hot wax to run down the outside of the candle.") The edges of pillar candles can be pressed (curled) inward while the wax is still soft, to keep pace as the wick burns down.

To avoid damage to candle holders as well as surfaces, it is advisable to extinguish your candles when they have burned to where there is only one to one-and-one-half inches of wax remaining. Candle snuffers are recommended to prevent smoking and sputtering, and are also philosophically more pleasing, as you are not extinguishing the flame with your breath of life.

When a jar candle has cooled sufficiently, you can use a cloth or tissue to remove soot from the inside of the glass. Also, replace jar candles' lids to prevent their scent from evaporating—but wait about thirty minutes after extinguishing them before covering.

With votive candles, some people prefer to remove the metal tabs at the bottom before burning; if not, it is recommended that you remove them before placing more votives in the same holders.

For the type of religious candles that come in tall glass containers, Genwax recommends that you do not burn them "for less than six hours at a time" because this "can cause the wick to tunnel down the candle and eventually prevent it from being relit."

To clean your candles, Wicks'n'Sticks recommends wiping them with a clean cloth, to which a few drops of mineral oil or baby oil have been added. They also note that, "Rubbing the candle with a nylon stocking will bring the finish to a high sheen."

Additional Health and Safety Concerns

Some health issues have been raised regarding candle soot and lead wicks. Candles do release a certain amount of soot and other chemical particulates into the air, although this varies depending on the brand and ingredients, with scented candles tending to produce more soot than unscented. However, National Candle Association spokesperson Valerie Cooper has pointed out that candles don't produce a significant amount of particulates under normal conditions—only when allowed to smolder.[2] This is something that can be minimized by keeping their wicks trimmed, keeping them out of drafts, and keeping debris out of the wax. If you are still concerned about your indoor air quality, you might want to avoid burning large amounts of candles in small, enclosed spaces. Also, some manufacturers advertise cleaner-burning candles. Soy candles, especially, are reputed to produce minimal soot and have longer burn times.

Most candles have cloth wicks, though some wicks are of tin or zinc. Only a very small percentage of candles may have lead wicks, which will release lead into the air. (Children are especially vulnerable to lead.) Although the U.S. Consumer Product Safety Commission is making plans to ban them, members of the National Candle Association (95 percent of U.S. candle makers) voluntarily agreed to stop using lead wicks back in 1974. Some imported candles may use lead wicks, including those from China and Taiwan, but a number of retailers have agreed not to sell these products. The National Candle Association says that you can test a candle wick by taking a piece of clean, white paper, and rubbing it on the tip of the wick of an unburned candle. A lead wick will make "a light-gray, pencil-like mark."[3]

There are also some health concerns regarding certain essential oils that are used for candle scents and anointing. Information on these is included at the end of appendix D.

Colors for Candles

Because most of the rites in this book are designed to be performed in response to immediate needs, they are not strict about requiring that specific colored candles be used. Many of these rites can be performed with just a white candle, (white being the general purpose color), or any color candle that you have on hand. However, different colors do have significant traditional and psychological associations, so if you have a selection of candles available, you can choose the ones that best align your mind and spirit with your purpose in burning the candles.

Of course, different people associate different qualities with different colors. For example, in burning the candle to give thanks for good fortune on page 115, one person may choose white to represent pure light and all of life's possibilities, another many prefer gold, silver, or green, and yet another may use red, which is the active color of luck in Asia. In recognition of these different approaches, each candle rite offers some color suggestions. Following is some additional information on color, based on various folk traditions, the lore of magic, heraldry, and psychology. Remember that different traditions, and even different authors of books on candle burning, will attribute different meanings to certain colors. Therefore, the choice of color is ultimately an intuitive one: select candles in whichever colors you sense will best express the mood that you wish to create.

Black: Total concentration, meditation, wisdom, self control, responsibility, constancy, impenetrability, protection, immovability, firm and somber resolve, mourning, absence of light, absorption of light.

Black and White combined: The cabalistic colors of knowledge—black representing understanding because it absorbs all light, and white representing the quintessence of Divine Light.

Blue: Depth of emotion, peace, serenity, relaxation, perception, honesty, fidelity, truth, kindness. In parts of Africa, sky blue is protective because it is the color of heaven, and evil spirits can't get into heaven.[4]

Blue, dark: Understanding, introspection, concentration, meditation, patience. Dark blue is the contractive (inward directed) aspect of intellect. This is the ceremonial color of philosophy faculties in American colleges.

Blue, light: Peace in the home, sincerity, loyalty, empathy, calm understanding, devotion, gentility, delicate charm, gracefulness.

Blue-green: Emotional soothing, healing and nourishment, regeneration; mystical unity with nature, the healing power of art, intuitive vision.

Blue-violet (indigo): Spiritual reflection, meditation, intuition, going deep within.

Brown: Pride in simple ways, pleasure in living close to the earth, the earth powers, strength rooted in the earth, groundedness, stability, supportiveness, business success, the security and emotional riches of home and hearth.

Gold: Personal pride and self-confidence, radiance, charisma, halo effect, attraction, expansiveness, generosity, creative activity and success, initiative, leadership, power and authority, prosperity, luck.

Gray: Neutrality (can be used to neutralize intense emotions, bad habits, or negative vibrations); groundedness, stability, constancy; certain types of corporate status and business success.

Green: Living Nature, the freedom of wilderness, youth, growth, fertility, resilience, emotional balance, adaptation, regeneration, bodily healing, the ceremonial color of medical faculties in American colleges; opportunity, steady work,[5] prosperity, money, comfort, success in business, financial security; the Druidic color of knowledge.

Lavender: Spirituality, spiritual relationships and connection with others, living according to your ideals, active dreaming and intuition, nostalgia; state of readiness, mindfulness, creativity, perception; a gentler expression of the regal, authoritative qualities of purple.

Mauve: Affectionate, sociable qualities of pink, but more retiring; desire for subtlety, dignity.

Orange: Warmth, vitality, social life, focused energy, self motivation, free expression, boldness, action directed by intellect, unity of mind and body (combining thought, will, and action), persuasion, endurance. Orange is used for a "change of plans" or "opening the way" in Hoodoo candle magic.[6] This is the ceremonial color assigned to engineering faculties in American colleges.

Orange-red: Assertiveness, activity, high energy, competitiveness, enthusiasm, wildness, force of will.

Peach: Warmth and softness, social harmony (it makes people feel safe and assured and enables people to connect well with each other). Peach takes the softness of pink, but adds the enthusiasm and energy of orange.

Pink, rose: Affection, romance, loving and nurturing, warm feelings, feeling good, well-being, sociability, pride in femininity, pleasure in self, good times, social favors. Everything looks better in the glow of pink or peach. Pink is the ceremonial color assigned to music faculties in American colleges.

Purple, violet: Altered states of consciousness, spirituality, psychism, inspiration, dynamic creativity (combines intuition with action), love of drama; dignity, focused power, authority, high stations in life, nobility, generosity, appreciation of variety and tolerance for differences. This is the color worn by law faculties in American colleges.

Red: Energy, vital force, life blood, enthusiasm, activity, impulse, tension, emotional expression, anger, immediate action, military action, victory, fast luck; human love, desire, passion, sexuality, eroticism, conception, childbearing and childbirth. In ancient times, red was a bridal color. In Asia, this is the color of active luck.

Red, dark (maroon and deeper shades): Sensitivity combined with the active and sensual qualities of red, a craving for the riches of life. This color brings love of power, wealth, and position to the intense drive of red. The Chinese describe deep red as the "heart" of red, and it inspires "deep respect."[7]

Red violet: Ambition, noble actions, adds more passion to the spiritual and mystical nature.

Silver: Subtle lunar energies, ethereal beauty, romantic feelings, mysterious charm, mystique, purity of understanding, the receptive aspects of creativity. Association with clarity and purity pertains to integrity, honesty, self-worth, and idealism.

White: Purification, purity of intentions, innocence of spirit, psychic energy, spiritual strength, purified emotions and absence of negative feeling; unity and harmony (because white is the result of all the colors in the spectrum combined). In America, a bridal color.

Yellow: Brightness, happiness, cheer, hopefulness, the solar power that stimulates growth, expectations, luck, success, prosperity (sharing qualities with gold); intellect, alertness, wit, wisdom, science; confidence, spontaneity, enjoyment of action, communication, questing for alternative experience. The active (outward directed) aspect of intelligence. In China, yellow is the color of longevity.[8]

Yellow-green: The calming and centered qualities of green, but more emphasis on intellect and activity; cool, but with the confidence and love of challenges of yellow; new growth.

Note that if you don't have a candle in the color you wish, a colored candle holder might help you create the desired effect.

Astral Candle Colors

Some candle burning rites may suggest that you use an "astral" or "essence" candle to represent yourself or any other person who is to benefit from the ritual; such candles are based on the color attributed to your (or his/her) sign of the zodiac—specifically the Sun sign. In this matter, you actually have a large choice of colors because there are different candle-burning traditions, and because astrologers have different opinions about the colors associated with the signs. The signs are Aries (March 21–April 19), Taurus (April 20–May 20), Gemini (May 21–June 21), Cancer (June 22–July 22), Leo (July 23–August 22), Virgo (August 23–September 22), Libra (September 23–October 22), Scorpio (October 23–November 21), Sagittarius (November 22–December 21), Capricorn (December 22–January 19), Aquarius (January 20–February 18), and Pisces (February 19–March 20).

The use of astral colors has largely been influenced by Henri Gamache, whose book, *The Master Book of Candle Burning,* set some trends back in the 1940s.[9] His color/sign attributions were white (as a primary color) and pink (as a secondary color) for Aries, red and yellow for Taurus, light blue and red for Gemini, green and brown for Cancer, green and red for Leo, gold and black for Virgo, crimson (primary) and black or light blue for Libra, golden brown and black for Scorpio, green and red for Sagittarius, red (primary) and brown, gray, or black for Capricorn, blue (primary) and pink or dark green for Aquarius, and pink (primary) and green, white, or black for Pisces. Gamache's system has been incorporated by Ray Buckland, D. J. Conway, and Patricia Telesco, among, no doubt, many others[10] (though they have also added to or modified it).

Some years ago, I did a survey (independent of the Gamache system) of colors that different astrologers have associated with the signs, and found the following to be among the more common:

Aries: red, white, yellow

Taurus: green, brown, pink, red-orange

Gemini: yellow, blue, light blue, orange

Cancer: white, silver, light blue, orange-yellow

Leo: gold, yellow, red

Virgo: yellow, green, orange, pale green, yellow-green

Libra: rose, blue, light blue, white

Scorpio: red, black, dark blue, blue-green

Sagittarius: purple, indigo, turquoise

Capricorn: black, brown, dark green, blue-violet

Aquarius: blue-green, metallic blue, white, purple

Pisces: foam green, blue-green, salmon pink, red-violet

Perhaps astrologers and others have ascribed so many different colors to different signs because some are thinking in terms of colors that amplify the qualities of a sign's personality, and others are thinking of colors that complement or balance them. The signs' associations with planets and elements, as well as gemstones attributed to them, may also be factors.

If you don't have an affinity for the colors ascribed to your sun sign, go ahead and use whichever color you feel to be most in harmony with who you are. It may be that you have a dominantly placed planet within another sign (as we all have many different planets and influences within our individual horoscopes).

By the way, some folk magic practitioners always light an astral candle in addition to whatever other candles are being burned. Although that is not necessary for the rituals in this book, it is a practice that you can incorporate if you would like to bring some extra focus to the rites.

Also, sometimes it is nice to light just a single candle in your chosen color (i.e., not as part of another rite), as a way of reminding yourself who you are. This is something you might want to do when the pressures of the world have been leaving you no time for personal reflection or the pursuit of your own interests. Many of us can use color as a way of rediscovering our Sun sign qualities when we reach middle age—as so many of us have repressed parts of ourselves in the process of accommodating the world.

Choices for Candle Fragrance, Anointing Oil, and Incense

Because most of the rites in this book are designed to be performed when you have an immediate need, you can use any candle that you have at hand—it is not necessary to choose a candle of any special fragrance, anoint your candle, or burn incense as a part of your rite. However, when you do have the time and opportunity to do these things, they can help focus your mind, align your energies, and enrich your ritual experience with extra layers of sensory meaning. Following are some suggestions on anointing a candle, the use of carrier oils, a list of some oils and other substances used in candle and incense burning traditions, and finally, some general precautions—including a listing of oils that are potentially hazardous under certain conditions.

Anointing

A major tradition associated with candle burning is the practice of "dressing" or "anointing" the candle with oil. This adds greater fragrance to the candle and also helps you focus on your intent. The oil is usually chosen for sensory associations that complement your purpose.

As I was taught, you pour a few drops of oil onto your fingertips, then rub them over the candle, starting at the middle and working outward toward the top, and then toward the bottom; also anoint the top, bottom, and wick of the candle. (Some folk magic practitioners suggest rubbing the candle from the wick downward to the base if you want to attract certain things into your life, or from the base upward to the wick if you want to let go of certain issues or dispel certain energies—however, there are also practitioners who suggest the opposite.) For jar candles, you can just anoint the exposed part. (Ray T. Malbrough suggests rubbing in a clockwise direction for attracting, and counterclockwise for dispelling.[11]) While you are anointing the candle, clear your mind and concentrate on your needs or desires. Some practitioners suggest re-anointing your candle if you put it out and want to relight it and repeat the rite, but for the rituals in this book, that is unnecessary unless you wish to do so for extra concentration.

Also: some of the rites may suggest incising certain symbols upon a candle. You would usually do this after dressing it.

Carrier Oils

You can apply some of your essential oils and other products for anointing directly to the candle. However, because essential oils are super concentrated and very potent, it is customary to dilute them by mixing them with "base" or "carrier" oils. By mixing your essential oils with carrier oils, you save money, the oil is spread more evenly, and it is less likely to irritate your skin. For the simple purpose of anointing a candle, high quality olive oil or other cooking oils are suitable. (For more sophisticated aromatherapeutic purposes, such as massage, some preferred carrier oils are almond, apricot kernel, avocado, coconut, grapeseed, jojoba, sunflower, and wheat germ.) For anointing a single candle, one drop of the essential oil mixed with one-eighth teaspoon of the base oil is probably enough.

Substances

In the list below are descriptions of substances that have popular or traditional uses in candle fragrance, anointing oils, or incense. Note that this is only a select list, due to space limitations. The products listed here are generally the ones that aren't too difficult to find (based on my survey of stores and Internet sites); most are reasonably priced. Because I have a preference for natural oils, I have not included those for which no genuine scent is likely to be available (such as freesia, magnolia, or plumeria). The list of natural fragrances that can be used in candle making and anointing is amazingly long: while vanilla, pine, and citronella-scented candles are familiar commercial products, one can also find special aromatherapy candles scented with anise, chamomile, juniper, marjoram, nutmeg, palmarosa, and the other oils listed here.

If I have omitted some of your favorite oils and scents, do not be dismayed—go ahead and use anything that pleases you—whatever you feel sets the right mood or helps you focus on your purpose. Also, many makers and purveyors of incenses and oils have special blends with names like, "Success," "Love and Happiness," "Spiritual Strength," "Healing Circle," "Sacred Offering," etc. which suggest their ideal uses, so you might give some of those a try. Remember that with the choices below, as well as those mentioned in the suggestions paragraphs that follow the individual rituals, the use of such ingredients is optional. They are only meant to provide some helpful ideas. Because people can have unique emotional image associations for different scents, you should follow your own instincts.

Anise or aniseed (*Pimpinella anisum*): The licorice-scented seeds of anise provide a common food flavoring as well as an essential oil. Anise is a staple in Hispanic folk-healing traditions, where in addition to its numerous medicinal benefits, it is used to soothe people who are "crazy with anxiety," and to cure "susto," which is a type of soul loss; anise is also used for ritual cleansing, and to counteract the evil eye.[12] In Afro-Caribbean devotional ceremonies, anise is used to please the ancestor spirits. Star anise is a different species (*Illicum verum*), but it has similar properties, and is used as an incense in Japan.[13]

Sweet basil (*Ocimum basilicum*): The characteristically fresh spicy scent of the oil from this annual herb promotes mental energy, clarity, and determination. Mary K. Greer recommends it for decision making.[14] In folk magic, it is used for attracting love, wealth, and success.

Allspice, pimento leaf or **pimento berry** (*Pimenta dioica*): The pimento tree, a Caribbean native, produces the familiar baking spice; it combines characteristics of cinnamon, nutmeg, and cloves, and can be used in incense. The leaves and berries yield somewhat different, but sweet and spicy-scented oils, which are cheering and refreshing. In folk magic, allspice is used to attract wealth.

Bay or **bay laurel** or **bay leaf oil** (*Laurus nobilis*): The pleasantly sweet, pungent scent of bay can clear the mind and turn it toward noble endeavors. The wreath of laurel is a symbol of success, used to crown those who strive for excellence; it was also believed to have a protective quality that ambitious people needed to counter aggressive energies.[15] The scent of bay also promotes spiritual and psychic awareness, and it is said to have inspired the Delphic Oracles of ancient Greece.

West Indian bay (*Pimenta racemosa*): Like the bayberry, the West Indian bay tree is a member of the myrtle family, and is not to be confused with the bay laurel, whose leaves are used in cooking. Oil from the leaves of this tree is the source of bay rum, a men's facial lotion with a robust, spicy, balsamic aroma. Some folk magic practitioners have used bay rum for candle dressing (probably for social favors, luck, and abundance).

Bayberry (*Myrica cerifera*): Early American colonists made candles from bayberry wax, which were valued for their rich natural fragrance and smokeless burning habit; however, it takes many pounds of bayberries to yield one pound of wax. Today, bayberry wax is usually mixed with beeswax (which is not as brittle); the less expensive candles use bayberry oil or synthetic bayberry oil. Bayberry is a prime scent for "money drawing" in popular magic.

Benzoin (*Styrax benzoin*): Benzoin's sweet, warm, vanilla-like odor combined with its refined spiritual vibration enhances a sense of awareness that spiritual forces are looking after us. Although this oil, which comes from the balsamic resin of certain southeast Asian trees, is used for blessing, meditation, and spiritual strength, it is also reputed to promote success and prosperity.

Bergamot (*Citrus bergamia*): Bergamot is a warm, refreshing, uplifting oil with a floral citrus scent. There is also a **bergamot mint** (*Mentha citrata*), which has many of the same aromatherapeutic qualities; however, the bergamot oil that is usually available commercially comes from the citrus fruit. Bergamot is such an all-purpose favorite that Colleen Dodt asserts that it is "a necessary essential in every household."[16] Its balancing powers are used to counteract stress, fatigue, anxiety, and depression, while promoting a sense of well being. On top of all that, bergamot is a folk magic staple, used for luck, happiness, protection, hex-breaking, money drawing, and help with legal matters.[17]

Cedar, Atlas cedarwood (*Cedrus atlantica*), or **red cedarwood** (*Juniperus virginiana*): There are several different types of wood oils labeled cedar or cedarwood. Some consider the scent of the Atlas more pleasant, but Scott Cunningham says that both the Atlas and the red "can be used with equal effectiveness in magical aromatherapy" (i.e. using aroma to enhance visualization and other techniques to bring about change).[18] Cedar was used as incense in many ancient cultures, as its warm, rich, woodsy scent enhances a spiritual focus and promotes strength and determination. In aromatherapy, it is used for calming and comforting, although aphrodisiac qualities have also been attributed to it.

German chamomile (*Matricaria recutica*), and **Roman chamomile** (*Chamaemelum nobile*): As an essential oil, chamomile is valued for the same soothing qualities that make it popular as an herbal tea. The oil is distilled from the sweet, fruity-scented white flower heads; oil from the German chamomile is unusual for its deep blue color. The scent of chamomile promotes sleep and dreaming, and it also evokes ideals of mothering.

Cinnamon (*Cinnamomum zeylanicum*): Cinnamon oil may come from the bark or leaves of a bushy evergreen tree native to Ceylon; however, the leaf oil is preferable for general use because the bark oil has greater skin irritant properties. In folk magic, cinnamon oil is reputed to have spiritual as well as aphrodisiac qualities, and also promotes luck, success, and wealth. Aromatherapists use it for mental energy. A related substance, **cassia** (*Cinnamomum cassia*) has similar uses as a spice as well as an essential oil, though its taste and scent are considered less refined; most of the spice sold as "cinnamon" in the United States is actually cassia.

Clary sage (*Salvia sclarea*): The oil that comes from the leaves and blossoms of the clary sage has a sweet, nutty, slightly musty aroma. It is becoming increasingly popular for its euphoric qualities, which banish stress and worry. Clary sage is reputed to stimulate deep sleep and vivid dreams, and it is also good for women's concerns. It is considered preferable to common sage, because it has lower toxicity levels.[19]

Clove, clove bud oil (*Eugenia aromatica* or *caryophyllata*): Clove oil comes from the dried brown flower buds of an Indonesian tree, (the familiar cloves we know as a kitchen spice), and sometimes also from the leaves and stems. Its strong, spicy scent has an energizing, mentally stimulating effect that boosts memory and concentration. According to Leydet Aromatics, it is good for "accessing higher brain functions [and] is centering for . . . someone on mental overload."[20] Folklore has it that oil of clove is also good for wealth, protection, and lust.

Citronella (*Cymbopogon nardus*): Citronella candles are well-known to people who enjoy outdoor living, as they are used to keep mosquitos away. Despite this repellant reputation, an aqueous solution of oil of citronella is known as "fast luck," and "brings luck in business by pulling customers into a store."[21] In aromatherapy, this pungent lemony scent (which comes from a variety of tropical grass related to lemon grass, vetivert, and palmarosa) is regarded as purifying and uplifting.

Coriander (*Coriandrum sativum*): This oil is steam distilled from the globular seeds (actually the dried, ripe fruits) of a Mediterranean plant. Its spicy, woody, slightly musty aroma has warming, stimulating qualities. HS Lim's "Guide to Essential Oils" suggests that coriander is good for "lack of motivation,"[22] and the Ancient Healing Arts website recommends it to "relieve doubt, fear of failure, feelings of vulnerability . . ."[23] The seeds are sometimes used in incense.

Cypress (*Cupressus sempervirens*): The smoky, evergreen aroma of cypress has perfumed many ancient temples (including the Tibetan); it is used as an incense to purify the air and fortify the spiritual atmosphere. In aromatherapy, its sedative, emotionally regenerative properties are used to help people deal with grief, regret, and the need for change (consistent with the traditional use of cypress trees in cemetery landscaping).

Eucalyptus (*Eucalyptus globulus, Eucalyptus radiata,* and related subspecies): This is possibly the most favored oil for promoting healing—on a psychic level, as a well as for practical medicinal uses, because its penetrating odor is as helpful for purifying and stimulating one's "energy body," as it is for improving respiratory conditions. (However, eucalyptus is fatal if ingested, and it is alleged to be bad for certain health conditions—see the safety section at the end of this listing.) Eucalyptus also boosts mental energy and focus.

Fir, balsam fir (*Abies balsamea*), **silver fir needle** (*Abies alba*): The sweet, rich, evergreen scent of fir evokes the winter holidays as well as the northern forests. The oil may be distilled from the resin of the balsam fir, or the needles, twigs, or cones of the silver fir, and it is valued for its grounding, calming, uplifting qualities. The folkloric associations of fir are similar to pine.

Frankincense (*Boswellia carteri*): Frankincense is best known for its biblical associations, but as an incense and an oil it is also valued by modern users for its power of blessing and protection, and its ability to turn the mind to the spiritual world. In therapeutic practices, it is used for slowing the breath and concentrating the mind. In folk magic, it is used for money drawing—an association enhanced by the richness of its sweet, warm, balsamic scent and its ancient associations with wealth.

Geranium or rose geranium (*Pelargonium graveolens*): In listings of essential oils, "geranium" usually refers to rose geranium, whose unique floral fragrance includes rosy and minty notes. It is so effective for generating a sense of well-being that Horst Rechelbacher, the founder of Aveda, says, is "like Prozac for the nose."[24] Its hormone-balancing qualities are widely recommended for female concerns. Geranium used to be one of the most popular perfume oils in the Deep South, where it was used for promoting peace at home, attracting luck and success (including business success for "sporting women"), and dispelling hexes.

Ginger (*Zingiber officinale*): Ginger is a fragrance that evokes the powers of elemental Fire. Because of its warming qualities, this spicy, pungent scent is often used in holiday candles. It is also used to warm the heart, sharpen the mind, and to stimulate communication, determination, and sexual drive. In folk magic, ginger is used to attract wealth and business success.

Grapefruit (*Citrus paradisi*): The light, euphoric scent of this sweet grapefruity oil conveys the ideal of morning in California: fresh and full of possibility.[25] HS Lim suggests that it is good for those "who dither and procrastinate."[26] It is also supposed to moderate the appetite.[27]

Jasmine (*Jasminum officinale, grandiflorum,* and *sambac*): Jasmine's alluring, exquisitely magical fragrance uplifts the spirits and promotes love and passion. Its warm, honeyed, floral scent helps women explore their feminine identities. Its association with the lunar mysteries also promotes dreams and intuitions. Because of the costly process required to extract the essence from its small, white, star-shaped flowers, commercial jasmine products are apt to be synthetic.

Juniper (*Juniperus communis*): Juniper is related to and shares some of the same properties as cedar; however, the fragrant evergreen scent of this oil (which may come from the wood or the berries) has a fresher, warmer, sweeter character, which adds some levity to its strong spiritual and mentally focusing qualities. Juniper has a long history of ritual use, as many cultures have included it in incense blends for blessing, purification, meditation, and protection. In therapy, it is used to ease stress and anxiety. It is also used to sustain concentration.

Lavender (*Lavandula augustifolia*): Lavender is the favorite all-purpose fragrance. The oil is distilled from the flowering tops of this evergreen shrub, and has a fresh, sweet, floral-herbaceous aroma. Due to its energy-balancing qualities, the scent of lavender is calming for those who are nervous and anxious, but it restores mental and physical energy to those who are fatigued. It is also used to promote peace and harmony, as well as love and attraction. Ann Moura says that it "attracts elves."[28]

Lemon (*Citrus limonum*): The characteristically lively scented oil of lemon is used for generating physical energy as well as mental awakening. In Hispanic folk-healing practices, lemon is one of the most commonly used substances, helping to banish lethargy and promote recovery after illness, among many other things. In aromatherapy as well as folk magic, the sunny scent of lemon promotes happiness.

Lemon balm, also called **melissa** (*Melissa officianalis*): Because the fresh lemony scent of this essential oil can banish worries while uplifting the spirit, it is used against depression, grief, and sleeplessness. It is sometimes also used in folk magic for healing, love, money, peace, purification, and success. Because this essential oil is expensive, it is often adulterated. (Note: sometimes lemon balm [*Melissa officianalis*] is confused with citronella [*Cymbopogon nardus*].)

Lemongrass (*Cymbopogon citratus* and related subspecies): Made from the tall, fast-growing leaves of a southeast Asian member of the sweet grass family, oil of lemongrass has a pungent earthy lemony scent. Its high-energy fragrance is used for revitalizing the mind (even clearing morning headaches, drivers' fatigue, and mental exhaustion), and promoting self-assurance. It is also reputed to boost the psychic senses. Oil of lemongrass in alcohol is known as Van Van Oil; it was very popular with people in old New Orleans,[29] both white and black, who used to perfume their baths, clothes, houses, and candles with it for luck and success (including success in gambling).

Lime (*Citrus aurantifolia*): The characteristically strong, bracing odor of lime is redolent of outdoor adventure, and conveys an ideal of personal confidence and potency. Its energizing effect "impels you into action."[30]

Mandarin (*Citrus nobilis* or *Citrus reticulata*): Mandarin is similar to tangerine (and sometimes identified with tangerine), but its scent is considered somewhat superior. As Julia Lawless points out, mandarin has an "intensely sweet, almost floral citrus scent," in contrast to tangerine's more orange-like aroma.[31] Mandarin is used to restore hope, cheer, and high spirits; it is widely recommended for children.

Marjoram, sweet marjoram (*Origanum marjorana*), **knotted marjoram** (*Marjorana hortensis*), **Spanish marjoram** (*Thymus mastichina*): The oil, which is distilled from the leaves, stems, and blossoms of this herb, has a somewhat camphoraceous aroma with warm, spicy, woody accents. It is especially appreciated for its soothing, sedative effects, and is sometimes used to numb the emotions in cases of great stress and grief.

Mint, peppermint (*Mentha piperita*), **spearmint** (*Mentha spicata*): The refreshing, penetrating odor of mint can stimulate mental and physical energy, as well as determination, focus, and clarity. Mint was scattered on the floor of ancient synagogues to produce a fresh scent when trod upon.[32] In folklore, mint is associated with wealth (an idea that is amplified by the word association with minted coinage). The oils of peppermint and spearmint are often combined. Spearmint has been in longer use; as its odor and its effects are milder, it is more energy balancing and better suited for children.

Myrrh (*Commiphora myrrha, Balsamodendron myrrha*): A small tree of Africa and Arabia produces the tear-like drops of resin that yield the oil of myrrh. Since ancient times, its rich, warm, spicy, bittersweet odor has been used to create a spiritual atmosphere. As Scott Cunningham has observed, inhaling its fragrance can "awaken your awareness of the spiritual reality behind our everyday existence."[33] In therapy, myrrh is used to boost motivation, self-confidence, and emotional strength.

Nutmeg (*Myristica fragrans, officinalis,* and *aromata; Nux moschata*): The oil of nutmeg comes from the kernels of an East Indian fruit, and has a characteristic sweet, spicy scent. Its warming qualities affect people differently, for some find it mentally stimulating and physically reinvigorating, while others find it calming and euphoric, good for inducing sleep and dreams. When abused, it is reputed to have narcotic and psychotropic effects.[34] In folk magic, nutmeg has money drawing[35] and aphrodisiac qualities.

Orange, bitter orange (*Citrus aurantium*), or **sweet orange** (*Citrus sinensis*): Oranges have long been considered lucky, and they are associated with the goddess Fortuna, one of whose symbols is a golden ball. The oil of orange has a sweet, tangy fragrance that restores cheer when a person is depressed and exhausted; it also relieves boredom and promotes creativity. Orange-scented candles are good for entertaining because they "promote open communication."[36]

Orange blossom or **neroli** (*Citrus aurantium*): This oil comes from the blossoms of the bitter orange, and its rich, floral fragrance is considered a very superior scent. (However, it is very costly because it requires a half-ton of blossoms to get one pound of the oil.) Neroli is used for easing anxieties, "transforming negative emotions,"[37] and promoting lightness of heart; it also has a tranquilizing effect. Because orange blossoms are worn by brides, neroli also suggests marital happiness and fulfillment.

Palmarosa (*Cymbopogon martini*): The leaves of a plant related to lemongrass and citronella are the source of palmarosa oil. Its light, sweet, exotic fragrance is complex: a citrusy floral scent with hints of rose and geranium (and sometimes confused with or mislabeled as rose geranium). Therapeutically, palmarosa is used to reduce stress, dispel grief, and promote a sense of well-being. In magical practice, it is used to attract love.

Patchouli (*Pogostemum cablin* and *Pogostemum patchouli*): Patchouli oil, which comes from the dried leaves of an East Indian shrub, is richly redolent of that scent of freshly turned earth that so delights the hearts of gardeners. Perhaps owing in part to this earth connection, patchouli has both relaxing and energizing qualities (sedative in lesser doses, stimulant in larger doses), and it is one of the most popular aphrodisiacs. It has additional folkloric uses for money and fertility.

Petitgrain (*Citrus aurantium*): Petitgrain is another oil that comes from the bitter orange, but it is distilled from the leaves and twigs. Its scent, which combines citrus, floral, woody, and herbaceous notes, promotes energy and alertness. Mary K. Greer observes that it is "surprisingly effective for strengthening your belief in yourself and your abilities."[38]

Pine (*Pinus sylvestris*): The refreshing, balsamic odor of pine is used in many commercial cleansers, which is in keeping with its traditional uses in rituals of purification,[39] but pine is also used for blessing, money drawing, fertility, and protection. In aromatherapy, pine is beneficial for respiratory ailments such as bronchitis, asthma, and sinusitis, and its antiseptic and detoxifying properties have the power to cleanse the mental and emotional environments. Also, pine trees "exude a lot of excess prana"[40] (life force), and the Bach flower remedies use pine to help people who are unable to let go of regrets,[41] so the fragrance may also convey these virtues.

Rose (*Rosa damascena, Rosa gallica, Rosa centifola*): Rose is one of the very best scents for love, romance, and charm. The oil described as "otto of rose" or "rose attar" is distilled from petals and is very expensive; a rose absolute extracted with solvents is less expensive, but still too costly for common use, so commercial products are usually synthetic.

Rosemary (*Rosemarinus officinalis*): Rosemary oil comes from the flowering tops of the herb, and it may well be the most popular substance in use for mental power as well as purification. Its penetrating, camphoraceous aroma clears the cobwebs out of the brain, improving memory and concentration. This clearing quality also affects the physical and spiritual atmosphere, which is why it is used for protection, banishing negativity, and healing.

Rosewood (*Aniba rosaedora*): With its rose-like fragrance, rosewood shares some of the same qualities as rose. However, the production of its oil is contributing to rain forest destruction, as it comes from a tree that only grows deep in the Amazonian wilderness.

Sage, common sage (*Salvia officinalis*), **Spanish sage** (Salvia lavandulifolia): Sage tends to have a strong, fresh, herbal, somewhat camphor-like odor, which has balancing qualities—energizing and mentally clearing and stimulating, but helping to calm and ease anxiety. It is also reputed to cleanse the spirit and promote spiritual vision. Sage is especially used for cleansing in Native American ceremonies, and some use it for attunement with the animal powers. Because common sage can have potentially toxic effects, Spanish sage and clary sage (see separate entry) are preferred.

Sandalwood (*Santalum album*): In the practice of Ayurveda (Indian medicine), sandalwood is used for "purifying the vital being and atmosphere."[42]

This warm, rich, sweet, exotic, woody scent also promotes meditation and spiritual peace and strength. Therapeutically, it is used for calming the nerves, and grounding and balancing one's energies. Sandalwood also has aphrodisiac qualities.

Spruce, hemlock spruce (*Tsuga, Pinus,* or *Abies canadensis*), **black spruce** (*Picea nigra*), **Norway spruce** (*Picea abies*), **white** or **Canadian spruce** (*Picea glauca*): Oil distilled from the needles and twigs of these northern trees has a fresh balsamic scent, and the same therapeutic qualities as pine and fir—that is, good for respiratory problems, as well as nervous disorders.

Tangerine (*Citrus reticulata*): The free-spirited fragrance of tangerine can be exhilarating and soothing at the same time, and it is widely recommended for children's concerns. The crisp, sweet, orange-scented oil is expressed from the outer peel of the fruit. It has traditional associations with luck, prosperity, and happiness. Tangerines (and oranges) are presented as gifts at Chinese New Year, because the word for tangerine resembles the word for luck or gold, and orange, the word for gold or wealth.[43]

Vanilla (*Vanilla planifolia*): The familiar scent of vanilla is warming and comforting, so it promotes well-being, sympathy, and domestic peace. However, it is also used in love magic, as one of the most popular fragrances for arousing lust. The vanilla used in aromatherapy and perfumery is not the extract used in the kitchen, but an "absolute," that is, a highly concentrated substance derived from vanilla pods through solvent extraction or carbon dioxide extraction.

Verbena, lemon verbena (*Aloysia triphylla, Lippia citriodora*): In herbalism, lemon verbena is valued for its uplifting effects. However, as the true essential oil is "virtually nonexistent,"[44] oil products sold under this name are apt to be mixtures of lemon, lemongrass, citronella, and an inferior oil from Spanish verbena.

Vetivert or vetiver (*Vetiveria zizanoides* and related subspecies): The heavy woodsmoke aroma of vetivert has been described as a very masculine scent. The oil comes from a tropical grass with thick, spreading (rhizomatic), long-reaching roots. With its ability to draw on the earth powers, vetivert can be used for summoning energy from very deep sources. Indeed, aromatherapists recommend it for conditions of extreme exhaustion, as well as other nervous complaints related to stress, anxiety, depression, and insomnia. Vetivert is a staple in folk magic, where it is used for luck, protection, hex-breaking, and money drawing.

Ylang ylang (*Cananga odorata*): This oil, whose delightful name means "flower of flowers," comes from the large flowers of a tree that grows in the South Seas islands. Its exotic floral aroma produces a euphoric state and induces romantic dreams. It is also one of the most popular aphrodisiacs, and is used for other purposes of attraction.

Other products: in addition to essential oils and cooking oils, many other products can be used for anointing candles, including perfumes and colognes, lotions, and other scented cosmetics. Anointing a candle with oil and then rolling it in fragrant herbs and spices (such as basil, cinnamon, ginger, etc.) is another practice, which has been described in Dorothy Morrison's *Everyday Magic*.

Essential Oils and Skin Sensitivity

Many essential oils can irritate the skin (and any essential oil is a potential irritant for certain very sensitive persons), so it is wise to dilute them in carrier oils and use care when applying them. Even though anointing candles is done with the fingertips, which are usually less sensitive, you could unthinkingly touch them to your face or other bodily surfaces, resulting in some stinging and reddening of the skin. Potential skin irritants include allspice, aniseed, basil, bay laurel, cedarwood, cinnamon and cassia, citronella, clove, eucalyptus, ginger, grapefruit, lemon, lemon balm (melissa), lemongrass, lemon verbena, lime, mandarin, mint, orange, peppermint, pine, sage, and spearmint. Note that citrus oils and the spicier oils are prominent on this list. Additionally, some oils that may irritate very sensitive skin, or that may lead to problems if used in large amounts or over long periods of time, are benzoin, bergamot, chamomile, clary sage, geranium, jasmine, juniper, nutmeg, rose, rosemary, palmarosa, patchouli, vanilla, and ylang ylang. There are also oils that cause photosensitivity (causing the skin to react to sun exposure), but dressing candles is unlikely to provoke that sort of problem.

Essential Oils and Other Safety Issues

Different books and websites devoted to essential oils and aromatherapy have made claims that certain essential oils are potentially toxic, and that others are potentially harmful for people who are pregnant, suffering from high blood pressure, or prone to seizures. However, there is considerable disagreement on this matter. Ironically, some of the essential oils accused of being highly toxic (such as basil and sage) are on the FDA's list of "Essential oils . . . that are generally recognized as safe for their intended use. . . ."[45]

As they may not always have scientific evidence or firsthand experience that certain oils are harmful, many writers may be passing along suspicions raised elsewhere. In their book *Aromatherapy for Health Professionals*, Shirley Price and Len Price state that some essential oils may have gotten a reputation for toxicity as the result of "gross misuse," and that, "when used in small doses (and for a restricted length of time), even the so-called toxic oils . . . do not normally present a hazard."[46] Perhaps some oils are rumored to be unsafe due to the anecdotal experiences of individuals with special sensitivities, or extrapolation from herbalism, where it is known that certain substances will have a toxic effect when ingested, others when ingested over a long period of time or in large doses. In his internet article on "Incorrect Safety," aromatherapist Martin Watt attacks a number of claims of toxicity, pointing out that many of the maligned substances (such as aniseed and peppermint) are common food flavorings, and that there is generally no evidence for most of these claims.

Although I suspect that many of the toxicity warnings are unfounded or exaggerated, and that the limited amount of contact with these oils and inhalation of their fragrances that is involved in anointing and burning candles is not likely to present health problems, I provide the following lists so that you can be aware that these allegations have been made. Due to a desire to keep things simple, I only include warnings against substances listed earlier in this appendix (and in the suggestions sections following the individual rituals), or substances that are close relatives and may be confused with those mentioned in this book. My sources include books by Shirley Price and Len Price, and Julia Lawless,[47] and the Sunspirit, Nature's Gift, LaVaughn's Celestial Healing, Elixarome, and Tradewinds' Organix-South websites. Note that this is not a comprehensive listing, and that these sources are not in complete agreement.

Different sources have listed these oils as potentially toxic (though actual levels of toxicity may vary): aniseed and star anise, basil, bay laurel, West Indian bay, cedarwood, cinnamon and cassia, clove, coriander, cypress (blue), eucalyptus, juniper, lavender (Spanish), dwarf pine, rosemary, and sage (common and Spanish). Children and pregnant women might especially want to avoid contact with these oils, particularly if they are undiluted.

Different sources have suggested that the following oils be avoided by pregnant women: aniseed and star anise, basil, bay laurel, cedarwood, chamomile, cinnamon and cassia, citronella, clary sage, clove, coriander, cypress, eucalyptus, geranium and rose geranium, jasmine, juniper, lavender (in the first trimester), lemon balm (melissa), marjoram, myrrh, nutmeg, palmarosa, peppermint, rose, rosemary, sage, spearmint, and vetiver. Many of these oils may affect hormone balance, which can be useful in regulating menstruation, but which, it is feared, might have a bad effect on women prone to miscarriages.

Different sources have listed these oils as potentially harmful for persons prone to seizures: basil, eucalyptus, rosemary, and sage.

Different sources have listed these oils as potentially capable of aggravating high blood pressure: eucalyptus, pine, rosemary, and sage.

In concluding this section on safety, it is important to bear in mind that because essential oils are so highly concentrated, it is common sense to avoid ingesting them, massaging undiluted oils onto your skin, or different forms of excess. Also, be aware that any substance may have the potential to cause adverse reactions in individuals with certain unique sensitivities. (For example, I had an acquaintance who was so sickened by the odor of peanuts that no one dared eat a peanut butter sandwich, or even open a bag of nuts, in his presence.) Don't let all of these warnings frighten you away from the pleasures of scent. However, if you notice that the scent of a candle, anointing oil, or incense is making you feel badly, just put it out and put it away; next time you may prefer an unscented candle, or perhaps you could try a different fragrance. (Extinguishing and removing such a candle will not negate the good intent expressed by whatever ritual you may have been performing.)

Eclectic Home Altars

People who enjoy candle-burning rituals often create home altar spaces for this purpose. Indeed, the practice of making personal altars or home shrines is becoming widespread, even among people who aren't conventionally religious and haven't been brought up in religious or ethnic groups with altar-making traditions. These new altars are often highly eclectic.[48] In addition to accessories like candles, incense, and crystals, home altars may be decorated with different types of sacred images, as well as an odd profusion of secular objects, such as personal and family mementos. Such altars can be used as sites for prayer, meditation, and reflection, and people may interact with them by adding new items, removing others, and rearranging them. Because of the thought and energy that go into them, altar decoration and maintenance also serve as ritual acts.

The word "altar" itself denotes something that is "raised up" (from the same root as "altitude"). On a home altar, you can raise up or focus upon significant personal images in a way that makes you more aware of your selfhood, your relationships to others, and the things you value. By juxtaposing personal objects with sacred images (or positioning personal objects in a manner traditionally reserved for symbols of the sacred), you are able to see your life symbols in relation to the divine order. Also, by performing short but frequent rituals at your altar, you can maintain a sense of your connection with this higher order.[49]

By putting meaningful personal symbols in high focus, a home altar can be used to explore different dimensions of selfhood. Self-integration is a concern, as we live in a society that requires us to adapt to changing circumstances. This engages a "fluid and many-sided" form of selfhood described by Robert Jay Lifton as the "protean self" (named after a mythical shape-shifter). He sees "American proteanism" as a way of "reconstituting the self in the midst of radical uncertainty," responding to a need "to be both fluid and grounded, however tenuous that combination."[50] By serving as a stable surface upon which one may add, remove, or rearrange symbols of personal identity and experience, and to which one may regularly come back, we can see that home altars contribute to a sense of being both fluid and grounded. You might want to reflect upon your own protean qualities by arranging photos of yourself at different stages in your life, along with objects associated with your personal transformations and growth.

Home altars also engage the "relational self," an inclusive sense of selfhood that identifies and empathizes with the other people in one's life, and is also shaped by the need to be different things to different people. People with a strong sense of relational selfhood include photos and mementos from friends and family in their altar arrangements, and may often burn candles while saying prayers on behalf of others. People whose altars display various natural objects (such as shells, rocks, and feathers) have a desire for relationship that reaches out to the creatures of nature.

Besides enhancing spiritual awareness and bringing the divine into the home, the display of sacred images is also a part of the home altar's celebration of relationship. Combining sacred and mundane objects reveals the spiritual order behind our daily life's activities, and associating personal and family photos and mementos with sacred images puts them in a sort of communication. As Kay Turner has observed in her studies of women's altars, "the home altar [is] where earthly and heavenly families are drawn together in rituals that prove their interdependence."[51] By displaying mementos, we also confer something of "symbolic immortality" to our loved ones and to our life's experiences.[52]

Another compelling feature of the more eclectic altars (as can be seen with some of those portrayed in Jean McMann's book *Altars and Icons: Sacred Spaces In Everyday Life*) is the tendency to blend images from different religious traditions. Thus, one may find statues of Catholic saints next to Hindu gods or serene Buddhas. This resonates to Lifton's theory that the protean self is engaged in "an effort to overcome spiritual homelessness," but that, "[i]n its aversion to dogma, the protean self tends to settle for a pluralistic spirituality that allows for doubt and uncertainty and includes a stress on personal responsibility."[53] Perhaps the combination of images from different religions also reflects peoples' desire to heal the religious differences that obstruct world peace.

There is much more that can be said about the symbolism of altars, as well as altar-making designs and techniques, but space limitations prevent me from including it here. However, there has been a recent spate of books on this subject, so you might want to look into Jean McMann's book as mentioned above, Kay Turner's *Beautiful Necessity: The Art and Meaning of Women's Altars*, Denise Linn's *Altars: Bringing Sacred Shrines Into Your Everyday Life*, and Edward Searl's *A Place of Your Own*, as well as all of the other excellent (and often colorful) books on this subject.

Candle Enhancements

Here are a few things you can do to personalize a candle and bring extra energy and concentration to your rite:

- Inscribe a candle for yourself with your name, birth date, the symbol for your sign of the zodiac, and other symbols with which you identify. This is a little easier if you heat the tip of your knife, pin, nail, or awl.

- Inscribe your candle with words or symbols related to your purpose. For example, to attract love into your life, you could carve a heart symbol.

- Encircle a candle with a beaded necklace or an assortment of gemstones in colors that are harmonious with your purpose.

- Tie a cord around the neck of a jar candle, with a symbolic pendant or charm attached to the cord.

- For a multiplied effect, position mirrors near the candle and/or set the candle on a mirrored base.

- When you are doing a rite to express certain feelings, help you achieve clarity on certain issues, or strengthen your resolve to change your behavior, write your intentions or concerns down on paper (either in a list or "freewrite" format), then fold the paper and place it under the candle.

Also: some dedicated candle burners have additional candles on their altar or focus area. One or two candles representing Divinity or the light of Spirit may be lit first, then used to light the other candles in an act symbolic of the extension of divine grace. These are often larger pillar candles that are set a bit behind the candle or candles that are the focus of the rite. (The "Rite to Affirm the Presence of Deity" on page 113 could be used for lighting such candles.) It is also common to include "astral" candles to represent the person or persons intended to benefit from the rite, whether yourself or someone who is not present. (See appendix C for more on astral candles.)

Notes

Endnotes are often passed over, viewed as comprising that part of the book that just supplies the obligatory information on source materials. However, I have tucked some interesting tidbits of information regarding folk customs, magic, and other curiosities—as well as some practical ideas and philosophical commentary—into these notes, because I didn't want to clutter the ritual sections with trivia that is not necessary for the performance of the rites (but which may be helpful in appreciating the metaphysical or multicultural traditions behind the ritual techniques or the accessories used).

For brevity, most book citations are limited to authors' last names and page numbers (and last name or title of article or web page for internet sources); for more complete information, refer to the Works Cited sections.

Introduction

1. Malbrough 69.
2. Williamson 33.
3. Talbot 117.
4. Stoddard 9.

Section I: Rites for the Rhythms and Routines of Daily Life

1. Lockwood 271–278.
2. See EOS, edited by Hatto.
3. Lauterbach 204–261.
4. Alexander 24–25. She suggests that this is a way that modern people can connect with Hestia, the goddess of hearth and home.
5. Carnegie 4.
6. McArthur 183.

7. Dodt 82–107. Colleen Dodt suggests blends and techniques for wake-up baths, cold-care baths, antidepressant baths, and more.

8. McArthur 183.

9. Refer to the sidebar in the Introductory Section, page xv, for a discussion of the term "unconscious."

10. Reed 66.

11. "Glamoury" is an archaic word for magic—especially the magic of fantasy and illusion.

12. Estés (*Riddle Mother*). A *cantadora* is a storyteller.

13. Mayes 129. While touring the herb garden at San Pietro in Perugia, Frances Mayes learned of a traditional belief that the leaves of the wild melissa "produce golden dreams."

Section II: Rites for Self-Improvement and Mind-Body Connection

1. Riva 108.

2. Greer 67.

3. Riva 9.

4. To learn more about visualization and self healing techniques, some popular works are Siegel's *Love, Medicine, and Miracles* and *Peace, Love, And Healing; Getting Well Again* by Simonton, Matthews-Simonton, and Creighton; *Stress, Diet, And Your Heart* by Ornish; *The Well Body Book* by Samuels and Bennett; and *Seeing with the Mind's Eye* by Samuels and Samuels. For more detailed and individualized techniques, see *Imagery in Healing* by Achterberg and *Rituals of Healing* by Achterberg, Dossey, and Kolkmeier. In the area of healing, there is an unlimited number of things we can do for ourselves, including designing or collecting a personal repertoire of rituals and visualizations, because as Jeanne Achterberg has noted, "it would be prudent to recruit as many neural patterns of health as possible," *Imagery* 132–34.

5. See Simonton, Matthews-Simonton, and Creighton, 140–63, on the necessity of picturing strong bodily defenses.

6. See Demiéville; see also Birnbaum 50.

Section III. Rites for the Working Life

1. Seneca and Carlyle are quoted in Stevenson.

2. For the use of ylang ylang in seeking employment, see Cunningham (*Aromatherapy*) 149, and Riva 173. The use of geranium was mentioned by Harry M. Hyatt's informants in the Deep South, circa 1920s and 30s, (*Hoodoo*).

3. Buckland (*Color*).

4. Carter 45.

Section IV. Rites for Problem Situations and Personal Sorrows

1. Scheffer 134.

2. Hunt 11.

3. Due to space limitations, I don't want to get into a discussion of the differences in definitions of soul, self, and spirit. In fact, my own definitions are fairly loose, because these
aren't tangible objects that we can describe and dissect, nor can we confidently delineate
where one begins and the other ends. Therefore, for the purposes of this rite, use your
own intuitive sense of what these words mean.

4. Linn 24.

5. Roeder 17, 235.

Section V. Some Candle Rites for Special Needs

1. Joralemon and Sharon.

2. Morita is quoted by Ryan-Madson 203.

3. Buckland (*Candle*) 152.

4. Cunningham (*Aromatherapy*) 58, and Moura 52.

Section VI. Rites for Your Spiritual Being

1. I have borrowed this line from the twelfth-century mystic, Hildegard of Bingen.

2. Some people find it easier to go into meditation by first doing relaxation exercises and/or
imagining themselves in some beautiful natural setting.

3. Bhikku Piyananda describes meditation as "concentrated awareness." On the subject of
using thoughts or mental states as meditation objects, he says that you apply your mind
"to the internal confusions and mental conflicts, and observe and pay attention to all the
changing states of your mind." In other words, "The task here is to become aware of the
thoughts that arise and pass away within the mind" [365–386].

4. Dyer 34.

5. When we see things from a higher perspective, what we might call a godlike ego state or
state of consciousness, we have compassion for others (including ourselves), and a readiness to take action when and where we are needed. However, we also maintain a state of
equanimity that frees us from fretting about things beyond our control.

6. Hay 219.

7. For some general information on how principles of hot and cold are modulated in purification rituals, see Richards.

Section VII. Rites for the Rhythms of Nature

1. Due to variations in local practice which emphasized some holidays and neglected others, there seems to be no evidence of a society that observed all eight of these year-marks as such, (that is, in a conscious and punctilious manner). However, that there may have been some ancient sense of this eight-fold division is indicated in an Armoric folk song which speaks of "the eight fires," with the "father fire" being lighted in May. Grimm 1465.

2. Hyatt (*Folklore*) 373.

3. Cardin 51–53.

4. Starhawk 79.

5. Budapest (*Grandmother Moon*) 199.

6. Of course, you can say affirmations any time you wish. However, the Full Moon period is an opportunity to ride a wave of energy.

7. Writing engages more areas of the brain.

8. St. Brigid's shrine in Kildare kept a perpetual flame, and was called "the House of Fire." It was formerly attended by nineteen priestesses.

9. St. Blaise's feast day (known in Germany as "Little Candlemas") has been celebrated with bonfires, women's parties, and a ritual of crossed candles, to protect against diseases. St. Agatha protects against fire and disease.

10. Although many Americans take their Christmas decorations down around New Years', many are now leaving them up longer—which seems natural if you live in an area that is blanketed with snow. Let the knowledge of this Candlemas tradition give you "permission" to enjoy your decorations through the end of January.

11. In the 1940s, folklorist Vance Randolph wrote that "there are thousands of people in Missouri and Arkansas who regard February 14 as Groundhog Day, and it is February 14, not February 2, that they consider in deciding the proper dates for plowing and planting," 27.

12. Celtic peoples do this on January 31, in the evening. It is a lucky portent if, the next morning, Bride's footprint is found in the ashes. See Carmichael 166–172.

13. If we aligned the seasonal festivals with the times of the day, we would place winter solstice at midnight and summer solstice at high noon, so spring equinox would be 6 a.m.

14. The Germanic Eostre/Austra/Ostara is related to the Roman Eos and the Vedic Ushas, goddesses of the dawn. Eggs and Easter hares (in America, rabbits) are her emblems, and her link with fertility is also seen in other words associated with her name:"estrus" and "estrogen."

15. Beltane is associated with the pan-Celtic god Belenos, whose name also means "bright fire," James 312. Also see Grimm 613–15, and Matthews 71.

16. James 169.

17. Dorothy Jacob cites this as a Danish belief, 97.

18. My relatives who vacation there have told me this is a spectacular sight.

19. In Europe, the word "corn" is a general term applied to grain (as opposed to maize, the stuff that Americans eat on the cob with salt and butter).

20. The Buddha cited this thought as one of the ten conditions for frequent contemplation. See internet sources: "reflections," and "Discourse on Ten Dhammas," or see Khemasanto 19.

21. For example, in different parts of Germany, St. Martin's celebrations, which begin at dusk on November 10 (St. Martin's Eve) may include (or have at one time included) bonfires, jumping over candles or bonfires, children's lantern processions (in the old days, the lanterns were like jack-o-lanterns, but hallowed out of beets or turnips), children going from door to door singing, begging, and receiving money and sweets, and sometimes even dressing up in costumes (Internet: Becker-Huberti, and Shea). St. Martin's is also a big day in France and Belgium. In Ireland, it is sometimes referred to as "Old Samhain."

22. This was my own experience: my first glimpse and memory of Halloween, which was the sight of costumed children crossing the street at night, thrilled me with the idea of a magical world.

23. The Scandinavian word for this holiday is Jul or Yule ("wheel"), denoting the completion of a year cycle and the beginning of a new one.

24. The roots of the Christmas tree are ancient, with symbolism echoing the tree of life motifs common to so many cultures. An antecedent of the Christmas tree is the old Norse world tree, which sheltered the human world, known as "Middle Earth," as well as eight other dimensions.

Section VIII. Rites for Special Days of the Year

1. Thomas 55–57. Also, see Adkins and Adkins, and Balsdon.

2. The celebration of the new year is a very important holiday in many countries. In France and some Latin countries, New Year moreso than Christmas is the time for giving and receiving presents. In Scotland, where it is called "Hogmanay," the year's transition is surrounded by rituals such as "first-footing," where a lucky person is invited to be the first person to enter the house. There are also superstitions surrounding special foods to be eaten for luck, such as my Texan friends' custom of serving black-eyed peas and bacon. Other beliefs include the need to have money in your pocket, that bread, silver, or salt should be brought into the house before anything is taken out, and that you should open the door at the stroke of midnight to let the old year out and the new year in.

3. There is a genuine American tradition of burning bayberry candles for luck and prosperity on New Year's Day or Eve (though some do this on Christmas). In a recent Internet discussion, some senior citizens and others described their families' practice—including one Italian-American family. See "BayberryCandles."

4. The reference to "the kingdom of culture" alludes to W. E. B. DuBois, one of King's inspirational mentors. In *The Souls Of Black Folk*, DuBois asserted, "This, then, is the end of his [the Negro's] striving: to be a co-worker in the kingdom of culture, to escape both death and isolation, to husband and use his best powers and his latent genius" 5.

5. Athanassakis 67.

6. Hyatt (*Hoodoo*) 670. Ceremonies involving the four directions seem to be universal, but I cite this example because I have been intrigued with the African practice of making "cosmograms," stylistic images of the earth through art and gestures, as a way of putting oneself in good relationship with the Earth.

7. Holmes, Internet.

8. Note that I had originally included "You, whose hearts have been touched with fire," after ". . . set apart by your experience." It refers to the most well-known line from Holmes' speech, "in our youth our hearts were touched with fire." This line has now been omitted, as in the wake of the events of September 11, 2001, I was concerned that some people might take this the wrong way and deem it insensitive. However, if you find this passage inspiring, you can certainly include it.

9. Jefferson, Internet. (Numerous websites have reproduced the text of the Declaration.)

10. Astrologer Donna Cunningham discusses continuing tensions related to the United States horoscope. Among the other results of its July 4, 1776, birth date, the U.S. has its Sun, Jupiter, Venus, and Mercury in Cancer, a sign concerned with security, nurturing, homemaking, and motherhood, while Uranus, the Planet of Revolutions, is sitting on its Gemini Ascendant, and also rules the United States Moon, because the Moon is in radical Aquarius. Cunningham explains that, "Aquarius does not combine easily with the Moon or with Cancer, and for a nation with four planets in Cancer to have an Aquarian Moon means there are great internal contradictions" 45.

11. Rappaport 138.

12. Ehrenreich 221. Among the problems that Ehrenreich's book reveals is how the very nature of low paid work (which includes long hours, changeable schedules, stress, fatigue, cumulative damage to the body, little [if anything] in the way of insurance and benefits, social isolation, and often the need to hold down more than one job) prevents members of the working poor from seeking a higher education or better jobs.

13. Performing this ceremony at eleven in the morning enables you to align your actions with the ceremonies at Arlington Cemetery, or with your local commemorations.

Section IX. Presentation Candles

1. Telesco 74.

Section X. Rites for Reaching out to Others in Spirit

1. Cunningham (*Aromatherapy*) 145.

2. Greer 65.

3. In Pali, the language of the Buddha, loving kindness is *metta* (may-tah), compassion is *karuna* (ka-roo-nah), sympathetic joy is *mudhita* (moo-dee-tah), and equanimity is *uppekha* (oo-peck-hah). At least this is the way these words sound to my ears, and the way I use them in practice. It is a common practice to recite these four words while going into and coming out of a meditative state, and while going to sleep at night and waking up in the morning. (Going into meditation you recite "metta, karuna, mudita, upekkha," and coming out you reverse this to say "upekkha, mudita, karuna, metta.") Also, *Brahmaviharas* is pronounced "brah-mah-wee-har-ahs." (The *w* is pronounced like a *v*.)

4. Barrie 143.

5. Achebe made this statement in an interview in which he was discussing his book, *Arrow Of God* (Cott 171).

6. Estés (*Women*) 478. Estés says that, "Ancestral worship, a term from classical anthropology, should more accurately be called ancestor kinship, ongoing relationship with those who have gone before."

7. Arrien 114, 126.

8. Somé 53.

9. Snyder (*Practice*) 75.

10. van Praagh 209.

11. Animal torture—particularly the killing of cats—is deeply embedded in the culture of American boys. Although we may regard animal torturers as "deviants," this definition has been stood on its head, so that young men who refuse to participate in torture are taunted as deviants by their peers. As one young man explained it to me, the peer group holds that "if you're not killing cats, it means that you must be f---ing them."

12. According to ASPCA president Larry M. Hawk, "Each year 2 to 3 million dogs and 6 to 9 million cats are relinquished to animal shelters across the nation. But up to 50% of the dogs and 70% of the cats that wind up in shelters will end up dying there because no one comes to adopt them." He says that if you could picture the 6 million dogs and cats that are destined to die each year, "the line would extend from New York city to Juneau, Alaska!" (newsletter, June 2001).

13. Confucius is quoted in Brown, 25.

14. Murray 131, 184.

Appendix

1. Some of the sources for these tips include pamphlets from Wicks'n'Sticks and the Bridgewater Candle Company, and online guides from House of Wicks & Wax and Genwax.

2. Cooper was citing the conclusions of an EPA study, (Watson, Internet).

3. National Candle Association, Internet; Vallese, Internet.

4. Thompson 118; Pinckney 72.

5. Yronwode, Internet.

6. Ibid.

7. Rossbach 121.

8. Ibid 121.

9. Gamache 8.

10. Buckland (*Candle*) 253; Telesco 149–51; Conway 28–29.

11. Malbrough 71.

12. Roeder 216–17.

13. Rosengarten 115.

14. Greer 100.

15. On the talismanic uses of laurel, see Burriss 154.

16. Dodt 23.

17. Riva 90; Malbrough 157, 160, 162.

18. Dodt 46; Cunningham (*Aromatherapy*) 72.

19. Lawless 213.

20. Leydet, Internet.

21. Hurston 284.

22. "HS Lim's," Internet.

23. Ancient Healing Art, Internet.

24. Rechelbacher 171.

25. Well, at least California as it was in the 70s and 80s.

26. "HS Lim's," Internet.

27. Dodt 26.

28. Moura 54.

29. When she did her folklore research during the Depression, Zora Neale Hurston described Van Van as "the most popular conjure drug in New Orleans" (284), and Hyatt's informants simply labeled it "luck" (*Hoodoo* 132, 509, 662.)

30. Greer 93.

31. Lawless 12.

32. Rosengarten 277.

33. Cunningham (*Aromatherapy*) 115.

34. Writing in 1969, Frederic Rosengarten claimed that "at 'nutmeg parties,' beatniks and hippies sometimes eat two or three tablespoonfuls of powdered nutmeg as a hallucinogenic drug" (301). These jags were followed by serious nausea, headaches, and other side effects. Overuse of the fragrance should be avoided, as it could produce toxic effects.

35. According to Leydet, "Inhaling the fragrance opens the conscious mind to attract money into your life" (Internet).

36. "Usage Ideas," Internet.

37. Mountain Home, Internet.

38. Greer 67.

39. The Roman poet Ovid saw a priestess use pine boughs in a purification ceremony (Nagle 58).

40. Sui 5.

41. Scheffer 134–38.

42. "Ayurvedic fragrances," Internet.

43. See Internet sources: "Customs in Celebration," "Chinese New Year Customs," and "Chinese New Year Feast."

44. Lawless 80.

45. See U.S. Food and Drug Administration, Internet. This pertains to "Essential oils, oleoresins (solvent-free), and natural extractives (including distillates) that are generally recognized as safe for their intended use, within the meaning of section 409 of the Act. . . ."

46. Price and Price 177.

47. Price and Price 35153, and Lawless 27.

48. Much of the material here is drawn from my short paper on "The Eclectic Home Altar as Icon of the Protean Self," 7 December 1999, unpublished.

49. Rappaport says that short but frequent rituals help to anchor the divine order in the mundane world, and they also enable the individual to stay focused on values, ethics, and identity when other cultural forces would tend to erode these things (202–205).

50. Lifton (*Protean*) 1, 3, 9.

51. Turner 44.

52. A major theme of Lifton's Book, *The Broken Connection,* is the self's search for images needed for the symbolic transcendence of death. Lifton comments that because our own cultural framework lacks "the connecting imagery of transcendence," religious seekers "construct, over time, the beginnings of new versions of immortalizing imagery, attempting to combine image-fragments into more enduring constellations" (209).

53. Lifton (*Protean*) 15, 127.

Works Cited

Printed Sources and Tapes

Achterberg, Jeanne. *Imagery in Healing: Shamanism and Modern Medicine*. Boston: Shambhala, 1985.

Achterberg, Jeanne, Barbara Dossey, and Leslie Kolkmeier. *Rituals of Healing: Using Imagery for Health And Wellness*. New York: Bantam, 1994.

Adkins, Lesley, and Roy A. Adkins. *Handbook to Life in Ancient Rome*. New York: Facts on File, 1994.

Alexander, Jane. *Sacred Rituals at Home*. Godsfield Press, 1999. New York: Sterling, 2000.

Arendt, Hannah. *The Human Condition*. Chicago: University of Chicago Press, 1958.

Arrien, Angeles. *The Four Fold Way: Walking the Paths of the Warrior, Teacher, Healer, and Visionary*. San Francisco: HarperSanFrancisco, 1993.

Aswyn, Freya. *Leaves of Yggdrasil*. St. Paul, Minnesota: Llewellyn, 1990.

Athanassakis, Apostolos N. ed. and trans., *The Homeric Hymns*. Baltimore, MD: Johns Hopkins University Press, 1976.

Balsdon, JPVD. *Life and Leisure in Ancient Rome*. New York: McGraw-Hill, 1969.

Barrie, Sir James M. *Peter Pan*. New York: Children's Classics-dilithium Press, 1987.

Basham, A. L. "Sanskrit," *Hatto* 140–47.

Birnbaum, Raoul. *The Healing Buddha*. Boulder, CO: Shambhala, 1979.

Bly, Robert. *Iron John: A Book About Men*. Reading, MA: Addison-Wesley, 1990.

Board of Tourist Industry, Japanese Government Railways, *Zinsya: Shinto Shrines*, n.d.

Borland, Hal. *Sundial of the Seasons: A Selection of Outdoor Editorials from the New York Times*. Philadelphia: Lippincott, 1964.

———. *Twelve Moons of the Year*. New York: Knopf, 1979.

Bridgewater Candle Company. "Time to learn . . . so you can burn," pamphlet. 1998.

Brown, Brian, ed. *The Wisdom of the Chinese*. New York: Brentanos, 1920.

Buckland, Ray. *Advanced Candle Magick*. St. Paul, MN: Llewellyn, 1996.

———. *Practical Color Magick*. St. Paul, MN: Llewellyn, 1983.

Budapest, Zsuzsanna E. *The Goddess in the Office: A Personal Energy Guide for the Spiritual Warrior at Work.* New York: HarperSanFrancisco, 1993.

———. *Grandmother Moon: Lunar Magic in Our Lives.* New York: HarperSanFrancisco-HarperCollins, 1991.

Burriss, Eli Edward. *Taboo, Magic, Spirits; A Study of Primitive Elements in Roman Religion.* 1931. Westport, CT: Greenwood, 1972.

Carmichael, Alexander. *Carmina Gadelica: Hymns and Incantations.* 1900. Edinburgh: Oliver and Boyd, 1928.

Carnegie, Dale. *How to Stop Worrying and Start Living.* 1944. New York: Pocket Books-Simon & Schuster, 1984.

Carter, Mildred. *Body Reflexology: Healing at Your Fingertips.* West Nyack, NY: Parker, 1983.

Conway, D. J. *A Little Book of Candle Magic.* Freedom, CA: Crossing Press, 2000.

Cott, Jonathan. *Piper at the Gates of Dawn: The Wisdom of Children's Literature.* New York: Random House, 1981.

Cunningham, Donna. *Being a Solar Type in a Lunar World: An Astrological View of Modern Life.* York Beach, ME: Weiser, 1982.

Cunningham, Scott. *The Complete Book of Incense, Oils, and Brews.* St. Paul: Llewellyn, 1989.

———. *Magical Aromatherapy.* St. Paul, MN: Llewellyn, 1989.

Demiéville, Paul. *Buddhism and Healing.* (Demiéville's article "Byo" from *Hobogirin*, 1937). Translated by Mark Tatz. Lanham, MD: University Press of America, 1985.

Dodt, Colleen K. *The Essential Oils Book: Creating Personal Blends for Mind & Body.* Pownal, Vermont: Storey Books, 1996.

DuBois, W. E. B. *The Souls of Black Folk.* 1903. New York: Penguin, 1989.

Dyer, Wayne D. *Real Magic: Creating Miracles in Everyday Life.* New York: HarperCollins, 1992.

Ehrenreich, Barbara. *Nickel Aand Dimed: On (not) Getting By in America.* New York: Metropolitan-Holt, 2001.

Estés, Clarissa Pinkola. "In the House of the Riddle Mother: Common Archetypal Motifs in Women's Dreams." Audiotape. Boulder, CO: Sounds True Recordings, 1991.

———. *Women Who Run with the Wolves: Myths and Stories of the Wild Woman Archetype.* New York: Ballantine, 1992.

Gamache, Henri. *The Master Book of Candle Burning,* ca. 1942. Plainview, New York: Original Publications, 1998.

Greer, Mary K. *The Essence of Magic: Tarot, Ritual, and Aromatherapy.* North Hollywood: Newcastle, 1993.

Grimm, Jakob. *Teutonic Mythology,* Volume 4, 1888. New York: Dover, 1966.

Hatto, A.T., ed. *Eos: An Enquiry into the Theme of Lovers' Meetings and Partings at Dawn in Poetry.* A. T. Hatto, ed. Mouton, 1965.

Hawk, Larry M. *ASPCA* newsletter, June 2001.

Hay, Louise. *Meditations to Heal Your Life.* Carson, CA: Hay House, 1994.

Hunt, Cecil, ed. *Uncommon Prayers.* Greenwich, CT: Seabury, 1955.

Hurston, Zora Neale. *Of Mules and Men.* Bloomington: University of Indiana Press, 1935.

Hyatt, Harry Middleton. *Folklore from Adams County Illinois.* 1935. Hannibal, MO: Alma Egan Hyatt Foundation, 1965.

———. *Hoodoo, Conjuration, Witchcraft, Rootwork,* vol. 1, Hannibal, Missouri: Western Publishing, 1935. Washington: American University Bookstore, 1970.

James, E. O. *Seasonal Feasts and Festivals.* New York: Barnes & Noble, 1961.

Johnston, Basil. *Ojibway Heritage.* Lincoln, NE: University of Nebraska Press, 1976.

Joralemon, Donald, and Douglas Sharon. *Sorcery and Shamanism: Curanderos and Clients in Northern Peru.* Salt Lake City, UT: University of Utah Press, 1993.

Khemasanto, Bhikku, compiler. *Anupubbasikkha: The Gradual Training.* Perry, MI: Wat Dhammasala, ca. 1999.

Lawless, Julia. *The Illustrated Encyclopedia of Essential Oils: The Complete Guide to the Use of Oils in Aromatherapy and Herbalism.* Shaftesbury, Dorset: Element, 1995.

Lifton, Robert Jay. *The Broken Connection: On Death and the Continuity of Life.* New York: Simon and Schuster, 1979.

———. *The Protean Self.* Chicago: University of Chicago Press, 1993.

Linn, Denise. *Altars: Bringing Sacred Shrines into Your Everyday Life.* New York: Ballantine-Random House, 1999.

Lauterbach, Joseph Z. "The Origin and Development of Two Sabbath Customs," *Beauty In Holiness: Studies in Jewish Customs and Ceremonial Art.* Ed. Joseph Gutman. n.p.: Ktav. 1970. 204–261.

Lockwood, John. "Classical, Later, and Medieval Latin." *Hatto,* 271–81.

Malbrough, Ray T. *The Magical Power of the Saints.* St. Paul, MN: Llewellyn, 1998.

McArthur, Margie. *Wiccacraft for Families.* Custer, WA: Phoenix, 1994.

McMann, Jean. *Altars and Icons: Sacred Spaces in Everyday Life.* San Francisco: Chronicle Books, 1998.

Matthews, Caitlin. *The Celtic Book of Days: A Guide to Celtic Spirituality and Wisdom.* Rochester, Vermont: Destiny Books, 1995.

Moore, Thomas. *Care of the Soul: A Guide for Cultivating Depth and Sacredness in Everyday Life.* New York: HarperPerennial-HarperCollins, 1992.

Morrison, Dorothy. *Everyday Magic: Spells and Rituals for Modern Living*. St. Paul, MN: Llewellyn, 1998.

Moura, Ann. *Green Witchcraft: Folk Magic, Fairy Lore, and Herb Craft*. St. Paul, MN: Llewellyn, 1998.

Murray, Alexander S. *Who's Who in Mythology: A Classic Guide to the Ancient World*. New York: Wings, 1989.

Ornish, Dean. *Stress, Diet, and Your Heart*. New York: Penguin, 1982.

Pinckney, Roger. *Blue Roots: African-American Folk Magic of the Gullah People*. St. Paul, MN: Llewellyn, 1998.

Piyananda, Bhikku. "Why Meditation?" *Gems of Buddhist Wisdom* [editor unknown]. Kuala Lumpur, Malaysia: Buddhist Missionary Society, 1983. rept. Taipei, Taiwan: Corporate Body of the Buddha Educational Foundation, pp. 365–386.

Price, Shirley, and Len Price. *Aromatherapy for Health Professionals*. Edinburgh: Churchill Livingstone, 1999.

Rappaport, Roy A. *Ritual and Religion in the Making of Humanity*. Cambridge, United Kingdom: Cambridge University Press, 1999.

RavenWolf, Silver. *To Stir A Magick Cauldron: A Witch's Guide to Casting and Conjuring*. St. Paul, MN: Llewellyn, 1996.

Rechelbacher, Horst. *Aveda Rituals: A Daily Guide to Natural Health and Beauty*. New York: Henry Holt-Owl Books, 1999.

Reed, Henry. *Edgar Cayce on Channeling Your Higher Self*. New York: Warner, 1989.

Richards, Richards. *Chisungu: A Girl's Initiation Ceremony Among the Bemba of Zambia*. 1956. London: Routledge, 1995.

Riva, Anna. *Golden Secrets of Mystic Oils*. Los Angeles: International Imports, 1990.

Roeder, Beatrice A. *Chicano Folk Medicine from Los Angeles, California*. University of California Publications Folklore and Mythology Studies, volume 34. Berkeley: University of California Press, 1988.

Rosengarten Jr., Frederic, *The Book of Spices*. 1969. New York: Pyramid Books, 1973.

Rossbach, Sarah. *Feng Shui: The Chinese Art of Placement*. New York: E.P. Dutton, 1983.

Ryan-Madson, Patricia. "Reality's Work" *Mindfulness and Meaningful Work*. Ed. Claude Whitmyer. Berkeley, CA: Parallax, 1994. 203-208.

Samuels, Mike, and Hal Bennet. *The Well Body Book*. New York: Random House-Bookwords, 1973.

Samuels, Mike, and Nancy Samuels. *Seeing with the Mind's Eye: The History, Techniques, and Uses of Visualization*. New York: Random House-Bookworks, 1975.

Scheffer, Mechthild. *Bach Flower Therapy: Theory and Practice,* A. R. Meuss trans. Rochester, VT: Healing Arts Press, 1988.

Searl, Edward. *A Place of Your Own.* New York: Berkley Books, 1998.

Siegel, Bernie *Medicine, and Miracles.* New York: Harper & Row, 1986.

———. *Peace, Love, and Healing.* New York, Harper & Row, 1989.

Simonton, O. Carl, Stephanie Matthews-Simonton, and James Creighton. *Getting Well Again: A Step-by-step, Self-help Guide to Overcoming Cancer for Patients and Their Families.* Los Angeles, J.P. Tarcher, 1978.

Snyder, Gary. *No Nature: New and Selected Poems.* New York: Pantheon, 1992.

———. *Practice of the Wild.* New York: Farrar, 1990.

Somé, Patrice Malidoma. *Ritual: Power, Healing, and Community.* New York: Arkana-Penguin, 1997.

Stevenson, Burton, ed. *The Macmillan Book of Proverbs, Maxims, and Famous Phrases.* New York: Macmillan, 1948.

Stoddard, Alexandra. *Living a Beautiful Life: 500 Ways to Add Elegance, Order, Beauty, and Joy to Every Day of Your Life.* New York: Random House, 1986.

Strehlow, Wighard, and Gottfried Hertzka. *Hildegard of Bingen's Medicine,* Karin Anderson Strehlow trans. Santa Fe: Bear & Co., 1988.

Talbot, Michael. *The Holographic Universe.* New York: HarperPerennial-HarperCollins, 1991.

Telesco, Patricia. *Exploring Candle Magick: Candle Spells, Charms, Rituals, and Divinations.* Franklin Lakes, New Jersey: New Page Books, 2001.

Thomas, Ruth Edith. *The Sacred Meal in the Older Roman Religion.* diss. University of Chicago, 1935. Chicago: University of Chicago Libraries, private edition. 1937.

Thompson, Robert Farris. "The Song that Named the Land: The Visionary Presence of African American Art." Dallas Museum of Art. *Black Art: Ancestral Legacy; The African Impulse In African-American Art.* New York: Abrams, 1989. 97–141.

Turner, Kay. *Beautiful Necessity: The Art and Meaning of Women's Altars.* New York: Thames and Hudson, 1999.

van Praagh, James. *Talking to Heaven: A Medium's Message of Life After Death.* New York: Putnam-Signet, 1997.

Versulius, Arthur. "Ficino's Garden," *Parabola,* Winter 1995, 68–71.

Walsh, William S. *Curiosities of Popular Customs and of Rites, Ceremonies, Observances, and Miscellaneous Antiquities.* Philadelphia: Lippincott, 1897.

Wicks'n'Sticks. "Wicks'n'Sticks Pocket Guide to Candles." Pamphlet. Houston, TX, n.d.

Williamson, Marianne. *Illuminata: A Return to Prayer.* New York: Riverhead, 1994.

Zukav, Gary. *The Seat of the Soul.* New York: Simon & Schuster, 1989.

Internet

For the convenience of readers with computer connections, I have grouped my internet sources separately. The big disadvantage of Internet sources is that they can disappear or become inaccessible, and there is no quality control to detect plagiarism or misinformation. However, Internet sources can offer information and ideas that are either too obscure or too new to have been published elsewhere. Also where the use of candles, essential oils, or certain folk customs are concerned, one can find real people discussing their own experience and participation in living practices.

Ancient Healing Art, "Essential Oil Details," www.halcyon.com/kway/details.htm, Accessed January 2002.

"Ayurvedic fragrances." godconsciousness.com/incense.htm. Accessed February 2001.

"Bayberry candles" at vegsource.com/earthsave/messages/9018/html. Accessed January 2002.

Becker-Huberti, Manfred. "Martin of Tours." with Christian Otterbach, trans. (Presseamt des Erzbistums Köln, 1997), rept. www.martin-von-tours.de/lexikon/englisch. Accessed October 2001.

Bethancourt III, W. J. "Halloween Myths, Monsters, and Devils." 1994. Illusions.com. Accessed October 2001.

"Burning Guide." houseofwicksnwax.com. 31 January 2000. Accessed February 2001.

"Chinese New Year Customs," www.asianinfo-by-cj.com/english/malaysia/culture/chinese/msp_chinese.html. Accessed February 2002.

"Chinese New Year Feast: Symbolic Foods to Celebrate the Year of the Horse," http://chinesefood.about.com/library/weekly. Accessed February 2002.

"Customs in Celebration." www.zoom.com/my/archive/customs/customs3.html. Accessed February 2002.

"Devonshire Incense." devonshireincense.com. Accessed February 2001.

"Discourse on Ten Dhammas." www.palikanon.com/english/arahats/arahants17.htm.

Elixarome Limited. "Safety." oils@aroma-oils.co.uk. Accessed January 2002.

Farsinet, "NoRuz, NoRooz, NowRuz (Persian New Year)." www.farsinet.com/norooz/. Accessed March 2002.

"Genny's Candle Tips." genwax.com/candle_tips/_0_gennytips.htm. Accessed January 2002.

Holmes Jr., Oliver Wendell. "Our Hearts were Touched with Fire." Memorial Day speech, 1884. www.people.virginia.edu/~mmd5f/memorial.htm. Accessed May 2001. The Internet material was taken from *The Essential Holmes: Selections from the Letters, Speeches, Judicial Opinions, and Other Writings of Oliver Wendell Holmes, Jr.*, Richard A. Posner, ed. Chicago: Univeristy of Chicago Press, 1992. Accessed May 2001.

"HS Lim's Guide to Essential Oils Page,"
    http://homex.coolconnect.com/user/1hs1701/1hsoil.htm. Accessed February 2001.

Jefferson, Thomas. *The Declaration of Independence. 04 July 1776.* reproduced at
    pagebypagebooks.com/Thomas_Jefferson/the Declaration_of_Independence. Accessed July
    2001.

"Kayagata-sati Sutta," accesstoinsight.org. Accessed February, 2001.

LaVaughn, Celestial Healing Arts. "Aromatherapy Benefits and Safety."
    www.celestialhealing.com/aromsafe.html. Accessed January 2002.

Leydet Aromatics. "Specials and Information." www.leydet.com/bargains/bargainshtm.
    Accessed February 2001. Also: leydet.com/products/oilslist.html. Accessed March 2002.

McBain's Etymological Dictionary of the Gaelic Language, Section 32, "samhuinn,"
    www.ceantar.org/Dicts/MB2/mb32.html#samhuinn. Accessed March 2002.

McConnell, John. "Why the March Equinox is the only true Earth Day,"
    www.wowzone.com/why-ed.htm. Accessed January 2002.

————. "The Real Earth Day," www.earthsite.org/real-ed.htm. Accessed January 2002.

Mountain Home Candles, "Sweet Neroli," www.homestead.com/mountainhomecandles. Ac-
    cessed March 2002.

"The Myth of Samhain: Celtic God of the Dead," www.religioustolerance.org/hallo_sa.htm.
    Accessed March 2002.

Nakhjavani, Farrokh, et al, "Noruz . . . Celebration that Would Not Die," Summer 1994,
    www.azer.com/aiweb/categories/magazine/22_folder/22_articles/22_noruz.html.
    Accessed March 2002.

National Candle Association, "Wicks," www.candles.org/Candlemaking/qa_wicks.htm. Ac-
    cessed March 2002.

Nature's Gift. "Contraindications." www.naturesgift.com/warning.htm. Accessed February
    2001.

Nelson, Gaylord "The History of Earth Day." users.erols.com/slym/org/edhis.html. Accessed
    January 2001.

Payvand's Iran News. "Noruz in Iran." www.payvand.com/news/01/mar/1105.html. Accessed
    March 2002.

Price, Massoume, "Iranian New Year No Ruz."
    http://parents.berkeley.edu/madar-pedar/noruz.html. Accessed March 2002.

"reflections." ("The Ten Conditions for Frequent Contemplation," from Pali A v.87-88).
    student.uq.edu.au/~351543/buddhism/budaword/reflect.html. Accessed December 2001.

Sunspirit Aromatherapy. "For Your Safety." www.sunspirit.com.au/safety.htm. Accessed Jan-
    uary 2002.

Shea, Robert. serve.com/shea/germusa/stmartin.htm. Accessed October 2001.

Tradewinds Aromatherapy. "Guidelines & Safety Measures for Using Essential Oils." *Organix Natural Health Reference Guide.* www.organix.net/organix/guidelines.htm. Accessed April 2002.

U.S. Food and Drug Administration. "Code of Federal Regulations Title 21-Food and Drugs." www.accessdata.fda.gov/scripts/cdrh/cfdocs/cfPCD/showCFR.cfm?FR=182.20. Accessed March 2002.

"Usage Ideas." house of wicksnwax.com.sg/ideas.htm. Accessed February 2001.

Vallese, Julie. "U.S. Regulators Vote to Ban Lead Wick Candles." February 2002. www.cnn.com/virtual/editions/europe/2000/roof/change.pop/frameset.exclude.html. Accessed March 2002.

Watson, Traci. "Candles Might be Polluting Your Home, EPA Says." *USA Today*, June 2001. www.usatoday.com/news/healthscience/health/2001-06-14-epa-candles.htm. Accessed March 2002.

Watt, Martin. "Incorrect Safety." www.aromamedical.demon.co.uk/new/incorrectsafety.htm. Accessed April 2002.

Yronwode, Catherine. "Hoodoo Candle Magic." www.luckymojo.com/candlemagic.html#history. Accessed April 2002.

"100% bayberry wax" at www.genwax.com/candles/_0_p0162374.htm. Accessed January 2002.

To Write to the Author

If you wish to contact the author or would like more information about this book, please write to the author in care of Llewellyn Worldwide and we will forward your request. Both the author and publisher appreciate hearing from you and learning of your enjoyment of this book and how it has helped you. Llewellyn Worldwide cannot guarantee that every letter written to the author can be answered, but all will be forwarded. Please write to:

Janina Renée
℅ Llewellyn Worldwide
P.O. Box 64383, Dept. 0-7387-417-2
St. Paul, MN 55164-0383, U.S.A.

Please enclose a self-addressed stamped envelope for reply,
or $1.00 to cover costs. If outside U.S.A., enclose
international postal reply coupon.

Many of Llewellyn's authors have websites with additional information
and resources. For more information, please visit our website at
http://www.llewellyn.com

CANDLES, MEDITATION, & HEALING

Charlene Whitaker

You don't need to run to a psychic to find out what's going on in your life! Now you can read and influence your own future through the magic of candles. It's easy! Candles are an extension of your consciousness—symbolic of persons, places, and things. When you ask that they represent something or someone in your life, they become very powerful. Light the candles and tap into a source of "enlightenment" and guidance on choices pertaining to career, romance, health, children, and personal growth. Do readings for yourself and friends, send healing energy to those in need, and amplify the power of your prayers and meditations. This book shows you how.

1-56718-818-4, 176 pp., 5³⁄₁₆ x 6   **$7.95**

PRACTICAL CANDLEBURNING RITUALS
Spells and Rituals for Every Purpose

Raymond Buckland, Ph.D.

Magick is a way in which to apply the full range of your hidden psychic powers to the problems we all face in daily life. We know that normally we use only five percent of our total powers. Magick taps powers from deep inside our psyche where we are in contact with the universe's limitless resources.

Magick need not be complex—it can be as simple as using a few candles to focus your mind, a simple ritual to give direction to your desire, a few words to give expression to your wish.

This book shows you how easy it can be. Here is magick for fun; magick as a craft; magick for success, love, luck, money, marriage, and healing. Practice magick to stop slander, to learn truth, to heal an unhappy marriage, to overcome a bad habit, to break up a love affair, etc.

Magick—with nothing fancier than ordinary candles, and the twenty-eight rituals in this book (given in both Christian and Old Religion versions)—can transform your life.

0-87542-048-6, 208 pp., 5¼ x 8, illus. $7.95

CHARMS, SPELLS
& FORMULAS

*For the Making and Use of Gris-Gris Bags,
Herb Candles, Doll Magick, Incenses,
Oils and Powders*

Ray T. Malbrough

Hoodoo magick is a blend of European techniques and the magick brought to the New World by slaves from Africa. Now you can learn the methods that have been used successfully by Hoodoo practitioners for nearly 200 years.

By using the simple materials available in nature, you can bring about the necessary changes to greatly benefit your life and that of your friends. You are given detailed instructions for making and using the "gris-gris" (charm) bags only casually or mysteriously mentioned by other writers. Malbrough not only shows how to make gris-gris bags for health, money, luck, love, and protection from evil and harm, but he also explains how these charms work. He also takes you into the world of doll magick to gain love, success, or prosperity. Complete instructions are given for making the dolls and setting up the ritual.

0-87542-501-1, 192 pp., 5¼ x 8, illus. $7.95

CANDLEMAS
Feast of Flames

Amber K & Azrael Arynn K

The only book devoted to Brigid's Festival of Returning Light—an ancient holiday filled with hope. Beyond the darkness of winter, there is an oasis of light and warmth on the journey from solstice to spring. Known as Candlemas, Imbolc, Brigantia, or Lupercus, it is a celebration held in early February to welcome the returning light. Celtic Goddess Brigid presides, and it's customary to light candles to observe the sun's rebirth.

Candlemas is filled with customs and traditions from a variety of cultures—Irish, British, Scots, Welsh, Norwegian, Greek, Roman, and Chinese. There are tales from medieval Ireland, delicious recipes, crafts, decorations, detailed rituals, and even magickal spells with candles you make yourself. Post-holiday blues, begone!

0-7387-0079-7, 360 pp., 7½ x 9⅛ $14.95